# Rulers of the Earth

# Rulers of the Earth

## Secrets of the Sons of God

Joe Lewels, Ph.D.

2007
Galde Press, Inc.
Lakeville, Minnesota, U.S.A.
www.galdepress.com

*Rulers of the Earth*
© Copyright 2007 by Joe Lewels
All rights reserved.
Printed in the United States of America

First Edition
First Printing, 2007

Cover design by Christopher Wells
The painting is *The Madonna* by Raphael (Gemäldegalerie, Dresden)

**Note:** The original painting does not contain a UFO. The object at the upper left of the
painting on this cover was added on the computer. However, other paintings shown in
this book and containing unidentified aerial objects have not been modified.

Galde Press, Inc.
PO Box 460
Lakeville, Minnesota 55044–0460
www.galdepress.com

# Dedication

This book is written in loving memory of Nicholas J. Lewels, my beloved son, whose grace, love, and spiritual nobility will be remembered by everyone whose lives he touched. It is also dedicated to the memory of John E. Mack, M.D., whose unprecedented courage as a scientist will always be remembered, and to the memory of Romeo DiBenedetto, Ed.D., whose friendship and guidance I will never forget.

# Contents

## Part Three: The Secret Teachings

# Acknowledgements

This book would never have been written without the help and advice of innumerable persons who confided their darkest secrets to me, most of whom I cannot identify by name. I totally understand and respect their wish to remain anonymous. These are the people who have had extraordinary personal experiences consisting of contact with nonhuman entities. Living their lives is difficult enough without having to deal with the judgment of their friends, neighbors, and the general public.

I do wish to express my appreciation to those whom I am able to identify. They are people who either consulted with me during my years of research or offered me valuable advice along the way. Some played a direct role in the project, while others, in a more indirect way, helped me to bring this project to fruition. They are: Roberta Fennig, D.O.; John E. Mack, M.D.; Romeo DiBenedetto, Ed.D.; Linda Moulton Howe; Walter Andrus; Leo Sprinkle, Ph.D.; Command Sgt. Major, Ret. Robert O. Dean; Rev. Barry H. Downing, Ph.D.; Whitley Strieber; Lou Farrish; Bob and Terry Brown; John White; and Phyllis Galde.

Wherever this manuscript is in error or is lacking in insight or proper perspective, it is the fault of the author alone.

JOE LEWELS
January 2007

# Author's Note

This is a true story. In some cases, names have been changed and identities obscured in order to protect the privacy of those involved. To make the text more readable and for the sake of brevity, conversations, interviews, and hypnosis sessions have been edited and condensed. Any errors or mis-statements in this book are entirely the fault of the author.

**An Apology**
I would like to apologize in advance to all my friends and loved ones, whether they are Jewish, Catholic, Protestant, or atheist. I love you all. Some of you will no doubt perceive this book as an attack on your faith. Please do not take it personally. This book is an attack on blind faith, on anti-intellectualism, and on fundamentalism, regardless of the religion. It is a book that proposes that spiritual knowledge trumps blind faith and also that it is too easy to have faith in the wrong thing. A look at the world around us teaches us that the human race is embroiled in a clash of religious doctrines. Each side believes that God is on its side. The only solution to this conflict is for each individual to seek spiritual truth within himself. I hope that this book will be helpful to those who believe it is time for a change and who will accept the notion that God is to be found within oneself, rather than in dogma taught by religious institutions.

## PART ONE

# Know Thyself

*"Lift up a song to the rider of the clouds.*
*His name is the Lord."*

—Psalm 68:4

## CHAPTER ONE

# Rediscovering the Rulers of the Earth

THE ANCIENT EGYPTIANS called them the guardians, the *Neteru*. The writings of the most ancient civilizations of Mesopotamia, those of Sumer and Babylon, called them the *Annunaki*. In the ancient Vedic literature of India the various gods had many names, but they always traveled the skies in their craft, which were called *vimana*. The ancient aborigines of Australia called them the creator gods: the *Wandjina*. They believed and still believe that it was these gods who created life on Earth. Early in the origin of Judaism, multiple gods were recognized as the *Elohim*, the plural of the word for God: *El*. Many times they are referred to as the sons of God. In the mystery texts of the Hebrews, the Books of Enoch (found among the Dead Sea Scrolls), they were called the Watchers. In the Gnostic texts of the first and second century Christian sect, they were recognized as Archons. In the Bible they are referred to as angels, archangels, and as Watchers, but regardless of which culture we study, from the Native Americans to the indigenous peoples of the Amazon, Central America, or even Africa, the concept is the same. It has always been known that there are beings more advanced than the human race who have been involved with the Earth and its inhabitants for all time. Today, we call these beings aliens or extraterrestrials and we call their craft unidentified flying objects: UFOs.

The nature of these beings has always been described in the same way. They are divine entities who serve a mysterious but necessary role between humans and God. They have awesome powers: they move back and forth between the earthly, material world and other more ethereal dimensions we know little about. When they wish to, they exercise total mind control over humans . They manipulate individuals and even entire nations from behind a veil of secrecy. They come to us in our dreams and communicate to us through mental telepathy, often giving us glimpses of the future or moving us out of harm's way from some imminent disaster. Sometimes they take humans with them on interplanetary journeys or even on inter-dimensional journeys. It is believed by many that they have altered the normal path of evolution by intervening, through genetic engineering, in the natural evolutionary process. They mate with us and create hybrid races that live in secret locations in outer space. They appear to us in various forms, sometimes as humans and other times as forms that are alien to us. They manipulate matter and are capable of passing through solid walls, or of vanishing before our eyes. They sometimes impart information that leads to important scientific discoveries, but sometimes they create powerful visions of some horrific global disaster that is to come. But perhaps the most unnerving thing about these creatures is their attitude. They seem to feel that they are in charge of the human race and of the Earth itself. They seem to feel they own us and they have a right to do with us what they wish.

Who are they? Where do they come from? Where do they go? Why are they here? How long has this been going on? How should we react to them? What should be our response to them as a society? Should we fear them, or should we revere and even worship them? No one has the answers. Because interaction with these beings is, for the most part, on an individual basis, each person reacts to contact on a deeply primal level, and most often that reaction is sheer terror. The human mind finds it nearly impossible to grasp the notion that there are others who are greater than us. We have been so sure for so long that we are the end product of billions of years of evolution, or that we are specially made in the image of God, that we truly believe we are at the top of the food chain. Discovering otherwise can be almost too much for us to handle.

**Religious Beliefs**

Consider for a moment the quote at the top of this chapter: "Lift up a song to the rider in the clouds. His name is the Lord." What in the world does this passage from the book of Psalms mean? Are we really meant to believe that the ancient Hebrews thought that God traveled in the sky on a cloud 2,500 years or so ago when the Psalms were written? The answer to that question must obviously be "yes." And we are also meant to believe that there was a mysterious unidentified object hovering over the town of Bethlehem on the night of Jesus's birth, commonly known today as the Star of Bethlehem. In fact, the Bible is full of references to mysterious aerial phenomena, powerful heavenly entities, and their contact with the human race.

Readers of my earlier book, *The God Hypothesis: Extraterrestrial Life and Its Implications for Science and Religion*, are aware of the extensive evidence I compiled in an effort to demonstrate that much of what is written in the Bible and other ancient texts regarding contact with beings which traveled through the sky is, in fact, to be taken literally. Readers of that book are also aware of the incredible journey I began when I first undertook an investigation into UFOs and so-called "alien abductions" in 1993—a journey that would lead me to a reassessment of the Bible and the Judeo/Christian beliefs that dominate our world today, as well as the true nature of reality.

When I began my research, I was ambivalent about the nature of the modern-day UFO phenomenon, but I leaned toward the notion that the Earth was being visited and studied by strange beings from other planets, and that they would no doubt reveal themselves to us some day when we were ready to deal with such a shock. (My own UFO sighting in 1969 pretty much eliminated any notion that they did not exist.) However, very early in my research, my perceptions about these so-called aliens and about our relationship to them began to be challenged by the data I was collecting. As the larger picture of this grand mystery was gradually revealed to me and my investigating team, it dawned on me that there was something far more profound going on—something that was somehow connected to our ideas of God, angels, heaven, and the spiritual nature of man.

It was in that book that I tried to put into writing the connections between the stories of angelic visitations in the Bible (and other ancient texts) and the modern-day UFO phenomenon. It was there also that I argued for a new definition for the true nature of reality—one guided by the amazing principles discovered through the study of quantum physics. It was in quantum physics that I discovered what I believed to be the link between UFOs and Bible stories and between angelic visitations and "alien abductions." I argued that instead of being visited by aliens, the human race is, in fact, involved in an ancient, symbiotic relationship with higher beings which are somehow capable of passing easily between our world and other unknown dimensions.

I tried to demonstrate that the ancient mystics were correct in their view of the world when they described a universe populated by beings of a higher order than the human race, who interact with us at their discretion for mysterious reasons, and who guide and influence us from behind a veil of secrecy. The differences between those stories and today's, I argued, are mostly cultural, based upon modern civilization's close relationship with technology and its obsession with the teachings of modern science. As a UFO theorist, I began to align myself with the ideas of many who came before me, such as the well-known researcher Dr. Jacques Vallee; Dr. Barry Downing, author of *The Bible and Flying Saucers*; Harvard psychiatrist Dr. John E. Mack, author of *Abduction: Human Encounters With Aliens*; Raymond Fowler, author of *The Watchers;* and long-time UFO researcher and lecturer, retired U.S. Army Command Sgt. Major Bob Dean, along with many others. These are the researchers who seek to place the UFO mystery into the context of human history and who, in doing so, are able to find a deeper meaning than the commonly accepted view that aliens are here studying the human race or possibly even to invade the Earth.

I began to see that the events described by the ancient peoples of all cultures, in which they interacted with beings they called gods, angels, or demons, were no different than events described today by UFO witnesses who describe "alien" visitations sprinkled with ecstatic visions, spiritual messages, mysterious impregnations, and life-changing revelations.

To my great amazement, what began as a search for answers to the UFO and alien abduction mysteries turned into a spiritual quest to discover the truth about the secrets of the soul and the true nature of God. In the process, my previously held beliefs began to change. With each step I took, I found it necessary to alter my beliefs (sometimes grudgingly) concerning just about everything I had ever known (or thought I knew) about science, religion, and reality itself. As part of this process, I was forced to accept that there were other ways to know than through the use of what scientists call the scientific method, or through our five physical senses. For someone with a strong social-science background and a tendency toward left-brained thinking, this last step was particularly difficult.

While using hypnosis on my subjects, it became apparent to me that they were somehow accessing information that came to them from somewhere other than their own memories or imaginations. It seemed as if the person's subconscious mind could tap into a vast storehouse of knowledge • from another dimension and also communicate telepathically with higher beings. In fact, it became fairly common for my research team to communicate indirectly with such beings and to receive knowledge from them. Spontaneous past-life recollections also became something to be expected from our subjects who were searching for answers about their UFO encounters. The healing benefit they received from these memories was so profound that past-life regressions became a standard part of our methodology. It was during these past-life, or in-between-life, remembrances that the greatest truths were revealed to us and to our subjects.

## The Jesus Enigma

Then there was the Christ connection—apparitions of Jesus or knowledge about Jesus and his connection to the UFO mystery—that kept popping up in my research. Many of my subjects, as well as those I interviewed in my travels to speak at conferences, demonstrated Christ-like psychic abilities, such as precognition, clairvoyance, and hands-on healing. Some reported past-life memories of having lived at the time of Jesus and having been touched profoundly by that experience. My own past-life regression experience left me wondering if I also had a connection to Jesus in a past life. The impact of this highly personal discovery left me astonished with its implications. Somehow, I was being drawn into a research project like a scientist into his laboratory maze. I wanted very much to be the objective observer, examining the UFO subject from a safe distance, but gradually I found that I was running the maze along with the other lab rats. I felt I was being guided to discover much more than I had bargained for. I was discovering that my search for answers about the universe had landed on my own doorstep.

Amazingly synchronous events began to happen to me that seemed to demonstrate over and over that there was an invisible intelligence guiding my work. People would call me with a piece of the puzzle just as I needed an answer to an important question, or I would stumble upon a book in the library as I was aimlessly browsing through the stacks in an area that I had no conscious need to search. Certain symbols would keep popping up in strange places as if placed by invisible helpers to mark my path in the journey toward some objective I could not yet discern.

Finally, I had to admit to myself that my research was leading me, seemingly of its own volition, in a direction I could hardly have imagined when I began. The story of Jesus and the mysterious sons of God was what I was supposed to be writing about. Not only that, but I also began to understand that it was my life's purpose. It was the reason that I was born in the first place. That revelation, when it hit me, shocked me as if someone had thrown a bucket of ice water in my face. In retrospect, I could see that everything I had ever done in my life seemed orchestrated to prepare me for this mission. The implications of this revelation caused me to re-evaluate my life, my career, my goals, and my worthiness for such a task.

But as soon as I seriously considered writing a book, I began to see that actually putting it all down in writing would be a daunting task. First, trying to connect all the various pieces of this grand puzzle—UFOs, abductions, the synchronicities, the Bible, hundreds of ancient texts—seemed overwhelming. Then there was the story of Jesus. There have been thousands of books written about Jesus (more than anyone else who ever lived), each one focusing on and revealing a different facet of the Jesus story and yet failing to reveal the whole story.

"Do we really need another one?" I asked myself. The answer that kept coming back to me through prayer and meditation was "Yes." This was where my research had been leading me all along. It led me to some extraordinary conclusions, which have provoked me to pose a series of questions:

How are these mysterious beings of the ancient past related to those described in today's UFO phenomenon?

Why did both Jewish and Christian church leaders delete or change references to these beings in the Bible?

Why were other sacred scriptures, such as the Books of Enoch and the gospels of the other apostles, suppressed by the leaders of both religions?

Why has it not been acknowledged by modern-day Christian institutions that Jesus and his relative, John the Baptist, were members of the Essene sect and that the Dead Sea Scrolls describe the true origins of Christianity?

Why did research into UFOs and alien abductions lead me, and many other researchers, to see in our data a connection to the origins of the Earth's great religions and the existence of a race of ancient beings who rule the Earth?

If Jesus is the only son of God, why are there multiple references in the Bible to other sons of God?

Why did Christian authorities, under the guidance of a Roman emperor who was not Christian, delete from the Gospels of the New Testament texts that referred to reincarnation and the importance of Mary Magdalene as one of Jesus' greatest disciples?

How is it that Edgar Cayce, known as America's "sleeping prophet," was able to determine while in trance that Jesus was an Essene and that important documents would soon be found proving this was true? Cayce died in 1945, two years before the Dead Sea Scrolls were discovered and before he could have known about the Gnostic Gospels, which were discovered the year he died, 1945.

Who are these strange beings who rule the Earth from behind a veil of secrecy and what is their agenda? How do they affect life on Earth? What role do they play in our individual lives and in our deaths?

In *Rulers of the Earth,* the answers to these and many other questions are discovered, in part, by tapping into what Edgar Cayce called "a river of knowledge" that is available to the human race. Cayce tapped into that river when he was in trance, allowing his consciousness to travel anywhere in the world to diagnose the illnesses of persons he had never met. He was also able to scan the past and to see in vivid detail the lives of those who lived in various ages, including those who lived at the time of Jesus. Amazingly, Cayce's readings revealed the connection between Jesus and the Essene sect at a time when few had ever heard the word "Essene." Cayce's imagery of a vast river of knowledge is useful in understanding how this book came to be.

It is helpful to visualize sacred truth as an underground stream that occasionally bubbles to the surface, offering its waters to those who have a thirst to know the truth only to retreat underground when it is discovered by those forces dedicated to keeping it submerged. The stream of truth is always flowing and, I have found, always available to those who seek to cleanse their spirit or quench their thirst for spiritual knowledge.

## Divine Connection

For ages, long before the life of Jesus, primitive peoples understood that there were invisible beings, or spirits, who guided and manipulated their lives. Contact with them in physical or spiritual form was an accepted truth, and they lived their lives accordingly. The ancient Egyptians and Greeks understood this also, and it was during this time that in the civilized world, secret mystery schools taught that man could commune with the gods through divine inspiration, and that each person could confirm this knowledge by asking for his own revelation.

Rather than being separate from God, the schools taught, everyone and everything in the universe is a part of the God force and cannot be separated—a view not dissimilar from that of the aboriginal peoples. It taught that the God force is neither male nor female, nor does it exist in a particular location. It is rather a sublime intelligence that pervades the entire universe, both the physical and the nonphysical realms.

Just as in primitive cultures, which use various methods to enter into trance-like states of consciousness, the secret schools taught their members how to access the spiritual realms through the use of states such as those achieved today through meditation and hypnosis. In ancient times, and even in some religions today, these were considered states of spiritual ecstasy, during which the secrets of the soul, the spiritual dimensions, and the guardians of the Earth were revealed.

Those persons who demonstrated psychic abilities, who had encounters with spirit or angelic beings, or who had near-death experiences were revered as shamans whose advice could be sought on every aspect of the society's problems. In many cultures around the world, certain plants were used to induce out-of-body experiences and to commune with nonphysical entities for the purpose of obtaining spiritual knowledge.

The secrets of the soul were an important part of the mystery schools of the first- and second-century Gnostics, which passed on what they believed to be the secret teachings of Jesus. It was the school's doctrine that the soul was, in fact, the true person and that the body was merely a temporary container, convenient for experiencing the physical plane. Once the body was shed, the soul returned to the nonphysical world, where angelic beings judged whether the soul was worthy of passing to a higher level or whether it must be born once again. This process was known as the resurrection of the soul, a joyful event, likened to a prisoner being released from a dark, cold prison. Such teachings would have been a major break from the orthodox churches, both Christian and Jewish, and would have been a cause of great concern for both religious and political authorities. They would also have exposed those who taught them to great danger.

In fact, some Gnostic leaders, both Jewish and Christian, did not believe that Yahweh/Jehovah was the true God of the universe, but merely an intermediary god—the god of the physical world. They believed there was a higher, more powerful force—the God of Light—who was the creative intelligence behind the physical and nonphysical universe and that it was this higher God to whom Jesus referred when he spoke of his heavenly Father. Such radical departures from the accepted doctrines put the Gnostics in direct opposition to the orthodox authorities and ultimately cost many of them their lives.

Their beliefs in karma, other lives, and the importance of the angelic realm were also buried, not to be discovered again for nearly 2,000 years, when they reemerged from under a rock in Upper Egypt in 1945.

### Demoting the Gods

For the past three thousand years or so, authorities in both the Christian and Jewish religions have sought to diminish the power and importance of inter-dimensional beings who seem to serve as intermediaries between humans and God. It will be shown that the belief in monotheism became so fanatical in early Hebrew culture that authorities went to great lengths to destroy references to these beings. The pantheon of gods, which defined the Sumerian, Babylonian, Canaanite, and other Mesopotamian cultures, was decreed to be not gods, but merely angels, and reduced to the level of mere messengers from heaven. Drawings and clay representations of the gods were outlawed, and those teaching about them were killed. Nevertheless, belief in them by the general public did not stop.

The Jewish sect known as the Elohists made sure their beliefs in multiple gods made it into the Old Testament, where we can still read about the gods who created the Earth and all of its life forms, including humankind. If read carefully, the Book of Genesis reveals the use of the plural gods when describing the creation. Such details somehow made it into the Bible and are left for modern readers to rationalize away the best we can.

In the New Testament we find the Apostle Paul writing at length to the Colossians about what he calls "the·heresy" being taught by some that angels had an important role in the birth, life, and death of Jesus. In spite of what is written in the Gospels about the role of the angel Gabriel in announcing to the Virgin Mary that she would bear a child, or the role of angels in the resurrection of Jesus, Paul wished to minimize Christian belief in angels for fear that it could diminish belief in the power of Jesus, as God, to accomplish His mission alone.

The importance of angelic beings and the aerial phenomena that accompany their earthly visitations are central in both *The God Hypothesis* and *Rulers of the Earth* because of the obvious parallel to the UFO sightings of today. Likewise the story of the virgin birth of Jesus and his mysterious ascension into heaven in a cloud are compared to the reports of mysterious impregnations in the modern alien abduction phenomenon and to the many reports of cloud-like UFOs. Just as it seems that in ancient times UFO sightings and encounters with nonhuman beings were, of necessity, put into a religious context, it appears that today they are put into a technological context. But that doesn't necessarily mean that our interpretation of these phenomena is any more accurate than that of our ancestors. Yes, it seems as if anyone in a flying saucer was considered to be a god in ancient times, but then anyone in a flying saucer today is considered an alien. In fact every age and culture seems to have had its own interpretation of such events. The deeper I delved into my subject, the more I came to see that I was faced with an uncomfortable choice: either angels use high technology and fly around in flying saucers, or aliens do all the same things angels and demons have been reported to do throughout the ages.

## UFOs and Religion

Early in my seven years of research, I began to find cases of persons who had experienced UFO-related phenomena and who also experienced miraculous healings or escapes from death. And many felt that they had been endowed with advanced psychic abilities, including the power to heal—just as Jesus did. There were those who were not sure whether their UFO experiences were alien or angelic or demonic and those who were certain that they were, in fact, in contact with angelic beings. I also discovered many women who believed they had been mysteriously impregnated at some time during their lives by these beings and that the fetuses were removed from them early in their pregnancies. Some actually believed that their own children, or they themselves, were the products of such intervention by higher beings, not unlike the story of the Virgin birth.

But as incredible as the amazing experiences of those having UFO contact today may seem, they make perfect sense when put into the context of religious experiences reported throughout the ages. Stories handed down from ancient times, such as Ezekiel's encounter with a metallic wheel within a wheel, the prophet Elijah's heavenly voyage in God's fiery chariot, and the many accounts of contact with angelic beings, take on new meaning when examined in the light of current-day encounters. Just as today's UFO stories lend credence to the factual reliability of biblical encounters, so too do the biblical encounters support the testimony of today's credible UFO witnesses. As stated recently by Monsignor Corrado Balducci, former chief exorcist of the Roman archdiocese and a highly connected Vatican insider, "UFO witness testimony must be taken seriously by all persons of faith, for it is on faith alone that Christians today accept the testimony of those who witnessed the Crucifixion and the Resurrection."

And, if religion is bound to take UFO stories seriously, then shouldn't UFO researchers also be equally bound to accept the involvement of UFOs in religious lore? Apparently not. Only a few researchers have dared to do so. Mostly ufologists have tried to steer clear of any religious connection, preferring to see the phenomenon through the lens of modern, atheistic science so as not to be seen as unscientific by the establishment. Yet any honest examination of the UFO mystery must conclude that UFOs are not a recent phenomenon, and that acknowledgement instantly destroys the common theory that aliens from other planets are here studying the human race. What kind of study takes thousands of years? And if they are not studying us, then what are they doing? These are the central issues at stake in this obscure field that few mainstream scientists are willing to venture into.

*Rulers of the Earth*, as a companion to *The God Hypothesis*, is one man's effort to fill the void left by those who dare not tread in that middle ground between science and religion, for it is this author's fervently held belief that the center point between these two seemingly mutually exclusive disciplines is defined best by the mystery of the unidentified flying object. For those willing to share this adventure with me, I invite you into the bizarre world of UFOs, alien abductions and angelic-like visitations that might possibly unlock the hidden mysteries of the ancient past. I invite you to join me in the rediscovery of the Rulers of the Earth and the secrets of the Sons of God.

*"If you bring forth what is within you, what you bring forth will save you. If you do not bring forth what is within you, what you do not bring forth will destroy you."*

The words of Jesus
The Lost Gospel of Thomas
The Nag Hammadi Texts

CHAPTER TWO

# Altered States
## The Gnostic Way of Self-Discovery

### Going Deeper and Deeper

YOU ARE FEELING very, very relaxed," the voice whispered in my ear. "Every muscle in your body is going perfectly limp, and as you go deeper and deeper, I want you to concentrate on my voice and also on your breathing. Allow yourself to go deeper and deeper into a state of peaceful relaxation."

As the words were spoken, I felt my body sinking into the easy chair, and my will to resist the hypnotherapist's suggestions seemed to drain from my mind, as if I were in a warm bath. I went deeper and deeper, just as I was directed, taking my first plunge into the bizarre world of the unconscious mind.

Earlier that warm June evening in 1995 I had set out to meet my associates, Dr. Roberta Fennig, a psychiatrist, and a woman whom I will call Molly. She was a social worker and a recently certified hypnotherapist at Roberta's medical-center office in central El Paso, Texas. Dr. Fennig, an osteopathic physician, and I had formed a team to investigate cases of so-called "alien abductions" in 1993. Roberta had recently completed her residency in psychiatric medicine at El Paso's Texas Tech University Health

17

Science Center and had begun her private practice. A native of Chicago, she attended Loyola University to obtain a nursing degree and then the Chicago College of Osteopathic Medicine to complete her Doctorate of Osteopathic Medicine. She had worked for eight years as a psychiatric nurse in Chicago, and she believed she had seen every kind of psychiatric disorder under the sun. But she knew nothing of UFOs and alien contact.

"I really believed that I would be able to resolve the matter of alien abductions easily by simply adhering to standard psychatric evaluations," she told me shortly after meeting her first abductees. "I thought I had seen it all, and that this phenomenon must be some type of psychosis that would fit neatly into one of the many disorders known to psychiatry. That's why I stuck very closely to the procedures we use to evaluate patients. I didn't want to miss anything." But clearly Roberta was puzzled by what she found early in our investigation. I could see the wonder in her inquisitive green eyes as she strained to make sense of it. Speaking of the first case she examined, a black woman who claimed, among other things, to have seen a small gray alien with big, black, almond-shaped eyes float across her bedroom toward her while she was fully conscious, she puzzled, "I couldn't find any of the signs of delusion or hallucination in her description of what happened to her. Instead, she was suitably skeptical and even questioned her own sanity. This is not what I expected.

"The only psychiatric condition I detected was what could be called Post-Traumatic Stress Disorder (PTSD). She suffered from high anxiety and insomnia. She was really stressed about her experiences, but she wasn't delusional. Even so, I tried hard to remain skeptical through about the first fifteen cases we examined. Finally, I had to admit there must be some kind of reality behind this phenomenon. Exactly what kind of reality we were dealing with was not clear, but it did seem to be associated with UFOs. That much seemed certain."

As for myself, I had become determined to discover the truth about UFOs and alien abductions after a lifetime of curiosity about the subject and after a bizarre nighttime encounter with a strange glowing sphere when

I was an army aviator in 1969. (See *The God Hypothesis*, chapter 2.) Even though I was only a businessman and not a working scientist, I felt my Ph.D. in journalism, my journalism experience, my strong background as a social scientist, and my military training gave me a good foundation for the project. As our investigation gained momentum, it became obvious to me that learning about hypnosis was absolutely necessary. It was through hypnosis that many persons who had experienced alien contact were able to recover memories that had been suppressed because of the traumatic nature of the encounters, just as with victims of crime, car accidents, or war. However, in the majority of cases, some portion of the contact experiences was remembered consciously without the need for hypnosis. We were using hypnosis to help fill in the blanks. Procedures were instituted to test the subject's ability to be led by the therapist, to assure that what was being recalled was not something suggested in any way by the person doing the hypnosis. It has also been discovered by many researchers (and verified by our own work) that the beings themselves are able to create amnesia in the person's mind, or to cover the memories with screen memories that are used to disguise the true events. For example, the same black woman who saw the gray alien while in a fully conscious state also remembered an earlier experience when, as a child, three little bears came into her bedroom one night. She always thought that was quite strange. Under hypnosis, she was able to remember the experience and describe the three little bears as being without hair, ears, and mouths, but with very large, black eyes and pale, white skin. They obviously were not bears.

In any case, to understand how hypnosis works, I completed a course of study, became certified as a hypnotherapist, and gradually became accustomed to performing hypnosis sessions myself. Usually, Roberta, Molly, Dr. Romeo Di Benedetto (a sociology professor who ran a hypnosis clinic), or I would conduct the hypnosis, while one of the others would sit in as observer. But tonight would be different. Instead of being the objective researcher, I was the one being examined. I had decided it was time to see what it felt like to be the guinea pig.

When we set the date for this session nearly two weeks ahead of time, I thought of it as an exciting journey. Now, as I drove the darkened streets near the medical center, the massive blackness of the Franklin Mountains looming before me, apprehension and nervousness set in. What would I find? What hidden memories would I uncover? Would I embarrass myself in front of my friends and colleagues? Or would I turn out to be one of those people who are unable to relax enough to reach an altered state? What if, unbeknownst to me, I had been abducted? This is inevitably a question an abduction researcher begins to ponder as he realizes the subtlety of the phenomenon. With their amazing capabilities and technology, the beings, I have found, find it incredibly easy to whisk anyone from just about anywhere and erase all memory of the event from the person's conscious mind—like the lady who came to tell us about the time she left the mall around 6:30 in the evening heading for her mother's house, and who found herself in the next instant in another part of town going a different direction. It was after 9:00p.m. and completely dark. Nearly three hours had passed and she had no idea what had happened. She thought she was going crazy.

Under hypnosis she remembered that a large saucer-shaped craft dropped down out of the sky and took her and her car in broad daylight while others were nearby. No one ever reported a UFO. Cases like this are so abundant that some researchers have speculated that some type of force field must be used to render the craft and the car invisible.

How many persons had I met who had absolutely no inkling of their lifetime of abductions until they were in middle age? A lot. Some abduction experiences are so cleverly hidden in the dark recesses of the mind and covered over by plausible "screen memories" that their discovery is most often a tremendous shock and is often met with denial and disbelief on the part of the experiencer. Many researchers, I believe, reach the point where they realize that this could happen to anyone, even themselves. Additionally, one begins to wonder if one's involvement in UFO research is really accidental. In my case, I was beginning to understand that very little in our lives is an accident. There was an underlying reason for my involvement in this work, of that I was sure. But what was it?

Yet, as I combed my personal history for events that fit the pattern I have come to know so well, I could find precious little. There were no missing-time experiences that I knew of, but I also knew that it is very hard to detect missing time in most cases, particularly when they happen in the middle of the night. Abductions can be seamless. That is, they can leave no impression on the conscious mind. I went through the extensive list of symptoms that researchers look for in their subjects. Yes, I had seen a UFO, but many abductees have never seen a UFO, and many persons who have seen one have never been abducted. I had no unusual scars on my body. I had precious little psychic ability. I had never had an out-of-body experience. I had never had vivid dreams of aliens or UFOs. I did not feel traumatized. I had no unusual fear of the dark or other such phobias associated with the phenomenon.

## Guardian Angels

There were, however, two areas that did ring a bell. Like many abductees, I seemed to have been watched over all of my life by guardian angels. I was saved from certain death on two occasions by mysterious forces, and I had a miraculous healing in childhood. And this last amazing experience did include the appearance in our home of a heavenly being that my mother understood to be Jesus. But the dream/vision of Jesus coming to our apartment to heal me of my rickets was my mother's vision, not mine. I remembered my illness—how my ankles would turn under me when I walked; how the doctors seemed concerned as they noted the soft bones in my skull resulting from a lack of vitamin D. But I had no recollection of the actual healing. My mother told me about her vision years later.

My mother has never wavered in her story or in her absolute belief that it really happened and was not a dream. At age ninety, her recollection of the event is the same as it was when we were all much younger.

"He was wearing a red robe and had light brown wavy hair, down to his shoulders," she said. "He sat on the bed, smiled and motioned with his hand for you to come to him. "He never spoke. Then he smiled at you and put his hand on your head." That, and a few other details, was all she could remember the next morning when she woke up knowing that I had been healed. She took me to the doctor that very day for confirmation of what she already knew to be true, and, in fact, the doctor found nothing wrong with me. I never again had the symptoms of rickets. I know that I was healed.

To say the least, that event has had a quiet but powerful influence in my life. I have always felt blessed. I have always felt a close, personal relationship with Jesus, albeit a difficult one. I have never been able to see Jesus the way my church wished me to—as God. No matter how hard I tried, I could only see Him as a great man, a great teacher. There were even times as I was growing up when I questioned whether such a man had ever even existed! I spent most of my time in Bible training as a child arguing with the teachers and questioning everything I was taught. Somehow I just knew that they had no idea what they were talking about and that the Bible did not tell the whole truth. My feelings about Jesus were very private and personal and seemed to come from some deep knowingness within me.

There was something else that I rarely verbalized about my relationship to Jesus. For some strange reason, I always felt protected. I also felt that I had been chosen to carry out a special mission that would someday be revealed to me. Whether justified or not, that feeling of protection and sense of mission freed me to act boldly throughout my life—taking personal and career risks that I might not otherwise have taken. As a teenager I began a lifetime interest in fast motorcycles. I finally gave up my last motorcycle while in my fifties, and then only after some frightening close calls with almost certain death. In the military I volunteered for Army flight training and chose to serve my tour in Vietnam as a reconnaissance pilot, flying single-engine Cessnas, known as "Bird Dogs," at tree-top level above triple-canopied jungle and through deep valleys, between high, jungle-covered mountains.

It was there that I had two miraculous escapes from death, something that is quite common in UFO contact cases. In the first case, my plane was shot down by small arms fire while I was on a mission that involved dropping propaganda leaflets over a remote mountain village in the II Corps area of the Republic of South Vietnam. The Korean-War vintage, single-engine Cessna I flew cruised at 80 to 90 knots, just above the jungle canopy. We flew with the windows open for air conditioning and often fired our M-16s out the window at the enemy during skirmishes.

In this instance, my crew chief, a corporal with the unlikely name of Davy Jones, sat in the back seat of the small aircraft and held a large bag of leaflets between his legs. At my command he flung handfuls of them out the open window as we made our pass over the few straw-thatched huts in a jungle clearing. Even though we flew just above treetop level, the wind swept the leaflets too far from the intended target. Looking down, I could see a frightened woman pick up an infant and dart into a hut, just as the papers fluttered away into the nearby jungle. "Damn! We'll have to go around and do it again," I yelled at my assistant.

"No sweat, lieutenant. I still have plenty of leaflets left," Jonesy answered.

As we came back over the village the second time there were no people to be seen. The footpaths around the village also seemed deserted. "Get ready, Jonsey," I warned.

But just as I was about to give the order to throw out the leaflets, I heard a terrific BANG and the aircraft shuddered.

"Sir," Jonesy said excitedly over the intercom, "I think I just got my first purple heart!"

"What are you talking about?" I asked incredulously.

"I just took a bullet through my left thigh," he answered. "And it went right up through the roof."

Since I was strapped in tightly, and he was sitting directly behind me, there was no way for me to look at his wound, much less help him. "How bad is it?" I asked.

"It's bleeding pretty good, sir. I'm going to have to get to a hospital pretty soon."

But of course there was no hospital anywhere nearby. We were a good hour or more away from the hospital at our home base, a small airfield on the South China Sea called Phu Hiep, and I had no idea what the bullet had done to the plane. I soon found out. As I attempted a few simple turns, it became obvious that the bullet had damaged the control cables that ran along the floor, encased in a metal pipe, to the back of the plane. I couldn't test the damage completely without making maneuvers that might endanger our lives. Worse yet, I would have to go over high mountains to get back to base. There was only one alternative. I would have to call for a medivac helicopter to come for my wounded crew chief and I would have to try to land as quickly as possible. I began to gently guide the aircraft toward the only landing strip in the vicinity—a small Special Forces compound carved out of the jungle about fifteen minutes away. Gently, I maneuvered the plane over the green jungle floor, following a line of rice paddies toward the clearing where the camp was situated. It wasn't much of an airstrip. It sat at the foot of what appeared to be a giant anthill, the red Earth dotted with sandbagged bunkers and trenches. The camp's fortified walls were laid out in a triangular pattern with minefields and barbed wire protecting the Green Beret forces inside. Guard towers stood in each corner of the triangle and a small airstrip ran parallel to the northern boundary. If the place had a name, it has been long forgotten.

It was only as I tried to land the plane on the small dirt strip that the full impact of the damaged controls became evident. Even using all my strength, I could not pull the control stick back more than a few inches. Only a hundred or so feet off the ground, the nose of the airplane was pointed down toward the runway, rather than up in its correct configuration. Trying to go around by giving the plane throttle was not an option, I thought. That would simply cause us to impact the ground at a higher rate of speed—we would never make it.

I had only a few seconds to solve the problem before impact. I looked around frantically for a solution, but could think of none. All I knew at that moment was that we were going to die. Then, as if guided by someone or something else, my left hand moved to the toggle switch that controlled the electric wing flaps. My index finger exerted forward pressure on it and slowly, the wing flaps began to drop. As they did, the nose of the airplane began to rise. As the flaps went down, more air was caught beneath the plane's wings, causing the nose to go up to the approximate position it needed to be in for a successful landing. When the wheels hit the runway, an instant later, I thought for a moment we had made it. Then, the nose of the plane, still in a slightly lower position than it should have been, began to drop again, until the propeller plowed into the ground, flipping the aircraft up on its nose and finally to a standstill.

I remember looking out the side windows and seeing gasoline pouring from the wing tanks above me onto the ground and seeing the two high explosive rockets mounted under each wing. But there was no explosion. My wounded crew chief and I scrambled away safely—in my view, miraculously. I was flying again within a few days and my unfortunate crew chief was back at work in a few weeks. Only I knew what had happened in the cockpit that day. Amazingly, my hand had found that toggle switch by itself. Of that I was sure. And that switch was the only thing that saved our lives.

## The Finger of God

My second miracle in Vietnam came only a few weeks later when I was flying a mail delivery mission alone in the mountains. This was a treacherous region for small aircraft due to the high mountain peaks covered with triple-canopy jungle that would swallow up a downed aircraft, leaving no visible trace. Radio contact was entirely lost while flying in the valleys below the mountain peaks. Many a downed pilot had been lost forever in the thick foliage.

This day I was flying a solo mission near the Cambodian border, enjoying the solitude and admiring the beautiful terrain. With the sun shining and the important part of my mission complete, I could sit back and enjoy the incredible scenery on the way back to base. Sometimes in the jungle below I could see wild animals through the trees. There were monkeys, baboons, oxen, and sometimes an elephant. Muddy rivers wound their way down the jungle-covered mountains to the valley floors below, with an occasional waterfall spraying mist into the sky. All I had to do to get back to my home base on the coast of the South China Sea was to fly due east. I would follow the highway through the mountains for most of the way, maintaining a thousand feet of altitude so as to be well out of range of small arms fire. But after about forty-five minutes, the cloud cover forced my plane down lower than I wished. Now I was flying above the road, but lower than the mountain peaks on either side of me. With mountains all around, I lost all radio contact and I realized the predicament I was in. Should I go down for any reason, no one would know where to look. It began to rain hard and the clouds coming from the east were getting darker and bigger, making me uneasy. Then I saw the mountain pass before me was blocked by clouds. I could go no further.

Although I was quite capable of flying on instruments, which would be necessary to get over the mountains, there was a problem. The "Bird Dogs" were old and their instruments unreliable. We were trained to fly by the seat of our pants rather than to rely on the aged altimeters and compasses or the antiquated gyros and radio homing devices. In fact, we were not permitted to fly on instruments at all for safety's sake. So, reluctantly, I turned the plane around and headed back. But after a short while, even that option had been eliminated. I was caught in a fast-moving storm that was quickly reducing my visibility to zero. There was only one thing to do—violate orders and risk going on instruments. I would have to take the plane through the clouds to the top, whatever altitude that might be. Since the plane was not equipped with oxygen, I hoped that the top would not be too high.

Banking the aircraft gently while applying throttle and pulling back on the control stick, I focused intently on my instruments. Slowly, the plane circled upward through the clouds for nearly thirty minutes before breaking out into glorious sunshine—the dazzling bright tops of the clouds created a snow-white wonderland all around me. My altitude was over ten thousand feet. I wouldn't need oxygen at this altitude, but I knew I was very lucky. It could have been twenty thousand or more than thirty thousand feet, and I didn't want to find out if conditions were going to change. I needed to get down soon.

At that altitude I was able to establish radio contact with my base and confirm my worst fears. This was no ordinary thunderstorm. It was a monsoon that had the whole country covered with clouds and torrential rains. The airfields were closed, and in any case, did not have instrument landing equipment. An Air Force base further north might be willing to help me with an instrument approach, but with my instruments, such an attempt would be crude and very dangerous. Additionally, I was hesitant to call attention to the fact that I had been forced to violate orders. Calling in for an instrument landing at an Air Force base could bring unnecessary attention. "Better leave that as a last resort," I thought to myself.

Instead, I continued my eastward path, toward the ocean, thinking that once I was over the ocean, I could begin a gradual descent without worrying about the jagged mountains below. If all went well, I would come out of the clouds, and I would see the ocean in time to level the plane out. Then I could fly back toward land and hopefully make landfall where there were no mountains or cliffs to run into. For now, all I could do was steer the plane eastward and pray for a miracle. Maybe there would be a break in the clouds that would allow me to descend. But if there were, it would have to be over the ocean, for any descent over land would be too dangerous. I flew on and hoped and prayed. As far as I could see in any direction there was a solid blanket of clouds covering the Earth. They seemed to stretch all the way to Japan.

Finally, my navigation instruments indicated that I was getting near the coast. I would fly another twenty minutes or so, just to be sure, and then begin my descent, I thought. In desperation I kept looking for a break in the clouds, but there was none. This was a big storm and it would last a long time—longer than my plane could stay in the air before running out of gas.

Then, suddenly, off to my right, I saw it. Could it be? I wondered incredulously. I banked the plane to the south and approached what seemed to be an impossible sight. There was a hole in the clouds—a perfectly round hole, maybe one hundred yards or so in diameter. As I flew over the hole, I could see straight down more than ten thousand feet. It was a perfectly round tunnel in the clouds, as if God himself had stuck his finger through them. And way down below, I could see an amazing thing. Not mountains or jungle and not ocean, but ocean waves breaking on the beach! It was the exact spot I needed to see to confirm that I should descend.

As they say in the movies, I didn't need an engraved invitation. I quickly pulled back on the throttle and simultaneously did a wing over, putting the plane into a steep, spinning dive. It was a daredevil act borne of sheer desperation. I kept the plane in a controlled dive, keeping the needle on the airspeed indicator pegged to its maximum allowable position and praying that the hole did not close in on me and that the wings stayed on the airplane. I spiraled downward and downward for what seemed an eternity, all the while watching as the sides of the tunnel held firmly. It was like the movie "The Ten Commandments," when Moses parted the Red Sea for the Israelites. Some mysterious force seemed to hold back the clouds for me as I plummeted to the ground.

Finally, I reached the bottom. I leveled out and found myself only a few miles south of my base with barely enough visibility below the clouds to make it to home base along the coast. As I looked up through the Plexiglass window above me to gaze once more at the amazing hole in the clouds, I saw the tunnel dissolve before my very eyes. The hole closed in a matter of seconds, leaving only dark, billowing clouds above me. Had I hesitated but a few seconds, I would surely have been caught in the clouds in the middle of a hair-raising spin. But I was safe. Within minutes I was landing on my unit's airstrip, near the village of Phu Hiep.

On arrival in the operations room the other pilots gathered around me. "How in the hell did you get in here?" they asked. "No one has been able to fly for most of the day!"

"Well," I said, "I didn't have any problems." I knew they would never believe my story. So I just left it at that. In either case, they would have been bewildered. I just let them believe the most believable of the two choices. Either there had been a miracle or I was an amazingly good aviator. It was probably a tossup which story they would have believed, given the choice, but this way seemed at the time the easiest way to leave it. It would serve as just one more instance, for those who knew me well, of my incredible luck. "That Joe," my friends and family have always said, "He's the luckiest guy!"

## Flying to the Past

In any case, my life's experiences did not seem to me to be comparable to those of the abductees I had studied or of those I had read about. I really did not fit the pattern that I recognized so easily in others. My real purpose for undergoing hypnosis, I told Roberta and Molly, was to see what it was like to be the one in the chair. That would help me do a better job as a hypnotherapist.

But what, specifically, did I want to deal with during this session, they asked. "Let's see if I have any hidden memories of the healing experience with Jesus," I said. "Then, if there is time, let's explore past-life memories."

Past-life memories were a topic that I had become interested in since learning to work with hypnosis. Time and again, our subjects, under hypnosis, would have spontaneous memories of previous lives. This was not something we were soliciting, and that made them all the more interesting and perplexing. I had never had strong feelings about reincarnation and, until I began sitting in on hypnosis sessions and witnessing the strong emotional content of the memories our subjects were uncovering, I had no reason to believe in it. But now, I had to admit, I was seeing it as a strong possibility.

Molly, who had worked with us on other cases, would do the hypnosis tonight, to get the experience. However, when it came to recovering past lives, we were all just learning, so I was feeling a bit apprehensive. Roberta would observe and scrawl questions and comments on a notepad for Molly to read as the session progressed. Using standard hypnotic induction techniques, Molly had me concentrate on my breathing and visualize a beautiful beach scene. Soon I was feeling very relaxed as she helped me to go deeper and deeper into the hypnotic state. Gradually, Molly began to approach the subject at hand.

"Go back in your memory to the time when you were a child and it was discovered that you had a bone disease," she suggested.

As she said the words, I could see the bedroom that we lived in at the time, in my mind's eye—my parents sleeping on a double bed in the middle of the bedroom, sheer curtains blowing gently in the breeze, near an open window. I was in my crib against the wall opposite the window. We lived in a one-bedroom apartment on the third floor of an old apartment building, across the street from the train depot. Behind the train tracks was the Rio Grande River and beyond that was the city of Juarez, Mexico. Small adobe shacks were sprinkled haphazardly over the barren hills rising on the other side of the river.

But try as I might, I could discover no memories of the healing event or of any other childhood event that might be associated with alien contact. So, having tried and failed to discover anything unusual, Molly went on to explore past lives.

"Imagine a beautiful garden," she said, employing once again a standard technique. The subject is asked to create a garden in his imagination and to create a path through the garden. The subject is allowed to walk leisurely down the path, admiring the flowers, trees, and foliage, until he comes to a doorway.

Behind the door, it is suggested, the subject will behold a scene or a symbol that will have meaning for him. He is to allow himself to reflect on the symbol or scene and to find meaning.

However, in my case, Molly didn't even have to finish her instructions. As soon as she mentioned the garden I consciously knew that we were beginning to deal with past lives. Immediately, an image appeared before my eyes. It was a cross—or more accurately, the silhouette of a crucifix. It was floating right in front of my face. Then, it began to move away from me, as if flying into the distance, pulling me with it.

Molly was still talking about the garden when I interrupted her. "I see a cross. It's flying away from me and pulling me along."

"Follow it," Molly said.

Then, the crucifix disappeared, and I saw a scene clearly before my eyes (or third eye) It was a beach. But unlike the beautiful beach I had imagined earlier during the relaxation exercise, this beach was bleak and void of vegetation and life.

"I see a beach with small waves and lots of salty foam in the water. It's like a desert—a desert with a beach."

"What else do you see?" Molly prodded.

I see some old clay jars—a row of jars. They're tall. They're lined up near the shoreline. They're very old."

"Where is this?" Molly asked.

"I don't know. Maybe it's the Sea of Galilee," I said, allowing my conscious mind to try to find a connection between the crucifix and the beach. But I quickly corrected myself, as if a part of me really knew where the beach was. "No, no, I think it must be the Dead Sea."

"Do you see yourself?" Molly asked.

"No, only the jars and the small waves." At this point my perspective was still from above. It was as if I were floating above the scene looking down. There were no people in the scene.

Then, Molly made a common mistake, one made by many hypnotherapists, which is normally quite harmless. She asked a leading question. (A person undergoing hypnotherapy, I have found, can hardly ever be led to believe something that is not in his or her memory.) In the excitement of the moment, Molly asked:

"Is this at the time of Christ?"

"I don't know," I said, feeling anxious.

Then, Molly asked two more leading questions which, unbeknownst to her, were powerful cues for me.

"Were you there? Did you know Him?"

The questions triggered no specific memory. The scene did not change. Yet the words did trigger something—something that came from deep within my soul.

It was as if a tidal wave of emotion had swept me away. I began to sob uncontrollably. I sobbed and sobbed until I became embarrassed and tried to open my eyes to come out of the trance. But I had no idea what I was crying about. I had never experienced such a thing before. I had no memory connecting the crying to anything. All I knew was that I was feeling a strange mixture of terrible sorrow and overwhelming love and a deep pain, and I didn't know where it came from. This was an emotional outburst from the darkest depth of my soul. I had touched a nerve I never knew I had. My session ended abruptly, and it would be many years before I would be willing to approach that threshold of pain and sorrow again. Yet I had learned a great deal about myself through that experience.

When I finally recovered and I was fully out of the trance, we sat for a long time and tried to figure it all out. I recounted the vision and what it could have meant.

"It was a cross, like a crucifix," I said. "And it was floating right in front of my face, like a 3-D picture in the movies. Then it took off, like it was flying fast into the distance and it was pulling me behind it. I felt as if I was flying into the past. Then the cross was gone and I saw a beach. It was a desert environment. It was sandy and there was no vegetation. There was salty foam on the water and small waves were lapping up on the beach. There was a row of tall clay urns, the color of the sand, standing on the beach. There were six or seven of them. Each of them had been sealed with a cap made of clay, like an inverted bowl."

I knew what they were. They were like the pictures I've seen of the jars that the Dead Sea Scrolls were buried in. "I think the scene was of the Dead Sea in ancient times, at the time of Christ."

"What is the connection between Jesus and the scrolls?" they asked.

"I don't know. No one seems to know. They were buried about the time of Christ, but from what I have read, they seem to have been written before," I said. I explained that I had a strange fascination with the scrolls since high school, and I had read a book or two about them. I knew that they were still a big mystery, even to the experts.

"There hasn't been any direct connection between Jesus and the Essenes who lived on the shore of the Dead Sea, as far as I know. They are the ones who are believed to have buried the jars in the caves above their compound. It is called Qumran."

"Who were they?" Molly asked.

"No one really knows. They are thought to have been a radical Jewish sect that believed in strict adherence to the laws of Moses. They shared everything and lived ascetic lives. They had no worldly possessions. They kept to themselves and apparently guarded a huge library of sacred texts. There were hundreds of scrolls discovered in several caves there in 1947. Many more are thought to exist still in caves yet to be uncovered."

"Then the scrolls don't mention Jesus?"

"No, they don't mention him. But there are many similarities between the Essenes as portrayed in the scrolls and the life of Christ. He too urged people to forsake the material world and he lived a life of poverty as an example to others. Jesus and the Essenes wore white robes, and the scrolls describe the community's ritual meal in which the accepted members of the group drink from a cup of wine and break bread together. That's a lot like what happened at the Last Supper."

"Weren't they all killed in the end?" asked Roberta.

"It's thought that they were massacred by the Romans, just like at Masada, in about A.D. 68, around the time of the destruction of Jerusalem. One thing is for sure, they never came back to get the scrolls. They were either killed or driven away for a long, long time."

"So what do you think this means?" Roberta asked. "What does it mean to you?"

"It makes me think there is a greater connection between Jesus and the Essenes than the experts know. It makes me think that I am somehow connected to that time. And it makes me think that my interest in UFOs is also connected somehow. I just wish I knew how to connect all the pieces. Maybe it's telling me to look deeper into the mystery of the scrolls."

"Well, we can try this again. We can have another session to try to get past that emotional block," Roberta suggested.

"I don't know," I said warily. "After what I've been through tonight I think it's going to be a while before I'm ready to go there again. We'll just have to see. I have never experienced emotions so powerful. It's hard to take. I'm beginning to understand why I always get emotional whenever I talk about Jesus or my belief in him. I get all choked up, even when I try to say a prayer out loud. That's why I don't like to say grace at the dinner table in front of others."

"How long has that gone on?" asked Roberta (always the psychiatrist).

"Since I was a kid. Oh, wow! I just remembered something else. When I was small, maybe four or five years old, there was a church on Montana Street, I think it's still there, but at that time it had a large sign in the shape of a cross, mounted perpendicular to the face of the wall. It was outlined in blue neon light, and at night, when we drove by, I thought it was the saddest thing I had ever seen. Every time I saw it I would get this terrible feeling of sadness. It was so bad that I would beg my parents not to go down that street. They would just laugh. They couldn't understand. Finally, they agreed to let me know ahead of time when we were near the cross so that I could hide on the floor of the car. I hated that cross, or at least the way it made me feel. I hid from it the rest of my childhood. Later, when I was older and had to drive past it, I would just not look at it. I still wouldn't want to see it if I could help it."

"Hmm, that's very interesting," said Roberta.

In the months and years after that night I contemplated the meaning of my vision and of my strong emotional outburst. I debated what it might signif,y with my rational mind not wanting to accept what my heart was telling me. I felt it was too great a responsibility to have taken part in perhaps the most important event in human history. I felt unworthy. I also felt embarrassed that anyone might find out about this for fear they would think I was trying to make myself seem important. But in fact, the last thing I wanted was to be important, at least not in this way. I began to list all the arguments against it.

First, I reasoned, if it wasn't my imagination at work, it might simply be that we are all able, under hypnosis, to tap into the so-called "collective unconscious" that Carl Jung wrote about. Maybe it's possible to tune into past events and see them through the eyes of those who lived through them. But the more I considered the possibility of reincarnation, the more it made sense to me. The idea of the evolution of the soul through trial and error over many lifetimes made infinitely more sense to me than having only one opportunity and being damned forever if you made a mistake. Besides, by then I had already read too many good books on the subject that documented case after case in which a person's past-life memories could be verified, down to minute details. Well then, if this was a past-life memory, I reasoned, many people must have been around Jesus during his lifetime. I could have been a passerby—someone of no importance. I could live with that idea.

But the biggest argument I kept coming back to was that I didn't have any specific memory of being with Jesus. In fact, after reviewing the audiotape of the hypnosis session, it was clear that my emotional reaction came just after the hypnotherapist asked me: "Were you there? Did you know Him?" Over the years I have learned that the much-maligned leading question in hypnotherapy is overly criticized. In fact, I have found that persons under hypnosis are very difficult to lead. Today I regularly try to lead my subjects intentionally away from aspects of the abduction phenomenon I know to be true. For example, I might ask them if the aliens have blue eyes or black hair when I know that most have black eyes and no hair. This is done just to check to see if the subject is suggestible. I have never found them to be. They always correct me and stay true to their memories.

Nevertheless, in this case, the questions resulted in the termination of the session and in no further information coming forth. (Years later, I took a course through the American Institute of Hypnotherapy and became certified as a past-life regression therapist. And many years later, I would work up the courage to delve once again into my own subconscious and to face that wall of emotion that assaulted me that memorable summer night.)

The experience left me with many unanswered questions. It left me wondering if my reaction could have been the result of my own personal feelings about Jesus, rather than a past-life memory. But if this was so, the teary outburst seemed way out of proportion to the questions asked. I was left thinking that I would feel more comfortable about linking my emotional reaction to a past life if I had a distinct memory to go with it. Clearly, further hypnotic regression was called for; however, I wasn't eager to face that inner part of myself again, and I wasn't sure that I would ever be ready.

I went home that night astonished that my research into UFOs had taken such a strange turn. Was it me? I kept wondering. Was I just inserting my own beliefs into the research, or was I being guided toward the truth? I thought about the prayer I recited regularly.

"Lord," I often prayed, "I want to know the truth, wherever it leads me. I promise I can take it. If you show it to me, I won't reject it, no matter how difficult it is to accept." But now that I was deep into my research, I found myself not wanting to accept what I found. My rational mind wanted to be objective and consider all possibilities. I needed confirmation from other sources to appease that side of me. What I resisted admitting, at first, was that I already had received confirmation of sorts from a case I had been working on. An inner voice kept asking: "What about Alicia? What about that?"

*"Then Jesus told all of the people to sit down on
the ground, and he took the seven loaves and the
fish, and gave thanks to God for them, and divided
them into pieces, and gave them to the disciples
who presented them to the crowd. And everyone
ate until full—4,000 men, besides the women and
children. And afterwards, when the scraps were
picked up, there were seven basketfuls left over."*
—Matthew 15:35–38

CHAPTER THREE

# The Case of Alicia
## A Lesson in Karmic Destiny

ALICIA (NOT HER REAL NAME) is a highly educated and successful health professional whom Roberta brought to a Mutual UFO Network meeting soon after the MUFON El Paso Chapter was organized in 1993. It was through these meetings that we met many of the UFO experiencers who became our subjects. But in this case, Alicia and Roberta had been friends for several years before Roberta became familiar with the symptoms and characteristics of those experiencing nonhuman contact.

It began when Alica confided in Roberta about difficulties she was having with her eight-year-old son. "He is terrified of the dark," she said. "He can't sleep alone in his room, so he's been sleeping with us at night. He complains that strange people or creatures come into his room when he's alone."

"So," Roberta asked, "what do you think is happening?"

"I don't know, but I don't think he is making it up. He is a very bright and sensible kid. Besides, there have been other things going on in the house for a long time."

"Like what?"

"Well, there have been strange banging noises and the sound of footsteps in the middle of the night. We've all heard them—my husband and my daughter too."

By then, Roberta was alert to the signs of what had come to be known as "alien abduction," but she never suspected that her good friend, or anyone she knew, for that matter, was involved. She decided to invite Alicia to a MUFON meeting and to introduce her to me.

I remember well the day Roberta brought Alicia to the meeting, which was held on a Saturday afternoon in a classroom at the El Paso Community College. Alicia arrived late and she slid into the room quietly, as I was introducing the topic of discussion. At the moment I didn't know who she was, because the meetings were open to the public and announced in the newspaper, so it could have been anyone. But the moment I saw her, I was sure I knew her from somewhere. Her demeanor, her big, brown eyes, and her olive skin all seemed very familiar. Those eyes seemed to me to hold deep secrets and innate wisdom. She appeared to be in her mid-thirties, and as I grew to know her, I found her to have a spirited, independent personality and an aura of compassion about her. I soon discovered she was not only a health professional, but she was also a natural healer.

Alicia was working in a hospital as a speech therapist, and she had a reputation among both doctors and nurses as something of a miracle worker. Often, doctors would bring her cases they had given up on—stroke victims, accident victims, persons with deformities and other "hopeless" cases. "See what you can do with him," they would plead.

While investigating her case, I went to observe her in her work so that I could understand fully what it was she did. Once, I observed as she taught a six-year-old boy to speak. He had been born deaf, and his parents were desperate to have him talk. I watched as she patiently held his jaw gently in her hand and helped him mouth different sounds. With love and humor she coaxed the first few sounds from him. Before long, he said his first word: "Mom." The delight in his face at his success was amazing to see, and it was very affecting to realize that his mother would soon hear her child say the one thing she had been longing to hear.

"How do you do it?" I asked her.

"I don't know," she said. "I've been trained, of course, but the truth is I just know what to do. Sometimes I can just 'see' into people and know what's wrong and what to do about it. Sometimes I just put my hands on them and they are better."

She went on to describe many of the patients she had healed by simply touching them and extending her energy toward them. At the time, I had not yet heard of cases where UFO contactees exhibited these same abilities, or if I had, it hadn't sunk in. But seeing it in person was something I couldn't brush aside easily.

We spoke at length about her life and her childhood, and soon I began to recognize the pattern of one who had contact with not-of-this-world forces.

"My son believes he can fly," she once confided in me. It was obvious she was very concerned about him.

"What did you tell him?"

"I told him he could, but I didn't know how."

"Why did you tell him that?"

"Because I have always known that I could fly. I know that sounds crazy, but since I was a child, I have had the same belief, although I realize it's impossible. I have vague memories of flying when I was a little girl. And, I have vivid dreams about it. I couldn't lie to him. I try to be honest with him, because he is so smart that he knows when I am not truthful."

I had heard other UFO experiencers tell me the same thing. One man I interviewed told me that he would jump off the roof of his house as a child because he was sure he could fly. UFO researchers have come across this belief often in their cases and they speculate that it comes from subconscious memories of being taken up to a spacecraft by aliens, often in a beam of light. Under hypnosis, contactees often remember having been floated through the air, high above the treetops and rooftops to an awaiting craft. Often they remember being taken right through the roof or through a wall, as if they, themselves, or the wall were not solid. Such memories often come out in dreams, along with others, such as surgical procedures and alien faces.

"If he is being taken," Alicia asked, "how can I help him? He's terrified. Can you do hypnosis on him?"

"No," I answered, "we don't do hypnosis on children. But we can do hypnosis on you."

Alicia's eyes widened. "Why me?"

"Well," I explained, "you seem to have had similar experiences. Researchers believe that this phenomenon runs through families. How can you help him if you don't understand your own experiences? Once you understand what your role is and what it's all about, then you will be able to help him by giving him the support and comfort he needs. Don't you agree?"

I could see Alicia pondering the idea and coming to grips with the dilemma. "Yes," she finally responded, "I see what you mean. I had never considered that this was something that involved me. I don't even believe in UFOs or aliens!"

"Well, I don't think it's necessary to believe in those things to undergo hypnosis. Actually, your skepticism is good. It shows you aren't fabricating this. If you're right, we won't find anything and we can rule UFOs out as a cause of the problem. Besides, Roberta is a psychiatrist and she will be there to make sure it is done correctly. She will be the judge about what is going on. You trust her, don't you?"

"Of course I do. She's one of my best friends. And I trust you too," she added. "But who would do the hypnosis?"

"Dr. Romeo Di Benedetto has volunteered to work with us. Do you know him?"

"Yes," she said, her eyes lighting up. "He's a wonderful man. I would trust him completely." And so, she ended up deciding that she would undergo hypnosis, even though she was obviously frightened of what she might find.

### Alicia's Hypnosis (March 3, 1994)

Alicia's case was one of the first cases of so-called"alien abduction I had the opportunity to study in depth, and it was the first time I had a chance to observe a hypnosis session. I had no inkling when we entered the simple, suburban home of Dr. Di Benedetto that evening in the spring of 1994 that the experience would jolt my senses and my perceptions of reality in profound ways.

Romeo volunteered to conduct the session as a favor to me and because he was, by nature, an open-minded and courageous explorer of the subconscious mind. He had been, many years before, a Catholic priest, but when he fell in love with his wife, Vicki, who was a nun at the time, they decided to leave the Church, marry, and raise a family. Together, they began exploring their spirituality through meditation, prayer, and eventually hypnosis. By the time I met him, he had received a doctorate in education and was a full-time professor at the El Paso Community College. He served as director of the college's Emerging Renaissance Lecture Series and cable TV program. His guest lecturers ranged from astronauts to psychics to Native American shamans, and all sorts of persons who had experienced unusual phenomena. He was also a certified hypnotherapist and owned the Southwest Hypnotherapy Clinic, which he operated at night and on weekends. His slight figure and graying beard, together with his humble demeanor, reminded me of Paul, the Apostle. He emanated empathy and a calm understanding and acceptance of his subject's experiences. But he had never had a subject who had alien experiences. In fact, as it turned out, he had never had a subject quite like Alicia.

Together with us that evening was my co-researcher, Dr. Roberta Fennig, who had already performed psychiatric examinations on several cases we were working on and was certain that Alicia was a highly functional and rational person. Her role in the investigation team was invaluable. She became involved in the project the night her architect husband had dragged her to a lecture on UFOs at the community college. She had no previous experience with those having nonhuman contact, but she had a curious mind and the sensibility of a true scientific explorer, so she quickly volunteered to provide free psychiatric screening for the case studies we were encountering. She was sure, at the time, that she would quickly uncover tell-tale signs of psychiatric disorders in our subjects, solve the mystery, and be on with her normal life. In the weeks and months ahead, however, she first became puzzled because she did not find evidence of hallucination, delusion or, in fact, any mental illness in our subjects, and then she became frustrated as she found that in order to fit these cases into her reality as a psychiatrist, her own paradigm had to be adjusted. Nevertheless, she was an excellent investigator.

She and her husband were not active in any religion at the time. She had been raised a Catholic, a religion strongly rooted on her father's side of the family, but her mother's roots were Jewish, originating along the Polish/Russian border, where her family had lived years before. At the time of our meeting, she found she was attracted to her Jewish roots. She had explored the local Jewish community, trying to find a comfortable place to search for spiritual growth. But, as we began our investigation, her scientific training took center stage, as did mine. However, deep down, we both felt a little more comfortable knowing we had a former priest on our team, just in case we turned up something for which we were not fully prepared.

By the time we undertook our investigation, I understood a great deal about the characteristics of alien abductions, and I could readily see that Alicia's case bore close resemblance to the many hundreds of well-documented cases studied by such experts as Dr. John Mack; Budd Hopkins, author of *Missing Time* and *Intruders*; and numerous other highly qualified researchers. The pattern I observed fit so many cases I had read about: poltergeist-like activity in the home, night terrors, vivid flying dreams, healing or psychic abilities, and even a strong skepticism about UFOs. Additionally, Alicia was exceptionally concerned that our investigation and our findings be kept in strictest confidence. She was horrified that it might get out that she or a member of her family had encountered UFOs or aliens, as were most of our subjects. As a result, we agreed not to reveal her name.

Interestingly, Alicia was a Mexican-American woman who, like Roberta, had been raised in a family in which one parent was Christian (in this case Catholic) and the other Jewish. That was one of the shared interests that had brought them together as friends in the first place. As an adult, she chose to practice Judaism and worked hard to bring up her two children in the Jewish tradition. She had long ago decided that Jesus was not God and, therefore, he was not relevant to her life.

## Screen Memories

When Alicia arrived at Romeo's modest, suburban home that evening, she appeared relatively calm, but expressed distress about going under hypnosis. "I am worried this is going to be a waste of your time. I don't think we are going to turn up any UFOs," she said as she sat on the living room couch. "But I've thought it over and I think I would like to find out something that has bothered me for years. It has to do with a recurring dream I have had since I was a little girl—since I was about five or six years old."

"Fine," said Romeo. "Tell us about it."

"Well," she began, "it always starts when I am being led by the hand by a little, skinny, white boy down a path that leads to an old house. Then, when we get inside, I find myself surrounded by a group of hooded men that I have always thought of as prophets. The next thing that happens is that there is an operation room and I witness some kind of operation. That's all I remember."

"Okay then," Romeo said. "That's where we will start. We will just see where that takes us. Are you ready?"

And with that, Alicia made herself comfortable, lying on the couch, as Romeo began the gradual process of putting her into a very relaxed state—one in which she felt totally safe and protected. Soon, her breathing slowed and she swooned into a deep state of hypnosis. Romeo then asked her to go back to the first time she had the dream in question and to begin by describing how it started.

"I'm with a boy, it seems like," she whispered. "He's a very skinny, white boy. He's not much taller than I am."

"How old are you?" asked Romeo.

"About five," she answered. "He's taking me down a path to an old cabin."

"Go ahead," Romeo said. "What happens next?"

"We go into a room. We're waiting for something to happen." (Being in a waiting room is a common event described in UFO cases.)

"Oh," she remarked with surprise, "there's a window that looks into another room. We're waiting for something to happen. The window is the kind you can see through, but the people on the other side can't see you. It looks like an operating room." (Operating rooms and even viewing areas behind windows are also common descriptions in UFO cases.)

I began to recognize that Alicia's story had another common element found in abduction cases. This has to do with what are called "screen memories." Often the person tries to fit the experience into what they know or have experienced. It is even thought that the aliens actually telepathically suggest they remember something commonplace, rather than a spaceship and aliens. Here, Alicia was remembering going into an old cabin with a small, white boy. But, amazingly, the interior of the cabin suggests something quite different. Old cabins generally do not have operating rooms and one-way glass. The beings disguise their appearance to the little girl. She thinks of the gray alien who is almost always the escort as a small, white, skinny boy, and the aliens are shrouded in hoods.

"There are a group of men with hoods gathered around an operating table. That's funny," she says with a bit of alarm in her voice. "They're holding shiny instruments in their hands. There's a man on the table. They're going to operate on his leg." She gasped, becoming agitated.

"It's okay," Romeo said, trying to calm her. "Just see what happens."

"Oh no!" she screamed. "They're taking off his leg! That's not how to do it! Let me do it; you don't have to cut him." Here, Alicia begins to sob and has to be calmed down by Romeo. It is obvious that she is reliving a real experience. No dream could elicit such emotion.

"What happens next?" Romeo coaxes her.

"They won't let me go in. There is blood all over the place. It's horrible. They took his leg off!" she cries.

"What happens next?" Romeo asks, trying to get her past the worst of the experience.

"Now a door opens with a whish, like it's electric or something, it just slides into the wall and a man with a hood comes in. He's their leader. He's a prophet. No, he's more than a prophet. He taught me how to heal people. I tell him, 'I wanted them to let me help do it the right way. They did it all wrong!'"

"What's his name?" Romeo asks.

"I can't say."

"Why?"

"It's a conflict."

"What kind of conflict?"

"It's just a conflict—a conflict."

"Okay then," Romeo asks. "Then what happens?"

"Oh, this doesn't seem right. Now I am lying on a table and the rest of them are all around me. I feel pressure down here," she said, touching her lower abdomen with both hands. "They're hurting me! They're hurting my ovaries! They like me. I'm a good mother. I've had many babies." (Alicia seems to be remembering other times when she was older. It is quite common for women to remember having given birth to babies aboard ships as part of some kind of genetic breeding program.)

"Can you see them clearly now? What do they look like?"

"No," Alicia answers. "They have hoods on; their faces are dark."

"Well concentrate on their faces. Just take a peek and see if you can see what they look like."

Suddenly, Alicia bolts straight up, eyes closed, and lets out a tremendous shriek—"Agghhhhhhhh!"

I nearly fell out of my chair as I recoiled with shock.

"They don't look the same anymore! They have bony, hollow faces and long fingers. They have white skin, no hair and big, black eyes!"

Now she begins to panic and she starts crying. Frightened, she speaks in the voice of a child, reverting back to her childhood experience on that table.

"You shouldn't look like that—you're scaring a little girl!"

Then she let out another long shriek and started to sit up again. Once again I was almost jolted out of my chair.

Romeo struggled to calm her down and to get her to lie down again. When she finally did, he suggested, "Okay, now you know everything came out all right, you're safe. You can go back and remember what happened."

But Alicia was gone. Instead, the person speaking was someone else. And she was speaking French, a language that Alicia did not know! Although I had taken a course in French in college and I could recognize it when I heard it, I couldn't understand the meaning, nor could Romeo or Roberta. The woman speaking was an old woman and she was going on about something we couldn't make sense of.

"Can you speak in English please?" Romeo asked. "We don't understand what you are saying. What's your name?"

The woman on the couch began to speak in halting English with a heavy accent. "I am Larrie Marquis du Bois," she said.

"Where do you live?"

"I live in the forest near Paris. I live in my father's house. He is the Marquis du Bois. He is a doctor. I am also a doctor, but not like him. I did not go to school to learn to heal. I heal with my hands."

"What year is it?"

"1700," she answered.

And so it went for the next half hour or so. She described in great detail her life in that time and the beautiful home she lived in. Finally, Romeo brought the session to an end by gradually bringing Alicia back to a conscious state and suggesting to her that she would be calm and fully awake. After a few minutes, Alicia was back, seeming relaxed and composed as we discussed the events of the evening.

"Wow," she exclaimed, "that was really weird. But it does explain why I have always felt compelled to go live in France. Now I know why."

"What about the prophet?" I asked. "You said he was more than a prophet. Who was he and what was the conflict you talked about?"

"I can't say," she responded, lowering her eyes. "There's a conflict for me. It's personal."

"Is it because you're Jewish?" I guessed.

"Yes."

"Was it Jesus?"

Alicia lowered her head and nodded in the affirmative. Finally, she said, "Yes, it was."

We all looked at one another expecting someone to say something, but no one did. We didn't know what to say or what to make of it. Was Jesus involved in the abduction phenomenon? Or was this also a screen memory, implanted in her mind to make her feel comfortable? Alicia's memories of having babies and being probed by nonhuman entities matched perfectly the abduction scenario, but Jesus? What was he doing there? Were her memories of that event intertwined with other past-life memories? I, for one, had to know more. So we ended the evening by scheduling another session for a few weeks later.

When we met the next time, it didn't take Romeo long to get Alicia into a deep trance. She also was anxious to learn more about her experiences. Romeo took her back to the old house where she had seen the prophet and asked about him. Suddenly, she was in another place and another time.

"This is a long, long time ago," she whispered. "I'm walking with him and there are hundreds of people sitting on the ground and on hillsides all around. I am told to take a basket and to give the people food. I'm walking through the crowd and as I walk I reach into the basket, under the cloth, and bring out bread. I give it to the people and then I walk some more, but the basket never gets empty. There's always more bread. I don't understand how this is happening. All the people get fed."

"Why are the people there?" Romeo asks.

"To hear him speak."

"Do you see him?"

"Yes, I see his face," she says, starting to weep.

She holds her hands up as if caressing something, an expression of love and compassion on her face, tears streaming down her cheeks. "I'm holding his face in my hands."

*"There were three who always walked with the*
*Lord: Mary, his mother, and his sister, and Mag-*
*dalene, the one who was called his companion.*
*Mary Magdalene, [he] loved her more than all the*
*disciples, and he used to kiss her often on the*
*[mouth]. The rest of the disciples...said to him,*
*'Why do you love her more than all of us?' "*

The Lost Gospel of Philip
The Nag Hammadi Texts

CHAPTER FOUR
# Strange Synchronicities Illuminate the Path

A FEW MONTHS after my own hypnosis session, in June 1995, I was asked to speak at the first International UFO Congress in Mexico City. It was to be a huge affair with thirty-six speakers from all over the world and a crowded auditorium at one of the city's large medical centers. Rita Perregrino (one of the subjects whom I had worked with in El Paso) and I were both invited to speak by the energetic organizer of the event, Zita Rodriquez, publisher of the popular UFO magazine, *Reporte Ovni*.

Among the many speakers at the weeklong conference was someone with whom I was anxious to speak. Robert O. Dean is one of the more popular and charismatic speakers on the UFO conference circuit, blending a government insider's knowledge of the UFO reality with a highly spiritual perspective on its implications. Dean is a highly-decorated Army veteran of two wars (Korea and Vietnam) who achieved the highest non-commissioned officer's rank, command sergeant major, before retiring to his home in Tucson, Arizona. Born on March 2, 1929, Dean was already sixty-three and retired from the U.S. Army for seventeen years when we first met. In retirement he grew to enjoy growing his silver hair down to his shoulders and maintained a matching silver beard and mustache that gave him the look of a Santa Claus figure, or even some kind of prophet. I had first heard him speak in 1993 at a conference in Gulf Breeze, Florida, where I found myself spellbound by his deep understanding of the implications for theology and the world's religions of a UFO reality.

"We are not alone and we have never been alone, " he said. As evidence for that statement he presented a long array of slides showing artifacts from the ancient past of a UFO presence. "These drawings from a cave in southern France are 20,000 years old, " he said, pointing to a photo of a cave wall with dozens of drawings of mastodons, wild boars, and other ancient animals. "But what are these doing here?" he asked pointing to numerous depictions of what seemed to be typical flying saucers, some with dotted lines behind them as if indicating that they were moving through the sky.

But the slides that intrigued me the most were the ones of medieval and Renaissance religious paintings and tapestries, some produced by students of the great masters, which clearly showed flying saucers in the background. One slide particularly provoked deep feelings of knowingness in me. It was a photo of a painting of the Madonna and Saint Giovannino by Italian 15th-century artist, Ghirlandaio. (See figures 1 and 2.) The painting hangs in the permanent collection of the Palazzo Vecchio in Florence. It depicts a traditional nativity scene with a close-up of the Madonna in the center. But in the background are a number of strange, anomalous items. In the sky to her left is the sun shining brightly, but just below the sun there are three small, round, bright objects that appear to have beams of light emanating from their bottoms. Then, even more incredibly, just over her left shoulder, to the right of her head, there is a round, metallic-looking object with rays of light emanating all around it. To leave no doubt that this object was thought by the artist to be something quite special—even astounding—he painted the figure of a man looking up at the object, his left hand shielding his eyes from the sun to get a better look, and his dog sitting beside him, barking at the mysterious orb.

"What is this metallic object?" Dean asked. "And why is this guy looking up at it?" I had no answers. I had never known that such paintings existed depicting what, by today's standards, could only be described as flying saucers. I felt that anyone looking at this painting with an open mind would be forced to conclude that UFOs were familiar to the artist and that he somehow saw a connection between them and the birth of Jesus. Somehow this painting triggered within me an understanding so deep that I had no words to describe it. The painting is irrefutable evidence that UFOs played an important role in the life of Jesus, at least in the mind of the artist.

Dean's presentation at that conference made such an impression on me that I soon invited him to speak in El Paso and helped to organize an event at the El Paso Community College where he spoke in March 1994 to a packed house. That weekend, Bob and I became good friends and began to realize just how much we had in common. We were both Vietnam veterans, we were both involved in UFO research, and we both agreed on many of the same conclusions about the meaning behind the UFO mystery. But most interesting for me was the fact that we both had a history of miraculous escapes from certain death. Bob also felt that he had guardian angels looking over him:

> I finished officer's candidate's school in October of 1950 and was commissioned a second lieutenant. The next thing I know is I'm on the front lines in Korea leading an infantry platoon in one of the bloodiest wars we've ever had. Then the company commander was killed, and I was promoted. It was then that a series of things began to occur. I seemed to live a charmed life. I was in places where I should not have survived. I walked away from helicopter crashes, the only survivor. Men were being killed all around me and all I got were nicks, a few scratches, and a little shrapnel. It got really eerie. The same thing happened years later in Vietnam, Laos, and Cambodia where I was involved in covert intelligence operations. One time I was sitting in a group with three other guys when a mortar shell dropped right next to us. All of them were killed, but I didn't have a scratch.

After Korea, the military downsized and many in the officer ranks were released. Dean stayed on as a non commissioned officer, an E-6, and gradually rose to the highest non-commissioned rank, that of command sergeant major. By the time Dean retired from active duty in 1976, he had been awarded a chest full of medals for bravery under combat and distinguished service. But it was when he was still just a master sergeant that Dean came face to face with incontrovertible evidence that the U.S. government had full knowledge of the UFO phenomenon.

## The Assessment

"In the early 1960s I served as an intelligence analyst with a 'cosmic top secret' clearance at NATO military headquarters just outside Paris," Dean explains. It was in this capacity that he had access to all the classified documents maintained in the vaults of the Supreme Headquarters Allied Powers Europe (SHAPE), to which he was attached. As Dean tells it, this became a turning point in his life:

> I arrived at SHAPE only to be made aware of a study that had been initiated in 1961 by a British Air Marshall by the name of Pike. This study was simply called "The Assessment." When this thing was published in 1964 and I had a chance to see it and read it, it changed my life. It was like a trigger. It not only triggered remembrances and awareness and understandings that I'd never had before, it was almost like a window had opened into my subconscious mind.

"The Assessment" was a military study conducted over a period of three years that concluded that although the Earth was being monitored by extraterrestrial intelligences, there was no apparent extraterrestrial threat. It concluded, Dean says, that this monitoring had been going on for a very, very long time, and that we were dealing with not just one but many extraterrestrial species. "The document, " Dean says, "was accessible only to those with the very highest clearance. In fact they gave it the highest classification we ever had, and still have, in NATO—'Cosmic Top Secret.' I spent many a long night reading it. It had special meaning for me because I had seen several UFOs during my military career. It launched me on a thirty-year study of everything from history, philosophy, and archaeology to mythology, theology, and physics."

It wasn't the "hardware," like spacecraft and propulsion systems, that fascinated Dean, nor was it the reality of an extraterrestrial intelligence, but rather "that we were dealing with a multi-dimensional source. I saw that there was an analogy to be found in death. I had always suspected that death was just a journey into another dimension, another reality, and that we come from there and go back there when we die. In a different way the SHAPE study concluded the same thing."

In other words, the most profound aspect of the document that affected him so much was the portion that addressed the theological implications. Here was an official government report that discussed, and produced evidence for, intelligent beings that materialized in our dimension at will and vanished into another reality just as easily. And the study made it clear that the phenomenon had been going on for perhaps thousands of years. In fact, an entire section of the report was devoted to a commentary on how such knowledge would impact religious beliefs and religious institutions. Obviously, if this were true, Dean thought, it would explain a lot about the Bible stories involving aerial phenomena, such as the Star of Bethlehem and the mysterious "cloud" from which Jehovah led the Hebrews through the wilderness.

"This, more than any other thing," Dean concluded, "is the reason that our government can never disclose what it knows about UFOs. No politician is willing to be the one who stirs up that nest of controversy."

The conclusion reached in the report is one that Dean accepts to this very day. "It concluded that the human race is a hybrid species that was created by extraterrestrials. Now I know evolution is a science that exists, but the human species is apparently not a part of it. The human race is a seeded race. We are not an accident. Furthermore, we have been genetically manipulated by intelligent beings that apparently combined some of their own genetic material with that of apes hundreds of thousands of years ago. That genetic manipulation is still going on today."

But Dean does not think it is all about genetics; he believes it also has to do with the soul. "I believe in the human spirit, in the soul, that it is an infinite spark of life. I believe we are a part of an infinite community of intelligent life and that the human potential is incredible. A young man from Galilee, two thousand years ago, said it very well when he said, 'Ye are gods,' and 'What I do, you can do and even more.' I believe that is where the human race is headed—toward a time when the human species will realize its full potential."

For Dean then, the quest for UFO information was more of a spiritual search. "The single most important issue here is that each and every one of us is an infinite, spiritual, living, conscious part of God. And once we grasp that, once we come to the point that the carpenter from Galilee tried so desperately to help us reach, we can make that transformation into another realm of reality," Dean says.

**Mexico City**

It was late when we finally got to the hotel across the street from the medical center, where the conference would be held, so there wasn't time to visit with any of the other speakers or organizers. Our gracious hostess had arranged a day of sightseeing for the speakers that would begin early in the morning with a bus ride to the ancient pyramids and ruins of Teotihuacan, about an hour and a half drive out of the city. It would be a great opportunity to get to know the speakers from Europe, China, South America, and the U.S. who had congregated to share their research and knowledge.

Early the next morning I arrived in the hotel coffee shop to get a quick breakfast before the long day's journey. As fate would have it, Bob Dean was sitting at a table by himself. He waved me over and I gladly joined him for an intimate chat. I was anxious to talk to him because when he had been in El Paso, he had confided in me that he was going to undergo hypnosis when he got back home to Tucson, Arizona.

At the time I thought that odd. I had not yet planned my own hypnosis session.

"Why are you doing that, Bob?" I asked.

"Well," he said, "I don't usually talk about this, but I have had some highly unusual experiences in my life, and I finally decided to find out more about them."

"Like what?" I prodded.

"Well," he said hesitantly, "like waking up in the morning and having memories of having been on an operating table and having 'people' around me performing medical procedures."

"Oh. "I can see why you don't tell many people."

"Unfortunately, if I were to talk about this aspect of my life, many people, particularly those in the UFO research community, would find me less credible. If I want people to listen to what I have to say, I feel I have to keep this quiet."

"Thank you for confiding in me, Bob," I said. "I certainly understand your concerns. But I can't wait to find out what you learned under hypnosis. You've got to promise me you'll fill me in."

"You are one of the few that I would tell," he said.

But months had passed since that conversation and, in the meantime, I had my own regression session. We had much to discuss now that we were together once more in Mexico City.

"Bob, it's so good to see you, I've been wanting to talk to you for so long," I said when I sat down at his table. "I can't wait to hear about the hypnosis session that you were going to do after the last time we were together in El Paso. But before you tell me, let me tell you about my hypnosis session. It was amazing."

I went on to tell him about the night of my regression and how the hypnotherapist had guided me through an imaginary garden and how she suggested that I would see a symbol or a scene that would be meaningful to me. When I began to tell him about the crucifix and how it led me to the shores of the Dead Sea and the clay jars like the ones the scrolls were found in, Bob's eyes grew large with surprise. By the time I finished telling him about the wave of emotion that overcame me and how I sobbed for nearly fifteen minutes, Bob was near tears.

"What's the matter, Bob?" I asked. "You seem shaken."

"I can't believe this. This is amazing. Almost the same thing happened to me!"

Now it was my turn to be astonished. "What do you mean, almost the same thing?"

"Well, I also remembered being there at the time of Jesus. I remembered being one of his followers and the terrible agony of losing him to the Crucifixion. It took me three hypnosis sessions to get past the emotional block that I had."

"Oh my God," I said. "I can't believe this!" It was an incredible experience to hear this news. It was like being shaken by the lapels by some invisible force that was saying, "See now! Do you get the idea?" I surely did.

## The Pyramids

I still regret that at that very moment two other of the speakers interrupted our conversation and asked to join us at our table. It would be a long time before I got to hear the details of Bob's incredible story. After breakfast around thirty of the speakers boarded the waiting bus to take us to the pyramids and Bob and I got separated, but his words stayed with me the entire way. It was hard to think about anything else.

It was mid-morning by the time we arrived at the pyramids and the sun was shining brightly on the beautiful, verdant valley north of Mexico City. The ruins of Teotihuacan lay before us like an alien landscape. The huge pyramid of the sun was at one end of a long concourse and the pyramid of the moon at the other end. It is still difficult to believe that no one really knows who built this magnificent city or what happened to them, but whoever did had an amazing command of science and astronomy. Researchers have discovered that the city was laid out in a precise fashion to mirror the night sky, just as, it is suspected, were the pyramids on the Giza plateau in

Egypt. What an amazing coincidence, I thought. Of course there were those who believed that extraterrestrial contact with the ancient peoples could account for the many parallels between the diverse cultures around the globe. I certainly was being led by my own research to that same conclusion.

The group meandered around the ancient city and some of us climbed the larger of the two massive pyramids at our leisure until early afternoon. Then it was time to gather together for the bus ride to a nearby restaurant for a late lunch. When the group arrived at the restaurant, the waiters hurried to push together enough tables to seat everyone together and we each hurried to find a place to sit. As fate would have it I was once again separated from Bob and instead I was seated next to another American speaker, John Carpenter, and his wife, Elizabeth. On the other side of me was a man I did not know and had not met. He was a stocky man of medium build who had the dark skin of his Aztec ancestors and a square, somber face. He had been introduced to the group on the bus as Dr. Ramirez and it was explained to us that he had volunteered his services as a physician to stay with the speakers and administer to their needs, should it become necessary— a thoughtful detail given the frequency with which tourists succumb to the dreaded "Montezuma's Revenge."

For most of the lunch I conversed with John and Elizabeth, only saying a polite *"buenas tardes"* to the Mexican doctor to my right. But as the meal was winding down, the doctor turned to me and told me in Spanish, "There is something I would like to tell you. I feel that what I have to say is meant for you to hear."

I couldn't possibly imagine what he was referring to. But, of course, I gave him my full attention.

"I have always been very psychic," he began, "and I feel that I am being guided to tell you my story for some reason. Please be patient and hear me out."

"Of course," I said. "Please go on."

"Several weeks ago I was watching television when a commercial came on advertising an exhibit of artifacts from the Holy Land that were coming to the museum here in Mexico City. One of the items being displayed was a box. It was carved out of stone and it had a lid that had engravings on it. In fact the whole box was decorated with engravings of some kind."

"What kind of box was it?" I asked.

"It was used to store the bones of someone. It was a funerary urn in the shape of a box."

"Oh, I see," I said.

"The moment I saw the box," he continued, "I recognized it, even though I had never seen it before."

"What do you mean? I don't understand."

"I knew that the box had been used to store the remains of a man named Caiaphas. Do you know who Caiaphas was?" he asked.

"Well, I remember the name, but I can't remember who he was," I answered.

And as I answered, I noticed that Dr. Ramirez's face was contorting, as if he were in pain. Tears began to well up in his eyes. "Caiaphas was the Jewish high priest who condemned Jesus to death," he said

Now I remembered the Bible story about how the high priests of the Jerusalem temple had conspired to have Jesus arrested by the Romans and how the high priest, a man named Caiaphas, was their leader.

"How did you know it was his box?" I asked.

"Because I knew at that moment that I had been Caiaphas in another lifetime," he said with tears streaming down his face. "I went to the museum to see the box and I found out that I was right. An archaeologist in Israel had found it." (Years later, while reading a magazine on Bible archeology I was stunned when I turned a page and saw a picture of that very stone box, called an "ossuary," which indeed had been discovered years before in Israel. The elaborately carved box bore the name "Caiaphas" on it and is to this day one of the few historical artifacts that verify the accuracy of some of the Gospels. (The ossuary of the high priest, Caiaphas, is a well-documented archaeological find and is commonly accepted as genuine. It remains one of the few artifacts confirming the historical accuracy of the New

Testament. Conversely, the much-publicized ossuary of James, brother of Jesus, discovered in 2003 residing in a private collection, has yet to be absolutely verified as genuine. In fact, experts now believe it to be a forgery.

Now, the doctor choked down his sobs and strained to control himself. "I condemned my savior to death!" he sobbed. "How could I do such a thing? Please help me understand!"

I was stunned.

I sat there in disbelief that this could be happening. I thought I had been stunned that morning at breakfast, but this was more than I could handle. *What is going on here?* I wondered to myself, staring in disbelief. Finally, I composed myself and asked him if he would like to go outside and speak with more privacy. He gladly accepted the offer. As we left the table I signaled to Bob Dean for him to come with us, and all three of us went out into the garden as a gentle afternoon rain began to fall.

Quickly I introduced Bob to the doctor and summarized the story I had been told. I watched Bob's eyes widen as I relayed the story to him and noted his look of bewilderment as I concluded.

Now he could understand the agony that was clearly apparent in Dr. Ramirez's face. Here was a devout Catholic who had learned that he had condemned his own Lord and Savior to death in a previous life. Here was a man who desperately needed answers to what it meant, and how such a thing could possibly happen. And he had chosen me, out of all of the speakers, in whom to confide.

We walked and spoke, finding shelter from the rain under a willow tree. For a long time, we tried to console the doctor. But what could we say? We were at a loss for words.

"You won't be judged forever for one lifetime," Bob argued. "That's why we have many chances to atone for our sins."

"The Crucifixion was necessary as a lesson for mankind," I added. "You were just playing a role, like a play."

But in the end, the best that we could do was to tell him that we understood and that he was forgiven. We put our arms around him and held him as he sobbed, looking at each other in amazement and noticing the tears welling in each other's eyes. The rain began to fall harder as the three of us embraced and cried together, letting the raindrops wash over us as if in the baptism we were all forgiven for our sins of long ago.

### The Rest of the Story

It was not until October 22, 1999, that I had another chance to speak privately with Bob about that day in Mexico by the pyramids. Much had happened since we had last spoken in earnest about those things closest to our hearts. My book had been published and now I was on the lecture circuit speaking about the religious and spiritual implications of UFOs and quantum physics. Bob had read it and called me to say, "You wrote the book I wanted to write! I recommend it to everyone." This was particularly endearing to me because I knew that Bob had struggled with his own manuscript for years, but his book never materialized for one reason or another.

Once again I invited him to speak in El Paso and he graciously accepted, even though at age seventy his health was beginning to fail him. Suffering from sleep apnea, walking with a cane because of a trick knee that sometimes gave out on him and, tiring easily, Bob struggled through his daily life. This time I made sure that we would have sufficient time to speak alone by scheduling an entire afternoon for the purpose of conducting an in-depth interview.

It was around 1:30 on a beautiful fall afternoon when we sat down under an umbrella next to the swimming pool at the Clarion Inn near El Paso's airport. Bob wore his long, white hair back in a ponytail, as was his custom, and he stoked on a long, black cigar that he claimed was one of only three vices he had. One of the others was an occasional glass of good Kentucky bourbon; the third, he said with a wink, was his own business.

"Bob," I began, "let's start out where we left off years ago in our discussion. When you first told me that you were going to have hypnosis you said you had memories of being taken at night and finding yourself on an operating table. What was that all about?"

"Joe, I have never spoken to anyone about this. It's very personal and very emotional for me. My life has been full of strange and supernatural events. For example, I remember being born. My mother didn't believe me, but I remember it vividly. I was above the scene looking down, very detached. The next thing I know, I'm in a body, squalling. I was a part of this body."

"So it was like an out-of-body experience?" I asked for clarification.

"Yes, that's what it was. But it was only the first of many strange things that happened to me. When I was only four years old, in Covington, Kentucky, I loved water and they couldn't keep me away from it. There was a nearby industrial canal and I was warned 'Don't go near it' by my mother. But one day I was out playing and I went to the canal. I loved throwing sticks and rocks into the water. It was a dangerous place with steep, slippery sides. Well, somehow, I got too close and I tumbled down into the water, and at first all I could think of was that I was really going to get my bottom tanned. I remember I was wearing a little playsuit and I was worried because it was soaking wet. Soon I realized that I couldn't hold on to the side. It was muddy and there wasn't anything to hold on to. As I was starting to give up I remember thinking, 'Well, this was a short trip.' There was no terror, just the acceptance of death.

"Then something happened. A powerful set of hands grasped me under the arms from behind and lifted me up to the top. But when I turned around to look, there was no one there. I scampered home, soaking wet and smeared with mud. When I got home I didn't tell anyone what had happened. I got the spanking I had expected. I never told my mother, even later in life."

Then there was the poltergeist activity. "As I was growing up there were always strange things happening in our house—strange noises and such. Once I was in the house all alone at night sitting on the toilet reading comic books when I heard the hall light click off. It was just a bare light bulb with a chain that made a 'kachink' sound whenever you turned the light on or off. I opened the bathroom door and the light was off so I turned it back on and went back into the bathroom. A little while later I hear this 'kachink' sound again and the light is out again. I checked around but no one was there. When it happened the third time I went out into the hall and yelled, 'Okay, you guys, cut it out!' but I don't know whom I was yelling at. There was always a feeling of a presence around the house, particularly at night in my room. It never bothered me much until my mom took me to see the original *King Kong* movie, and that scared the hell out of me. After that I was scared of the dark."

## UFO Events

Then there were the UFO events. "I was stationed at Fort Huachuca, Arizona, in 1960 with the public information office and we were sent out to cover the launch of a combat-surveillance, unmanned-drone aircraft. Early in the morning we went out onto the west test range. They had a theodolite system out there, which was a high-speed motion picture camera that would track the flight of the propeller-driven drone. But, before the launch, the camera swung around about ninety degrees to our right and everyone turned to see what was there. There, about five hundred yards away, was a silvery object hovering about two hundred feet off the ground. It was very beautiful. It was elongated almost like a teardrop, with the sun glinting off of it. It was kind of bobbing up and down in place. It began to move slowly, and then it just took off and disappeared. No one had any idea what they had just seen, but a colonel came over to us and told us that this was top secret and we were not to tell anyone about it. 'What you've just seen didn't happen!' he said. I thought it had been some kind of secret project they were testing. It wasn't till I got to SHAPE headquarters and read that report on UFOs that I realized what it was."

It was at SHAPE, outside of Paris, that Dean had another sighting in broad daylight. "This was right outside the headquarters building. I saw everyone looking up into the sky, so I looked up and there was a very large, very high metallic object with an elongated body just hovering there. One end of it was covered with a strange blue-violet glow. I noticed my boss, four-star general Lyman Lemnitzer, standing there looking up at the object. He saw me looking at him and he smiled and raised his eyebrows, then he got in his car and drove off."

But one of the strangest events in Dean's life occurred when he was working for the department of emergency services in Pima County, Arizon, after retiring from the Army. He and a coworker drove from their homes in Tucson to the town of Ajo for a search-and-rescue seminar. That night they headed back around 11:00 m. for the one and a half-hour drive back.

"The road crosses the Indian reservation near the town of Sells. Just before we got to Sells I remember we drove into a thick, white fog. My coworker was sound asleep. I remember slowing down in the fog and suddenly there was a flash of white light, like a flash bulb going off in front of me. I jumped and sat up straight. The next thing I know I see a sign that says 'Tucson 25 miles.' I don't remember going through Sells at all. There was about a thirty-mile stretch of highway missing from my memory, and instead of getting back at 12:30, it was 1:30 a.m. We had an hour of missing time. Years later Budd Hopkins tried to hypnotize me to find out what happened, but I just couldn't relax enough to be hypnotized."

It was during these years that Dean was living in Tucson. On two occasions, he woke up with memories of having been on an operating table during the night.

"The first time, I remembered the table being cold and hard and complaining about it. There was a bright, white light and people standing around. The next time it happened I remembered that it felt nice and warm. I remember wiggling my butt and shoulders on the padded table and saying, 'This is an improvement.' There was a tall, thin man with a large nose standing next to me. He was running his hands over my body without touching me. I could feel the warmth from his hands. Then a voice said, 'We thought you would like it.' "

## The Hypnosis

When Bob decided once again to seek help from a hypnotherapist, he searched for someone who was well qualified and who came highly recommended. Eventually he settled on Dr. Phyllis Barrons, who held a Ph.D. in psychology and taught at the University of Arizona near where he lived at the time.

"I wanted to deal with some of the strange phenomena that had occurred throughout my life, including the UFO stuff," Bob said, "but also the
strange memories and flashes of memories I had for many years. For years
I seemed to remember past lives and I was drawn very much to certain periods in ancient history, such as the Etruscan and the Roman empires, as
well as the time of Christ. I wanted to know if it was just my imagination
or if there was really something there worth looking into. But I was in no
way prepared for what happened.

"The first thing that happened was that I went back to times when I
lived as both an Etruscan and a Roman. They were difficult and brutal lives
and very painful to remember. Then she said, 'Go to a past life where you
were happy.' The emotions were so powerful that I just began to sob and I
couldn't stop. I cried for fifteen minutes and it took two more sessions to
break through the emotional barrier. When I did I suddenly found myself
at the Crucifixion." Bob's chest was now heaving, his eyes filled with tears.
He struggled to control himself by taking some deep breaths.

When he finally recovered, he went on. "I saw a place where the Romans had a number of permanent stakes in the ground about eight feet tall.
They used them all the time. There were no cross pieces on them. There
was a large crowd—people took their kids to see this, it was a spectacle, like
what they did in the arenas—the coliseum. It was like entertainment. Then
I saw them bring this young man in who was a friend of mine, he was forced
to carry a cross piece over his shoulder. [Bob started to cry again.] They
had beaten him half to death. He could hardly walk. He had something
around his head and blood was dripping into his eyes. He was bleeding all
over, front and back. He looked at me and the rest of his friends with such
love and sympathy as if to say, 'It's all right.' But it wasn't all right. He threw
the cross piece down and fell to his knees. His back was all lacerated where
they had beaten him. He had greenish eyes and chestnut hair with reddish
highlights—beautiful. Some of us wanted to save him, to start a fight, but
he motioned us to hold still. Then they put his arms out on the crosspiece
and nailed him to it through the wrists. He cried! He was a man. That's the

way I knew him. He didn't say he was the only Son of God, he said we are all sons of God. He would say I am a son of Man—I'm human. He would feel pain; he would feel the cold. He didn't say he was special, but unexplainable things would happen around him all the time. He was the best friend I ever had.

"They tied ropes around the cross beam and wound them around his chest, then they put the ropes up on one of the stakes which had a groove in the middle and they hauled him up. He was in pain—his legs were kicking. One of the Romans grabbed his legs and held his feet together. He took a long spike and a hammer and with one quick blow, drove the spike through his feet into the post. It was fast. He knew what he was doing. They tied the ropes to the post. That's what kept the cross beam in place. There was only a small part of the post above the cross beam, not how you see the crucifix depicted in paintings.

"He wasn't at all how he is depicted in the Bible. He was married and had children, like any other rabbi. His wife was named Miriam, but in the Bible she was called Mary of Magdala, and has been made out to be a harlot. She wasn't a harlot; she was a priestess. He was from a very pious sect with strict rules who set themselves apart, but he did not isolate himself. He was friends with everyone, even Romans. His teachings were like those of the Gnostics. He taught that God is within and that people don't need priests or churches to find God. The Jews at the time taught that the priests were intermediaries to God for average people. But he said, 'Your Father is wherever you are. Your Father is always listening.'

"Then Dr. Barrons asked me, 'Did you have a name?' And I answered, 'Yes, I had a name.' I'm not sure if I accept this even now, but when she asked me what it was, I answered, 'Philip.'

"Then she asked me, 'Were you one of the ones who were closest to him?' And I answered, 'Yes.' Later I questioned this. You always hear about people who remember being Napoleon or Cleopatra. It sounds crazy."

"What about the Resurrection?" I asked. "Did it really happen?"

"Yes, but don't ask me how. I saw him again. But I wasn't there when he ascended. He was resurrected and he ascended with their help," Bob said, pointing up into the sky. "But don't ask me who 'they' are. A cloud came down from the sky and took him and he said he would come back the same way. I think that will happen. I just want to be here when it does. I think what you and I are doing is helping to get people ready. I think it's going to be soon."

*"So the soldiers came and broke the legs of the two men crucified with Jesus, but when they came to him, they saw that he was dead already, so they didn't break his. However, one of the soldiers pierced his side with a spear, and blood and water flowed out."*

Matthew 19:32–34

## CHAPTER FIVE

# Witness to the Crucifixion
## More Synchronicity

YOU'RE NOT GOING to believe what happened last night," Roberta said excitedly as soon as I picked up the phone one morning in late December 1998.

"What happened?" I asked, curious about any new tidbit of information she might have. Roberta and I had been working together as research associates for about five years, and together we had grown to accept that life and the universe were much stranger than most people suspect. We had interviewed and performed hypnosis on dozens of persons who seemed to be having alien contact. We had traveled to conventions and workshops together and taken classes in hypnotherapy. We confided in each other and shared our thoughts, dreams, and fears.

"You're going to love this. It's really amazing because it's just what you need for your research."

"Well, what is it?" I asked impatiently.

"I did a hypnosis session last night on a patient of mine and he had the most incredible past life memory of witnessing the Crucifixion."

"You're kidding!" I exclaimed. "Tell me about it."

"Well, we have it all on tape and he has agreed to allow me to share it with you. He's the quiet guy who comes to the MUFON meetings and doesn't say anything. His name is Jack [not his real name]."

"Oh yeah, I think I know which one you mean. Well, what did he remember?"

"It's too long to tell you on the phone. You'll just have to listen to it yourself. It's over an hour long. He told a very detailed story. It was very emotional. It's probably a good thing that you weren't involved in the session. It would have been hard for you to handle."

"When can I get the tape from you?"

"I told him I would set up lunch for next week and the three of us could talk. I'll give you the tape and you can make copies for us. How does that sound?"

"That sounds good to me. I can't wait."

With that we hung up and I was left in deep thought. *Well, here's another one*, I thought to myself. Ever since my own hypnosis session there had been a procession of people with past-life memories of being with Jesus or who had Jesus-like figures involved in their so-called alien encounters. Roberta was fully aware of this and was fascinated by the seeming series of coincidences. As someone who was actively trying to reacquaint herself with her Jewish roots, Roberta was finding the spate of Jesus cases interesting and puzzling. She was also beginning to realize that the story of Jesus was one that pertained to her search as well, for the study of Jesus was also a study of ancient Judaism. Our research into UFOs had caused us both to seek additional information about the true origins of Christianity.

### A Man Named Jack

Born in 1947 in El Paso, Texas, Jack is a quiet, almost somber man of medium build who seems to prefer to listen rather than to speak during conversation. An elementary schoolteacher, he lives with his wife and son in suburban El Paso. His appearance is clean-cut and down-to-earth. His demeanor is gentle, honest, serious, and pensive, perhaps due to the heavy burden he has subconsciously carried for his entire life—a burden so heavy that even recovering its hidden secrets could not relieve the stress those memories imposed.

"I've always been, I guess you'd say, a depressive personality," Jack confided in me. "I have a lot of trouble with depression and I've taken medication for it, but I don't see that it has done much good. I think it's more likely that I'm depressed about something. I think there's some kind of spiritual or emotional thing there." So when a family counselor referred him to Dr. Fennig, he gladly went to see her. "I had no idea that she was involved in UFO research. I just needed help in understanding why I felt the way I did." As it turned out, Jack and Roberta had something in common—an intense interest in UFOs and other New Age subjects.

Jack, who studied in Italy for four years, came back to El Paso and earned a bachelor's degree and a master's degree in education from the University of Texas at El Paso. By the time he met Roberta, he had been fascinated for more than twenty years with UFOs, reincarnation, and related topics, even though he considered himself a devout Catholic and much of this information conflicted with the Church's teachings.

"I was a Presbyterian as a child, but in the late 1960s I had a chance to go to Italy with some friends. While I was in Rome I had an opportunity to see where all these things described in the Bible took place. I used to go have lunch at the Roman Forum and just sit there and think about the things that happened there. I saw a lot of places where the saints were martyred, and that blew me away. I converted to Catholicism at the American church, St. Susana's. I was in my twenties."

"How have you reconciled your interests in such things as reincarnation and UFOs with your Catholic teachings?" I asked.

"It's like holding two contradictory views in your mind at the same time," he laughed. "I have an open mind about such things, yet I believe that Jesus was the Son of God and that much of what is in the Bible is true.

"As for reincarnation, the books he had read caused him to consider, and even become apprehensive about, the possibility that the Church had left out some things or changed some things for political reasons, going back to the time of the Roman Empire.

As for his interest in UFOs, seeing is believing. On two occasions Jack saw UFOs in broad daylight.

"Once I was driving west on the freeway near the university and I saw these two round objects that looked bright silver, traveling side by side, against the wind. The wind was blowing out of the west about thirty to forty miles per hour, very steady, very strong."

Another time when he and his son were working together in their backyard, they both observed a strange object in the sky directly above them. "It was four or five in the afternoon. I looked up and there was this object. It was shaped like a dart—like an arrow point. It was dark brown and had a structured surface, like long lines and different planes on it. There was this enormous, brilliant, red-orange flame coming out of the back of it—like an Atlas rocket taking off, but there was no sound and it was going very slowly. What was even stranger to me was what appeared to be civilian, private planes, like three or four, circling around this thing. But again there was no sound from their engines. It seemed to be several thousand feet up, so that would have made it very big, about two hundred feet or so long, and the plume was maybe three to four times the length of the object. All this assemblage of things was floating across the sky very slowly. We must have looked at it for about twenty minutes and neither of us thought about going to get a camera; we were so astonished by it. We finally followed it out of sight. There were planes going back and forth at different altitudes that appeared not to notice it at all." Jack was amazed that no one else seemed to see this object. To him it seemed as if all of El Paso should have been able to see it.

The more Jack thought about his UFO experiences and the more he read, the more he became concerned that there might be some connection between UFOs and other strange events in his life.

"I had read about missing time experiences in the UFO literature and it made me wonder if that might be the reason I can't remember my childhood," he confided. "A lot of people can say, 'Oh yeah, I remember that,' but I can't remember a lot of stuff."

"At what age do your memories begin?" I asked.

"I guess when I was a teenager, about fifteen or sixteen years old. But before that I can't remember."

"That's interesting," I commented, "I run into that a lot."

"You do? Wow."

Many of those who had UFO encounters reported the same thing, and I suspected it had to do with suppressing the trauma associated with their experiences. In some cases, I had found, some form of parental abuse may have also been a contributing factor, although that did not appear to be in this case.

"Then there was the time when I was living in Italy," Jack continued, "when I got very ill and I thought I had pneumonia. I was bedridden. The apartment that I shared with another student didn't have any heat, so we suffered a lot when it got cold. I think that had something to do with it. During that time there were several days that I can't account for."

"Where was your roommate?"

"He had taken a trip. It must have been four or five days. I don't know what happened. I don't know if I was unconscious or what. When I started reading about missing time, I started wondering if there was some connection to my experiences. I still don't know. I haven't come to any conclusion about that."

Jack then went on to explain another aspect of his experiences that rang a distinct bell with me. Many UFO experiencers have told me that they have always felt they were from someplace else, not from the Earth. Some have recovered past-life memories of being on other planets in nonhuman form.

"I've always had the idea that I'm not like other people," Jack went on, "that I don't like the things other people like and that I'm sort of living in this civilization and I'm seeing it from the outside, like I don't enter into it. It's strange to me. It's strange and alien to me and I don't really subscribe to a lot of beliefs that other people do. When I got into the Catholic Church there was a set of beliefs and dogma that you had to accept. I found that comforting. I still do."

"Kind of like an anchor?"

"Yeah, like an anchor. There was so little before that I could believe in."

### The Hypnosis

Nevertheless, when Jack first decided to undergo hypnotherapy, it wasn't his missing time he was most concerned with. "I wanted to explore the possibilities of past lives. I thought that might be the reason I was always so depressed. I didn't seem to suffer from depression caused by chemical imbalances. To me it seemed I was depressed *about* something. I just didn't know what."

After completing a psychological evaluation and using traditional counseling techniques, Roberta agreed to the use of hypnosis as a means of uncovering clues that would help Jack with his depression.

Without having the slightest inkling as to the nature of his burden, Jack arrived at his first hypnotherapy appointment with Roberta in December 1998 with a heavy sense of expectation. What would he learn? What new facet of himself would be uncovered?

"In the first session, what came up was a life back at the time of the Civil War. I was a ten-year-old girl who was killed by a stray bullet at the battle of Antietam in Maryland. Then, the next life after that I was a Nazi SS sergeant. I think my name was Klaus. I was executed at the end of World War II in 1945."

"You were born in 1947?"

"Yes, that's right."

"Were those memories shocking to you?"

"You bet they were. Especially the one about the SS sergeant. I clearly remembered shooting an old French man in the head. He was lying to me about partisans. I remember taking a pistol out and shooting him in the side of the head. I could see the plume of blood and smell the blood in the air. Fragments of skull adhered to my uniform. It was horrendous."

"I don't think anyone would imagine or fantasize about something like that," I said. "That's the last thing in the world we would want to think about ourselves."

"You're right. But it did explain why I had always been fascinated with the Civil War and particularly what it was like for the people who lived through it. It also explained my fascination with the Nazis. One of my few early memories is of watching television in the 1950s and seeing films of Nazi concentration camps and Hitler. I remember getting a very strange feeling. I was repulsed by it, but I was also attracted and fascinated by it. Joe, don't you think it's possible, even more probable, that what people are doing when they go under hypnosis is that they're tapping into what Jung called the universal unconscious? I really have doubts that I experienced all these things myself. Maybe I just tapped into the memories of other people."

"That's exactly what came to my mind after my hypnosis session," I said. "I've thought about that a lot. I don't think we will ever be able to know for sure. I guess each person has to decide that for himself. Yet, the more I study this issue, the more I lean toward the reincarnation theory. It makes sense to me that souls need many lifetimes and many perspectives to grow and mature. One lifetime could hardly be enough."

### The Crucifixion

As incredible as his first session was in its detail and realism, it did not seem to relieve Jack of his depression. There seemed to be something deeper that had yet to be uncovered.

On the day of his second session Jack accommodated himself in the large, turquoise reclining chair in Dr. Fennig's medical-center office and easily drifted into a trance. Using a time-tested technique for past-life therapy, Fennig asked him to envision a lovely garden with a golden door. Once he passed through the door, he would, she suggested, be able to see a scene that would give him clues about a past life:

**R.F.** [Roberta Fennig] As you walk through the doorway you can tell me what it is that you notice as you look at your surroundings and you start to look around you.

Jack answered in the hushed, faltering tones, familiar to hypnotherapists, of a person in deep hypnotic trance.

**J.X.** [Jack X] I see a narrow street, with paving stones. There's a lot of noise—people talking and yelling, buying and selling, jostling against me. This is a long time ago. Everyone is wearing robes; even the children are wearing tunics and sandals. I'm wearing sandals. I smell many animals. Their droppings are everywhere. Donkeys, horses, and oxen. I see Roman soldiers.

**R.F.** Do you know what this place is called?

**J.X.** Jerusalem. They're [the soldiers] speaking a strange language that's different from the people.

**R.F.** Do you know what language the people speak?

**J.X.** Hebrew and Greek.

**R.F.** What language do you speak?

**J.X.** Greek. But I'm not Greek.

**R.F.** What are you doing there?

**J.X.** I've come to find him. The man I've heard about.

**R.F.** Do you know his name?

**J.X.** Jesus.

**R.F.** What have you heard?

**J.X.** That he works miracles. I want to know about what he teaches…I have heard he is here. I came from Syria.

**R.F.** Do you have a miracle you want him to perform?

**J.X.** No.

**R.F.** What happens now?

**J.X.** A soldier pushes me with his spear saying (in Hebrew), "Get away, get away. "I can see coming up the street a group of soldiers. They're marching. I can hear them. Their sandals have iron studs that make noise when they march. There's no one speaking now. There's silence. I can see a group of prisoners coming now. Some of the people are weeping. Some look away. I can see three men coming behind the soldiers.

A tall man is walking with great difficulty. He's covered with blood. He is wearing a red cloak and underneath is a white garment. It's soaked with blood. His face is covered in blood. He looks horrific. I wonder how he can keep walking. He looks dead. His skin is pale and gray looking. He's bleeding so much that as he walks, drops of blood are falling on the pavement. I look away too because I can't stand to see it.

Behind him there are two men coming. Each one is carrying a wooden piece on his shoulder. More soldiers are coming up behind them. I can hear women crying and yelling. Some of the men are laughing. One steps out from the crowd and spits on them.

The Romans hit him. Knock him down to the ground.

What did these men do? I have to find out.

I walk up behind them. They walk out through the city gate. A Roman turns to me and pushes me with his spear. "Get away! You can't come here," he says.

"But I know this man," I said...But I don't know him. What does this mean? [Jack wonders to himself.]

So the soldier says, "Well, go with them." There are other men and women behind me following the soldiers with their heads bowed and crying.

This is Jesus. This must be him. But what has he done? I must find out. Nothing he has done could deserve this. Nothing.

They are coming to a hill. It's a round hill. The soldiers are shouting to each other. What are they going to do? There are three posts set up. The soldiers make the men drop their wooden pieces and push them back. They are made to lie down on the cross beams and the soldiers are nailing their hands, their arms to the cross beams.

What did these men do? [incredulously]

The tall man...they strip him naked and nail him to the cross beam. He doesn't cry out. There is great pain in his face. [Jack begins to weep.] God, God, why are they doing this? [Now, barely able to speak.] They're nailing him to the cross beam through the wrists. The other men cry out "Help, help, we didn't do anything." But he doesn't say anything. He doesn't cry out. How can he do this? [Jack breaks down crying.]

[Recovering his composure.] They attach ropes to the cross beams and drag the men across underneath the posts then they attach them to pulleys and they haul them up onto the posts. I can hear the creaking of the pulleys. They're iron.

Blood is flowing out of their wrists. They're yelling and screaming, but the tall man is not saying anything. How can he bear the pain? I can't believe it. He is between the two other men. Blood is flowing down the posts. How can they do this? They are savages. My God! [weeping] If I had a weapon I would hit them. I would cut off their hands. How can they do this?

It's growing dark. There's a thunderstorm coming. The ground is shaking! An earthquake! People are screaming. The soldiers are running around. Their leaders yell at them to stop and to stand up straight. The clouds above are glowing. They're black and green. I've never seen a sky like that! What's happening? It's the end of the world!

Most of us are down on the ground, holding the ground. Lightning is crashing everywhere. Everybody's terrified. The rain is washing the blood down. It's standing in pools underneath the crosses. [panting now] Now the ground has stopped shaking. It's raining. There's no more lighening…It's cold. I can see our breath.

The man in the middle has his head down. He's hanging just by his arms. The soldiers rush up to him. They drive a nail through his feet into the post. How can he bear that? He doesn't let out a sound, but he's alive. His body is writhing in pain. How can he do this? Those savages, animals! [breathing heavily]

The women are sobbing. I can hear soldiers talking. One moves behind the cross in the middle. He's tying the rope that holds the cross beam up. I don't understand them. Everyone is standing in silence. Some of the men are sitting on the ground. They have their heads in their hands.

One of the soldiers has climbed up and put a sign over the head of the man in the middle. It is crude writing, scratched out on a board. I don't understand what it says—it's in their language.

**A Boiling Sky**

It's very dark and cold, everyone is huddled, and everyone is numb. They can't believe what has happened. The clouds above are boiling. They look like—I've never seen the sky like that. It looks strange—terrifying—green—dark green sky—gray—black. The clouds look alive. They are moving. It's horrible.

The man in the middle is writhing. Blood is coming out of his hands—every part of his body is pouring blood. They've beaten him and cut his skin all over. I can't look at it. I can't look. I hope they die soon. At least it would be over for them.

Now the wind is coming up. It's an icy, cold wind. Everyone is wet. It's freezing. The man in the middle is saying something. I can't hear what he is saying. One of the soldiers takes a sponge with something in it, some liquid, and puts it up to the man's lips, but he doesn't want it.

The soldiers are laughing and joking. I see them. They're throwing pieces of bones on his garments. I don't know what they are doing. Now they seem to be fighting over them. The officer comes over and strikes them both and takes the garments himself and wraps them up.

The man in the middle is saying something to the man on the left. All three of the men are talking, but I can't hear what they say. It's like we're watching a ceremony that means something. But what does it mean?

It's a rite…it's a ritual. But only the soldiers are not aware of this.

The man in the middle pushes himself up with his feet and he cries out. Then he sinks back down. [sobbing] How can he do this? [breaks down sobbing.] Oh Jesus, Oh Jesus! [After recovering] Everybody is waiting. Nobody is speaking…It's getting colder. [panting heavily] Why don't they die? Why don't they die quickly?

Something else is happening. It means something…Everybody can feel that. There is something else happening. It means something. Everybody can feel that…Something we don't see. I don't know what it is. There are spirits around. I can sense it.

Even the soldiers are quiet now. They're sitting down on the ground. After a while a Roman rides up on a horse and says something to the commander and he goes over and says something to a soldier and the soldier takes a big wooden beam and he goes over to the man on the right and he breaks his legs. The man screams out. He breaks one leg and then moves to the other side and breaks the other leg. How can he do this? [crying] I can see the bones sticking out. Now the soldier goes over to the man on the left and breaks his legs.

They don't break the legs of the man in the middle. He pushes himself up and yells out in a language I don't understand. It's not Hebrew. His whole body trembles. He yells out till he falls down. [crying] There's a huge crash of thunder. He's dead. [breaking into sobs] How can they do this? Forgive me! Forgive me! God forgive me! Why am I saying that? It seems to come from deep inside me.

One of the soldiers has a lance. Ahhh! He moves around. He drives his spear into the side of the man. And the man doesn't move. He's dead. Water is coming out. Water. A lot of water and blood is coming out of that wound. Water. How can that be? Why is there water and blood? Water is flowing down underneath the cross. [sobbing] Forgive me!

Everybody's starting to move away. They're walking back. Their heads are all bowed, but no one is saying anything. A soldier pushes me with his spear. "Get out of here," he says in Hebrew. I look back and I see that they're taking the man down—the man in the middle. It's finished. They're taking them down. All three of them.

When we come back through the gate there is no one there. The city seems deserted. I can see lamps in the windows, but the streets are empty.

Oh my God! I was too late. Now I'll never know what he said or what he meant. I have to find a place to stay. I keep walking through the city, out the other gate. There is no one out. It's the Passover. I'm not a Jew so I don't observe the Passover. I must find an inn. I look down and find I don't have any money. Someone in the crowd must have taken it from me. I don't care. I just keep walking.

Something has happened to the world. The world is different. There is no one I can talk to about this. No one. I find a cave. I'll sleep there tonight. I wrap up in my cloak. I try not to think about the cold. What does all this mean? Who was that man?

## The Resurrection

In the morning I can see there's a red sky. It's still cloudy. There's fog. I walk up the road. I meet people coming toward the city. One of them stops and asks, "Have you been in the city?"

"Yes," I say.

"What of Jesus of Nazareth?" he asks.

"He's dead. The Romans killed him."

"You saw it."

"Yes," I say. "I was there."

"We came to hear him. What shall we do now?"

"I don't know." I don't care. I'm hungry. I keep walking. I haven't eaten for two days. The sun is rising now. It's getting warmer. It's so cold. I'm shivering.

More people are coming. They ask me the same questions...I don't want to talk about it. "Leave me alone." There are many people on the road. They must have all been coming to hear him.

What possessed me to do this—to come down here with no provisions? I must have been mad.

I meet a man. He smiles at me. He says, "You must be hungry. Here, have some food and some wine and some bread."

"Thank you," I say. "Who are you?"

"I'm a friend," he says.

"Forgive me," I said.

"What did you say?"

"I said, forgive me."

"You haven't done anything to me."

"I don't know why I say that, I just keep saying it over and over again. I don't know why."

Then he puts his hand on my shoulder. "You will know why," he says. Then he walks on.

I turn to thank him again, but he's gone.

Forgive me!

I eat and I feel much better. Who was that man?

**R.F.** What did he look like?

**J.X.** He was tall, but I had never seen him before. I have more than I can eat here. I keep walking. The sun is setting. Why am I going back? [to Syria] There's nothing left for me there. I don't know anything else to do.

I meet more people on their way to Jerusalem to hear Jesus speak. I tell them, "Don't go. He's dead." But the man tells me, "We have no food." I tell them, "Here, take this food, I have all that I need." They thank me and I leave. I gave them all the food that I have. That's foolish of me. Why did I do that?

I meet other people. I tell them, "You won't find him there, he's dead." They too say they have to go on. I say, "Take this food." I had more food. Where did that come from? I don't have any food. [perplexed] I keep walking and this happens over and over again. More come, and more water and more bread. Where is it coming from? What is this?

Finally, I get back to Syria. I still have food with me. I have to tell the people here about what happened—that I have food and I don't have food— that a man gave me food and now I have food all the time. I never run out! And I tell people and they say I'm mad. They turn from me and they laugh. "You're mad, get away from us," they say.

I get back to my home. I'm a cobbler. I make shoes. I get to work. I have more food again. What does this mean…I have food all the time? I see a poor man in the street. I go out and give him food. I see another and I give him food. I close up my shop. I can't work any more today. I sleep. I dream a man in white clothes comes to me and says, "Get up, you must go back to Jerusalem"'

"Why? What is there?"

I wake up. It's the middle of the night. Am I going mad? I must be going mad. The voice inside of me keeps saying, "You must go back." In the morning there is a horse outside my shop. No one has a horse here. It has a Roman saddle. Someone will think I stole it. The Romans will kill me!

I ask people whose horse it is. They say it just walked up to my house by itself. I close my shop. I get on the horse and I go back down the road. I keep wondering as I ride, what's in Jerusalem? It doesn't take so long to get back.

It's dark. The streets are empty. There's a pall of sadness that has settled over the city. No one is out—only the Romans in twos and threes. Now I'm afraid to get off the horse because they will see it has a Roman saddle. I ride out to the hill where they crucified him and I hit the horse on the rump, setting him free. There is nothing but three posts here. They're going to crucify more people.

I sit there on that hill for some time, and then I see the man who met me on the road. He walks up to me.

"Do you know me now?" he asks me.

"What are you talking about?"

"Do you know why you had that food?"

"No, can you tell me?"

He smiles. "Not yet," he says and he walks away.

"What do you mean, not yet? Who are you?"

He turns to me and says, "Do you not recognize me?"

And then I did. It was the man— the man who was killed. And I fall down in front of him on my face. "You're Jesus! You're the Lord!" But then I get up and he's gone. Where did he go? He couldn't have walked away. It was him! It was him! Oh my God, forgive me! I'm so blind, I cannot see anything.

I go back into the town. People are coming out of their houses. But why? It's night. They should be inside. There are a lot of people with torches, talking. They're saying, "He is risen! He is risen from the dead as he said!" And I walk up to them and say, "Yes, yes, he is risen! I just saw him!" People are singing and laughing. They're all happy. I'm carried along by the crowd. It's dark. Where are they going? They're going to Herod's palace. We must tell Herod he is risen from the dead. Suddenly, a group of Roman soldiers on horseback come into the crowd and start beating people. Some they jabbed with their spears and killed right there in front of me. Others are shooting arrows into the crowd and slashing at them with swords. People are scream-ing and running in all directions. I'm running along with the rest of them.

Animals! They're like animals. Herod is the worst of all of them. He's a Roman as much as they are. Beast! The soldiers withdraw. The dead are lying, bleeding in the street…This is beyond humanity to do this.

Here, Dr.Fennig wraps up the session due to time constraints.

**R.F.** Do you ever see him again after that?

**J.X.** No.

**R.F.** Okay. I want you to go to the last day of that lifetime. Where are you?

**J.X.** I'm in Rome. I'm with Christians. I have become a Christian. Peter has been seized by the Romans. He is to be crucified tomorrow.

### Analyzing the Case

As I listened to the audiotape of Jacks' hypnosis session with Roberta, I could feel the excruciating agony he experienced as he relived the horren-dous torture and death of Jesus. Roberta had been right. It was a good thing I wasn't the one doing the hypnosis. I would have had a difficult time deal-ing with the emotions. As it was, tears streamed down my cheeks as I felt the pain and frustration that Jack was feeling.

It was truly as if Jack was reliving the experience. His emotional reac-tions were severe and his description of the people, the smells, and the ac-tion was in great detail. He seemed to have a physical reaction to the strong odors around him. During the interview, he told me that he could smell the blood that was everywhere and the strong body odor of the Roman sol-diers. This is not uncommon among those who recover memories under hypnosis, whether they are of events in this life or in a past one.

Some subjects have the ability to enter into such a deep trance that they relive the entire experience and, as reported in the case of Alicia, even speak in a foreign tongue that is unfamiliar to them in their present life. After listening to the tape and meeting with Jack and Roberta, I had the strong sense that Jack was not fantasizing or imagining these events. First, he did not seem to me to be fantasy-prone or highly imaginative. Neither did Roberta see him this way. In fact, in every respect, Jack seemed like a person who was well grounded, highly intelligent, and totally sincere. If anything, it was he who was questioning the authenticity of his memories. In fact, in later conversations with Jack, he stated that he still did not believe that they were past-life memories. He seemed to have a hard time believing in reincarnation in spite of the intensity of the emotions he uncovered and the detailed story he told. I thought perhaps it was because his religion does not accept the concept, and the fact that he holds a great loyalty to his Church.

But I did not believe that this information came from his imagination. It was coming from someplace else. If it was not coming from a past-life experience, then perhaps he was tuning into some collective unconscious, as some theorize. But more importantly for me was the question of why I was listening to the tape in the first place. Jack had not sought Roberta out because of her involvement in UFO research or even because she sometimes used past-life regression in her therapy. He had been referred to her through normal means. He went to her as a psychiatrist who might help him with his depression. There were many qualified psychotherapists that he might have gone to or been referred to. But of all of the choices, he ended up with the only one in town who knew of my peculiar research interests.

Here was another case of an amazing coincidence that brought new knowledge and important information my way. I should have been used to it by now, but each time it happened I was just as amazed as the time before. It seemed as if a higher power kept arranging events in such a way that I would be propelled further in my search for answers. Well, I had asked for it. I had prayed for the truth and now it was coming to me faster and in more bizarre ways than I could ever have imagined. I felt as if I were on one of those moving sidewalks they use at airports to transport pedestrians, only I couldn't get off of this one. I had made a commitment—a promise to God that I would follow his guidance no matter where it took me and I intended to honor that promise.

I thought about Jack's account of the Crucifixion regularly after listening to the tape, but the thought of it was particularly in my mind as I interviewed Bob Dean nearly ten months later. The similarities were uncanny. First, I was struck by the raw emotions that both exhibited. Such emotions are not made up or imagined. Secondly, I was struck by the similar imagery in their descriptions. Both men described Jesus as bleeding profusely from all over his body, front and back. They both noted that the posts for the crucifixes were already in place when the procession reached the place of execution, a detail not mentioned in the gospels. They both described the driving of spikes through the wrists of Jesus, rather than through the hands, as is commonly depicted in religious paintings. This is the way that the famous Shroud of Turin depicts the wounds of the man on the shroud. Experts today agree that this is the only way the spikes could actually hold up the weight of a body in such a position. Driving spikes through the hands would result in the weight of the body tearing through the fragile bones of the hands.

Finally, both men agreed that the Romans used ropes, tied to the cross beam, to hoist the man onto the upright post that was already in the ground. Bob's description of this differed slightly in that he remembered the ropes being placed in a groove at the top of the post, while Jack remembered that the Romans used pulleys and he could even hear the creaking of the pulleys as they hoisted Jesus up. This difference, I thought, was a minor one. I wished that I had a copy of the audiotape of Bob's hypnosis session, but it had been lost in his move from Tucson to Phoenix, along with many of his prized possessions. His story of the Crucifixion was from his memory of the hypnosis session. To really check the details, I would have to hear the missing tape, but that was impossible.

In any case, I had heard enough to see that there was a lot of agreement between the two versions of the story. Differences in details might be accounted for by the fact that hypnosis is not perfect. Undoubtedly some of the person's conscious memories and beliefs creep into any hypnosis session. I never believed that hypnosis was infallible or magical, only that it was a doorway to a multidimensional universe and that it could serve as an aid in research and therapy.

## An Emerging Pattern

I was much more fascinated by the pattern that was emerging from the many synchronous cases that were coming to me in which Jesus played an important role. I was also fascinated by the impact that these past lives had made on the present lives of the experiencers. It seemed to me that all of us carried with us traumas from past lives into our present lives and that these ancient experiences were, in many ways, responsible for how we were choosing to live our lives today. The first element in the pattern that I noticed was that all of us, myself, Bob, the doctor in Mexico, Alicia, and Jack, all carried with us a deep well of emotion that, when tapped, erupted into seizures that included sadness and love, as well what seemed like a good deal of guilt, that could not be accounted for by any of us. I recognized in all of them the same reaction that I experienced when recalling my scant past-life memories—the sudden tears welling in the eyes, the choking down of emotions, and a heaving chest indicative of a strong reaction to some memory.

Secondly, it was obvious that in all of these cases, including my own, there was a direct connection to UFOs. Either the person had seen UFOs, had an intense interest in the subject, or believed he or she had actually had alien contact experiences. The UFO mystery was the common link. Somehow, it was our interest in the UFO mystery that had brought us together in amazingly synchronistic ways.

Thirdly, I began to see that past-life memories were affecting our current lives in various ways. Bob Dean had memories of being a warrior in past lives and the pattern repeated itself in this one. He was also dedicating his current life toward enlightening the public about the relationship between the current UFO mystery and the origins of the Judeo-Christian religions. Alicia was struggling to make sense of her Jewish roots, but was finding that her religion, rather than teaching spirituality, was merely teaching dogma and traditions. Her innate understanding of spirituality, in fact, was much more akin to the true teachings of Jesus as described in later chapters of this book.

In my own case, I had growing suspicions that I might have had something to do with the ancient and mysterious Jewish sect known as the Essenes in a past life, and that I might have even been involved in maintaining and studying, or even teaching, some of the Dead Sea Scrolls. I wondered if my fascination with writing and with the true origins of Christianity came from my subconscious past-life memories. The doctor in Mexico, who believed he had been responsible for the death of Jesus, chose to become a healer and a helper of people in his current life. And Jack's fascination with the Civil War and ancient Rome led him to become a history teacher and a devout Catholic. If these things were true, then I was gaining a valuable lesson in the evolution of the soul and the importance of understanding past-life memories in the treatment of mental illness.

How, I wondered, could any psychologist or psychiatrist today even begin to treat his patients without understanding this basic concept of human existence? Without understanding that (1) the soul exists, (2) that it pre-exists the body, (3) that it has lived many times before, (4) that it is on an eternal journey of growth, and (5) that past-life experiences continue to affect people in their present lives, how could a mental-health professional even begin to help his patients? I began to conclude that psychology has a long way to go before it crosses most of these controversial barriers of understanding, and that many practitioners feel inhibited, or restrained by their peers and by the professional organizations to which they belong.

PART TWO

# The Search

*"(We shall separate ourselves) from the men of perversion in order to go to the wilderness to prepare the way of HIM, as it is written: 'In the wilderness prepare the way of (the Lord), make straight in the desert a road for our God.' "*

The Essene Manual of Discipline
The Dead Sea Scrolls

## CHAPTER SIX

# Journey to Qumran

### The Dead Sea

THERE ARE TWO common ways for tourists to get to Qumran when they visit the Holy Land, as I did in the spring of 1999. You can get there from the north by way of the highway that today drops down from the hills upon which Jerusalem was built, passing first through the narrow, twisting streets, crowded with tourist buses, and then on to the highway toward the arid lowlands to the east, leaving behind the ancient city with its glistening domes and the acres of olives trees that cling to every available hillside on the city's outskirts.

Soon, the road turns southward toward the shores of the Dead Sea, dropping to more than one thousand feet below sea level in the process. The narrow, two-lane road winds down and down into the wilderness where nothing grows of its own accord, passing near the town of Jericho where John the Baptist was said to have preached, near the place on the Jordan River where the Gospels say he baptized Jesus, and then finally to a turn in the road where the vast expanse of what was called, in Jesus' time, the "Sea of Salt," comes into view. From that point the ancient ruins of Qumran, indicated by the sign labeled "Khirbat Qumeran," are only a few more miles. (The word *khirbat* means "ruins" and the Israeli spelling of the name Qumran is slightly different.) The total distance traveled is less than twenty miles, but that is deceiving. Much more so than in Jerusalem itself, one feels that in Qumran one has journeyed back in time, back to the days when Jesus himself traveled these ancient lands.

Across the sea in the distance, one can see the mountains of Jordan, the ancient land called Moab in the Bible, which borders the sea the entire length of its eastern shoreline, about fifty miles. Named after the grandson of Lot (of Sodom and Gomorrah fame), whose descendants settled in the region, the nation of Moab blocked the entry of the Israelites into the Promised Land and was subsequently conquered by King David and cursed by Israeli prophets, fueling a bitter hostility that continues into modern times.

The sea itself is deceptively beautiful, its blueness stretching as far south as the eye can see, south toward the mountain fortress of Masada, king Herod's ancient palace. Masada was later the site of the mass suicide of Jewish zealots who were the last to be slaughtered in the Roman army's bloody suppression of the first-century Jewish uprising that saw the destruction of Jerusalem.

Bordering the sea on the west for the length of its frothy shores are arid mountains and precipitous cliffs dotted with hidden crevices, canyons (*wadi*) and many hundreds of caves, where the ancient scrolls were found. The sea itself is so full of minerals (about thirty percent) that nothing can grow or live in it, and any metal parts of boats corrode and rust away in practically no time at all. Tourists come to bathe in the water, not so much to spend a day at the beach, but to test its legendary buoyancy. It is virtually impossible to sink or drown in water with such a high mineral content. So the sea is not only barren of fish and plant life, but also of the boats that are common to most other bodies of water its size. The effect on the senses is to make it seem like a desert—a desert of water, where nothing lives and nothing ventures. At 1,200 feet below sea level the air is heavy and oppressive for most of the year and on most days the temperatures are ten degrees hotter than at sea level. One wonders why anyone would want to live in such a hostile environment.

The second common way to get to Qumran is from the south. The high-way from the port of Ashdod (where elegant cruise ships would dock to disembark their wealthy tourists) takes the tour buses across the lush land-scape of the land of milk and honey—orchards of olives, oranges, grape-fruit, dates, and flowers paint the landscape in bright pinks, yellows, and reds. Then, after about an hour, the terrain begins to get rockier and dryer, the olive trees scarcer. Soon, the road begins winding down through desert terrain to the only road below the lush heights—the one that runs the length of the Dead Sea all the way to Jerusalem. From this southern entry the tour buses first stop at the imposing three-thousand-foot cliffs of Masada, where a gondola carries tourists to the top of the massive citadel to see the ruins of Herod's luxurious palace and to imagine what it must have been like for the nearly seven hundred Jewish men, women, and children who commit-ted suicide rather than be taken alive by the Roman legion that was about to storm over the fortress walls.

Here too, just as at Qumran, ancient scrolls were discovered that seem to link the victims of Masada to the Essene community. If in fact there was a connection, it would seem that the shores of the Dead Sea were suitable for habitation by the most unpopular religious groups of the time, driven to the wilderness as a place of isolation and refuge they sought against not only the despotic Roman rulers, but also the authorities of orthodox Ju-daism, whom they opposed for their collaboration with the Romans. First-century Palestine was all about religion. A person's religious beliefs defined who he or she was. Religion and politics could not be separated from each other. One was either aligned with the group in power or risked annihila-tion. What is truly amazing is that not much has changed in the interven-ing two thousand years. Religion is still what it is all about in that region.

**The Wilderness**
There is a third way to get to Qumran, however, that most tourists don't know about. The third way is not for the squeamish or the faint of heart, but it is the way that many would have taken in the days of first-century

Palestine. It is a way that now requires a four-wheel-drive vehicle, a plentiful stock of provisions and water and, above all, an experienced guide. This is the way our small party decided to take in April 1999 on our journey to Qumran, a journey my soul had yearned for since my hypnosis session four years earlier. I had to go to Qumran and see it for myself; I had to discover the connection between that mysterious place and my vision of the crucifix and the beach with the jars, and between the story of Jesus and the Dead Sea Scrolls.

To make the trek across the Judean desert where few tourists ever venture, we hired a forty-nine-year-old Jewish guide named Yossi who had served in the Israeli army and had lived in a kibbutz for nearly twenty years. He divorced and set out to make a new life for himself as an adventure guide, taking tourists deep-sea diving in the Red Sea and on camel-back rides to the ancient city of Petra in the Jordanian desert. His excellent English, his intimate knowledge of the country, and his easy, self-assured manner made him a good choice for our small group of slightly nervous adventurers.

"It's not so dangerous," he assured us when we made the arrangements. "I will bring a SUV with four-wheel drive and we will cut across the desert so that you can see what it was like in ancient times. Nothing has changed out there in thousands of years." The idea had great appeal to me, for it was a connection to those ancient times that I was seeking.

"Yes, but don't we have to go through Palestinian territory?" I questioned nervously.

"That is true," he said. "We also go through Bedouin territory. But don't worry; I speak their languages and I do this frequently."

"Okay," we finally agreed. The lure of experiencing the Judean wilderness of Biblical times was just too great. "Let's do it," we said, and the bargain was sealed.

True to his word, Yossi arrived early in the morning on the appointed date in a beige Isuzu to pick up our party of four—my wife and I, and another couple who had joined us on our voyage to the Holy Land. Right away he began to put us at ease about the trip by telling us about himself and his life in Israel.

His casual conversation soon put us at ease. It was clear that what we considered to be a dangerous adventure, he merely considered a routine drive, as if he were on the way to the mall. His demeanor, along with the beautiful spring weather, a cloudless blue sky, and a balmy seventy-degree temperature, combined to put us into an adventurous spirit. By the time we passed through the last Arab village, stopping at a gas station to use the holes in the floor that passed for commodes, the media stories of terrorist attacks and frequent Palestinian-Israeli clashes began to fade from memory and visions of camel caravans and holy magi following a mysterious star began to take their place.

Very soon all signs of civilization disappeared and even the dirt road faded into a rutted, winding path, which climbed abruptly into the barren Judean mountains where not even occasional weeds can grow and where sand and rocks stretch as far as the eye can see. Now I understood all too well what the authors of the Bible meant when they said about Jesus, "… and he was taken into the wilderness for forty days to be tested," after his baptism in the Jordan River.

*Spending forty days out here would be quite a test. Nothing can live out here*, I thought. We climbed higher and higher, the car jostling precariously close to the treacherous precipice to our right. Just then, we turned a bend and before us was what appeared to be a shack with a black tarp draped over a doorway. The tiny hut lay down in a ravine, smoke coming from a makeshift chimney.

"What is that?" we asked excitedly.

"That's a Bedouin house," Yossi calmly explained. "They are the nomadic people who have lived here for thousands of years. They don't like staying in one place. To them, the land belongs to everyone. Ownership of land is a foreign concept to them. All they want is to be left alone. So the government leaves them alone. Besides, who else would want to live out here?"

"How do they get food and water?" we asked.

"They have wells and they raise goats and camels," he answered.

When we reached the top of the mountain there was a more-or-less level area where Yossi parked the car next to a cement encasement resting on the ground.

"We'll eat lunch here, next to this Bedouin well," Yossi said. We were grateful for a chance to get out and stretch our legs and take some pictures. The view of the expansive desert was magnificent from our vantage point. With binoculars we could track the flight path of a lone hawk high above us, searching for his noon meal. *Lots of luck*, I thought. It didn't seem to me that there was anything for him to find.

Looking eastward we could see the mountain range that borders the Dead Sea, and to the northwest the vague outline of the city of Jerusalem in the far distance. It was easy to visualize this as the spot where Jesus came to be tested, sitting on a rock on the mountaintop and confronting Satan. "Turn the rock into a loaf of bread," Satan taunted. "I'll give you riches if you follow me. I wondered how true that story really was or if it was merely one of the many embellishments to the Jesus story added by overzealous followers in later years. Even though I believed that much of the Bible was true, I was also highly suspicious that it had been embroidered and changed over the many intervening years. *I guess we will never know for sure about that*, I thought.

## Living in Isolation

While Yossi heated the water for the tea and emptied the ice chest containing the lunch of cheese and pita bread he had prepared for us, we peered down into the darkness of the Bedouin well, where, about twenty feet down, we could see a pool of water. A long rope attached to a bucket, dangled from a metal rod protruding from the cement. The side of the cement encasement was shaped like a trough used for watering animals. This was the source of sustenance for the intrepid Bedouin people who insist on living their lives just as their ancestors did for unknown thousands of years, resisting all temptation to become civilized. *How odd*, I reflected, *that there were people who could not only resist the lure of technology and modern conveniences, but who actually went to great lengths to run away from it. What do they know that we don't know?* My thoughts were cut short by Yossi's signal to us that we had to stay on schedule.

Back in the car we began our downward trek along the rugged mountain road, winding back and forth between mountain peaks, crossing over rocky ravines and washed-out gullies. After a few miles, we reached a deep canyon that dropped a good thousand feet sharply to the floor below. We followed the canyon for several miles before we were suddenly caught by an incredible surprise. Clinging to the other side of the canyon wall, beginning at the canyon rim and meandering all the way down to the valley floor, was a sight straight out of a fairy tale. My first thought was that we had stumbled upon the lost city of Shangri-La, the mythical city where no one ever ages. It looked like a fortress built on the side of a precipice with thirty-foot high walls and a labyrinth of hundreds of rooms on at least ten different, ramshackle levels. Yossi seemed to enjoy the surprise on our faces as we finally thought to ask, "What in the heck is that?"

"That," he answered, "is the monastery of Mar Saba. For five centuries as many as five hundred Greek Orthodox Christian monks have lived here in total isolation from the rest of the world. But now, there are only sixteen monks left. If you look carefully, you might see some of them walking about."

Gazing down upon the improbable sight, I found it incredible that even today there is still a religious group dwelling in seclusion near the Dead Sea, living a life of piety, just as the Essenes did two thousand years ago. Mar Saba stands today as a testament (just as Qumran and Masada did in their day) to the extreme measures taken by those searching for enlightenment and salvation. I remembered that in one of the many books I had read about ancient texts I discovered that it was here, at Mar Saba, that a fragment of the earliest known copies of the book of Mark was discovered. How I longed to be able to rummage through their collection of sacred texts!

I was also reminded of a line from one of the Dead Sea Scrolls that I was studying just before the trip. It comes from a scroll called "The Manual of Discipline," or sometimes "The Community Rule." It is one of the documents that describes the beliefs, rituals, and practices of the mysterious Essenes. In this organizational document we are told that the people of Qumran must separate themselves "from the dwelling place of the men of perversion [meaning the Jewish priests who controlled the Jerusalem Temple and those who followed them] in order to go to the wilderness to prepare the way of Him, as it is written [quoting from Isaiah 40:3]: 'In the wilderness prepare the way of the... [the name of God is indicated by four dots], make straight in the desert a road for our God."

This ancient document makes it clear why the Qumran community existed. It was because the Essene sect believed that its mission was to fulfill the prophetic words of one of Judaism's greatest prophets. Isaiah, they believed, directed them to live in the wilderness to prepare a proper reception for the coming of the savior—a messiah. Their role would be to prepare a proper place for Him, a pure place where he would be received and nurtured so that he could fulfill his mission on Earth.

Now it all began to make sense to me. I began to understand the mindset that was behind the mystery of Qumran and the sacred scrolls. The Essenes believed that they alone were worthy of receiving the Messiah and that the orthodox Jews, known as the Pharisees, had corrupted Judaism by consorting with the Romans and abusing their power to gain personal wealth. They referred to the priests of Jerusalem as "seekers of smooth things."

Those who occupied the Qumran community had very much the same idea in mind as the monks of Mar Saba—to get as far away from civilization and government authority as possible so as not to be influenced by negative forces from the corrupt world. In fact, the Essenes saw the world and the universe around them as being a constant battle between good and evil. These dark forces, they believed, were unleashed upon the world when angelic beings violated the laws of God by coming down from the skies and corrupting humans by having sexual intercourse with them and creating a race of hybrid offspring, called Nephilim in the Bible. The Essenes had in their library of sacred books a little known text called the Books of Enoch, which detail the existence of angelic beings, who were given the task by God to watch over life on Earth. Such beings were known as "Watchers."

The Books of Enoch describe the ensuing battle between the good Watchers (the defenders of the light), led by the archangels Michael, Rafael, Sariel, and Gabriel, and the bad Watchers who "had begun to go unto the daughters of men, so they became impure." As punishment for their sins, God destroyed humanity and the hybrid offspring by causing a great flood. The Essenes saw themselves as the human representatives of the good Watchers and referred to themselves as "The Sons of Light," indicating that they were in league with the good Watchers in their continuing battle with the evil ones. The more I studied about the Dead Sea Scrolls, the more I realized that they represented an entire library of secret books that contained a vast array of knowledge ranging from the secret location of an immense treasure of gold and silver to the history of mankind's ancient relationship to God and His angelic messengers.

All of these thoughts were running through my head as we came closer and closer to the shores of the Dead Sea on our slow trek through the Judean Desert. After pausing to get out of the car to take in the astonishing sight of the Mar Saba monastery, we resumed our descent on the rutted path, down a series of winding turns to the valley floor. Suddenly, we could see before us another unexpected sight—not an ancient fortress, but a modern one. It was a high-security, highly fortified military compound, completely surrounded by tall, barbed wire fences and with lookout towers in each of its corners. Slipping past it, we began to notice the burnt-out bodies of old cars and trucks strewn along the sandy road. "Where are we?" we queried our guide nervously.

"Oh, don't worry," he answered calmly, "This is just an Israeli Army training area," as if such explanation could possibly calm our nerves.

Then we noticed, on the dunes in the distance, an Israeli tank traveling roughly parallel to the road. Soon, we saw two, then three, then numerous tanks in the distance. Yossi seemed unperturbed by their presence and acted as if he were driving down the street in Tel Aviv. We, on the other hand, expected to hear the whistle and explosion of a tank shell at any moment. We were sure the tanks would find our Isuzu an enticing moving target for their daily practice. But no shells came our way and the tanks continued milling about as if we were invisible. Before long we came to a paved road and Yossi turned the car to the right, toward the east and the shores of the Dead Sea where the Qumran ruins lay. Within twenty minutes we came into view of that lifeless body of water and we made our way to the sign reading "Qumeran next exit."

**Qumran**

From the highway, Qumran lies only two hundred yards up an incline toward the cliffs where the scrolls were found. My heart raced in anticipation of seeing them and the ruins, but the view was obstructed partially by a modern building that served as an information office, gift shop, and restaurant. We parked the car in a large parking lot, now beginning to fill with tourist buses, and made our way to the entrance gate where we bought our tickets and were directed toward the main building. To my surprise, instead of getting to go directly to the ruins, we had to go through a door into a small theater where visitors are first made to sit through a film about the history of the historical site.

"Isn't there any way to skip this part?" I impatiently asked Yossi.

"No," he answered. "We have to wait here until we are guided to the next exhibit."

"Oh God," I groaned to myself. "Not another exhibit!" All I wanted to do was to get to the ruins, and if there had been a way, I would have bolted there and then.

But then, the lights dimmed and the movie began and I quickly found myself being enraptured by what I saw. There were three movie screens aligned in a semicircle and three projectors were used to give the audience an intimate view of what life might have been like in the ancient village.

The movie started by showing a group of men all wearing long, white linen robes, walking about a desert compound, the walls glistening with white plaster. The buildings were crowded together, with a few open areas for outside gatherings and for pools of water, which were connected by a series of canals that diverted rainwater from the cliffs down to the cisterns in the compound.

I thought it was a good re-creation of the ruins I had studied so carefully in books and journals. The men all had long, dark hair and beards and looked very Christ-like, I thought. I found myself being drawn more and more into the film.

Then the camera focused on a group of men who were entering a room in single file and removing their robes to expose long, lean bodies, covered only with white loincloths. The narrator explained that the Essenes practiced ritual bathing as part of their religion. By performing this ritual of submersion, those who were spiritually pure would maintain their purity. The bath was meant to cleanse the soul as well as the body and was a sacred ritual that had been practiced for at least fifty to one hundred years before the time of Jesus. So, the narrator concluded casually, this is where the idea of baptism was born.

I was struck by the matter-of-fact way this information was presented, as if this fact was common knowledge. But, in fact, this information is only common knowledge to Dead Sea Scroll scholars. Indeed, orthodox Christianity does not accept, nor does it teach, that baptism and other Christian practices originated with the Essenes. Catholics and Protestants alike do not hear this information during Sunday sermons or Bible training. Christianity simply ignores the Essenes and fails to convey to its constituents the importance of the scrolls to the Christian faith.

This is one of the problems I find with organized religion. The more I researched the subject, the more I saw religious institutions as censoring bodies, which kept the intense debates about the authenticity of the Gospels and the true origins of Christianity isolated to scholarly journals. True, there are clerics from different denominations who are deeply involved in these debates and who are highly knowledgeable about the serious implications of the scrolls and other recently discovered texts, but somehow this information never makes it to the pulpit or to Bible study groups.

As a result, modern Christians still adhere to the beliefs that were formulated for them by one segment of the early Christian church several hundred years after the death of Jesus.

As I watched the men soaking in the sacred pool, cleansing their souls, I became intensely aware that there had been another form of Christianity long ago, and from deep within me began to well up strong pangs of emotion. The men began to climb the steps one by one, pressing the water from their hair with cloths and reaching for their robes. The camera zoomed in on one of the men who was slowly drying himself, and I suddenly felt a strong kinship to him. A fleeting hint of recognition swept over me and the emotion clamped down on my chest and throat like a savage beast, cutting off my air passage and stifling my breath.

I struggled to maintain my self-control, but in the darkness of the theater my eyes filled with tears and I choked down the sobs that wanted to burst forth from deep within. Something in the reenactment of this ancient ritual had quite unexpectedly provoked within me a deep emotional response. I recognized right away that I had felt this emotion many times before, but not often this intensely.

By the time the movie ended and the lights were brightening, my chest was heaving and I was trying desperately to gain control of my emotions and to dry my eyes. To prevent anyone from noticing, I trailed behind the others as we filed down toward the front of the theater, wiping my eyes with a handkerchief. I didn't want to have to explain my tears to anyone. How could I?

Then, another surprise. The center portion of the movie screen suddenly began to retract up into the ceiling, gradually revealing behind it a darkened passageway that looked like a cave. Slowly, at the back of the passageway, a scene became illuminated. What I saw there only served to provoke my emotions once again. The faint illumination revealed a cave-like setting and a group of earthen jars, identical to the ones the scrolls were found in, strewn on the floor, looking much as they must have when they were found by a Bedouin goat herder in 1947.

Yossi began to lead our group through the passageway toward the exhibit, and I followed behind, amazed that the clever designers of the theater would devise such an unusual exit. We walked up the darkened passageway to the display, the jars tantalizingly out of reach, and the power of they the jars once held overwhelmed me. It was hard to imagine that information could be preserved and transmitted over such a long time, overcoming such great odds. After all, the entire power of the Roman Empire and that of the Pharisaic priesthood had at one time been intent on finding and destroying all such documents. How amazing, I thought, that they would be preserved for all of these years, and then stumbled upon by an innocent goat herder just in time for the information to be made available to the world at the end of the second millennium.

My group had gone ahead, leaving me in deep thought, gazing upon the replicas of the old jars. At last I had to pull away from the display, my heart in my throat, tears streaming down my cheeks. I followed silently through the few other exhibits of photographs and artifacts, all the time trying to regain my composure. Then, finally, we walked through a door and we were out in the bright sunshine. For a moment my eyes strained to adapt to the glare, and then I could take in the expanse that lay before me. We stood near the base of the rugged mountain, much taller than I had imagined from the many photos I had seen. A trail led up the steep cliffs to a number of cave openings high above.

To our immediate left, up a slight incline, I could see the ruins of an old tower with thick walls made of smooth stones. A few short steps and we found ourselves on top of a large plateau overlooking the Dead Sea, which was only a few hundred meters to the west. The Qumran ruins lay spread before us like a war-torn village from a long-forgotten war. Rock walls protruded from the ground, exposing the design of the old community, which appeared to be a jumble of rooms of various sizes with passageways leading here and there.

I took a deep breath, filling my lungs with the air from that long-ago time, my heart thumping in my chest from the rush it gave me. Then I took my first step into the place where, I was certain, Jesus himself once walked and worked and taught. I was finally here. I had made it back.

*"We now understand that many of the beliefs and practices of the early Church, that were once thought to be unique, were in many cases prefigured at Qumran"*
—James Vanderkan, Bible scholar

*"...this structure of stone that endures between the bitter waters [of the Dead Sea] and precipitous cliffs...is perhaps, more than Bethlehem or Nazareth, the cradle of Christianity."*
—Edmund Wilson
*The New Yorker*, May 1955

*"We must now affirm that, in the Essene communities, we discover antecedents of Christian forms and concepts."*
—Frank Cross,
Harvard University Dead Sea Scroll scholar

CHAPTER SEVEN
# The Sons of Light
## The Secret Books of the Essenes

A S I STOOD atop the plateau overlooking the Dead Sea, amid the stone ruins of what had once been the home of the mysterious Essenes, I struggled to stifle the strong emotions welling up from deep within my chest. Why was this happening? Was this a reaction to something I had read or to my religious training as a child? I remembered my childhood and my grandmother's strong devotion to Jesus and to the Catholic Church. She kept a large print, depicting Jesus with a yellow halo around his head, eyes cast to the sky above, in a wooden frame above her bed. But, in fact, we rarely went to church when I was a small boy and by the time my parents converted to Presbyterianism, when I was eight, the teachings of the Catholic Church had been lost on me. I had never attended catechism class, nor taken my first communion. All I remembered about the Catholic masses was how somber and frightening they were.

**Religion or Spirituality?**
The Church of the Holy Family, which we attended, was dark and cold inside. Old ladies in long black dresses, scarves wrapped around their heads, knelt before flickering candles, mumbling prayers while clasping rosaries tightly in their gnarled hands. Some waited patiently in line before old wooden booths for their turn to enter for some mysterious purpose. The mass itself, wreathed in swirling incense, had an ominous tone for a small, wide-eyed boy. In those days the mass was in Latin, not the familiar Spanish of my childhood, and this had the effect of heightening the mystery of the strange rituals being performed. I didn't know what was being said, but it was clear that the focus of attention was the statue of the man who hung on a cross behind the altar, blood dripping from his head and side and from where the nails had punctured his feet and hands. His eyes, barely open, were cast downward, giving him a strange expression of both supreme sadness and exquisite peacefulness at the same time. The life-size effigy seemed to cast a pallor of sadness and, it seemed to me, fear, which left the people depressed and saddened by the experience.

But most remarkable to me was the priest, whose unquestioned authority on issues of spirituality and morality made him a person to be feared and respected within the poor border community in which we lived. "*Vente! Escondete! Hay viene el padre!*" ("Come on! Hide! Here comes the priest!"), my grandfather (always the joker) would jest, whenever the priest would come to visit my grandmother who was ill. Even with a bad heart, my grandmother could not help but laugh at his antics as we pretended to run and hide from the priest. My *abuelito* (grandfather) was not enamored of the Church.

The Protestant church we later attended, however, was cheerful and bright in comparison to the darkness of the Catholic Church; the minister, friendly and jovial, was respected, but not considered more holy than anyone else. His sermons, however, were deadly serious and quoted liberally from the Old and New Testaments in words I could understand. After all, he held a doctor of theology degree from the Dallas Theological Seminary and was a devout fundamentalist. The Bible was the divine and holy word of God, and that was it, as far as he was concerned. He never saw any contradictions in the Bible, and his expertise was never questioned.

That is until some members of the congregation tired of his rigidity. One day, they simply voted him out and hired a new minister! Which issues of doctrine were in dispute, I did not understand, but the disagreement caused great anger and bitterness between members of the congregation, half of whom left and founded a new congregation.

Bible study and Sunday school are what I remember most about the early teen years I spent at the Hillside Bible Presbyterian Church near our home. Yet there was nothing I could think of that could have provoked such a dramatic response in me so many years later when I underwent hypnosis. By the time I was eighteen, I simply refused to go to church anymore, and even though I attended services occasionally in later years, the dogma of the religion did not appeal to me. To put it more clearly, I was not one who could accept what was in the Bible on the basis of faith alone.

In later years, I was particularly dismayed when, as an Army officer stationed in Georgia in the 1960s, I discovered that there was a Presbyterian church for whites and another for blacks. (The practice was common in all the denominations at the time, as far as I could tell.) When I asked the minister to explain how such a practice lived up to the spirit of Jesus, he simply smiled and said, "Son, you'll find out that we do things a bit differently here in the South." Needless to say, that answer did not satisfactorily resolve the issue in my mind.

After much contemplation I realized that it wasn't my religious upbringing that caused the strong emotions I was feeling. Neither church ever managed to gather me into its fold, even though both had made distinct impressions upon my psyche. My spiritual path was destined to take me in a much more circuitous route to God.

*Maybe,* I thought to myself as I surveyed the Qumran ruins, *it is just the drama of the place itself that is making me feel this way.* Maybe it was the cliffs, the caves, or the mysteries of the scrolls themselves. But if that was the case, then why didn't I have emotional responses to the other dramatic sights we had seen? In the course of our visit to Israel we walked the shores of the Sea of Galilee, just as Jesus had. We visited Nazareth and Bethlehem and were shown the place of the nativity and where the Holy Family lived. We walked the cobblestone streets of the Via Dolorosa where it is said that Jesus carried the cross on the way to Calvary, and we visited Golgotha where he met his death on that fateful day. But in none of those places did I experience much, if any, emotion. Yet here, next to the caves where the scrolls were found, and among the ruins of what until recent years had been thought to be an old Roman fort, my heart was in my throat.

Maybe it was the hypnosis session that somehow programmed me to feel this way, I considered. But it was clear from listening to the tape recording of that session that the hypnotherapist had not suggested anything about Qumran, the caves, the Essenes, or the scrolls. She had not suggested that I visualize a crucifix or a beach or a row of earthen jars. These were images that came to me from somewhere else, as if of their own volition. All I knew for certain was that from that moment on, I became obsessed with discovering the message that those visions held for me and with uncovering the connection between the scrolls and the life of Jesus.

## The Paths of Qumran

That driving force caused me to read everything I could find on the subject and ultimately find some way to go to Qumran to see for myself. What had I hoped to find here? All I could hope for was to walk among the few remaining walls and to glimpse from afar the caves that held the sacred writings. I knew I would not discover a new artifact or scroll fragment that had gone undetected by the archaeologists who have pored over every square inch of the site for half a century. No, it wasn't artifacts or new discoveries I was after. It was closure. Somehow I had to satisfy a yearning deep within my soul. I needed to touch the rock walls, to walk the paths, and to see the caves. (How I would have loved to climb the hills and explore the dark interior of any one of them.) I needed to feel the energy of the place and to let it wash over me and penetrate my every cell.

And now that I was here, the stones were speaking to me. An emotional energy was surging through me like waves crashing on a sandy beach. There was a connection for me in this place that I could not explain in a rational way. I continued to trail behind the group as we walked the narrow paths between the crumbling buildings while our guide gave us a history of the excavations. But I needed no lecture. I recognized the ruined buildings from the many photos I had studied. I knew the layout of the structures by memory—the drainage canals carved from the rocky ground, the cisterns and the bathing pools, the oven used for baking pottery and working metals, and the large room thought to be where the scrolls were copied and written.

I knew this place better than most guides could know it and I didn't need more information—at least not at this moment. All I wanted to do was to soak it in and to let it fill my senses. I wanted to smell the salt in the air, to feel the warm breeze in my face and to listen to its song as the wind brushed against the ancient walls. My senses were heightened and they were telling me that this was sacred ground, that this place was special, that it was important.

For years now I had been praying for guidance and to be shown the truth. I had now learned to pay attention to even the slightest details, particularly when it came to my emotions. I had learned that, in my case, intuitive feelings were accompanied by emotional sensations. I began to see that this was how I sensed subtle energies; I was beginning to learn to use my innate psychic abilities. But at this particular moment, I had to push these energies aside. My group had stopped to peer down into one of the now-empty ritual pools, and I took the opportunity to ask my friend to take my picture. I sat on the stone edge of the pool and draped my leg over the side as if I were dipping my foot into the healing waters. It was easy for me to imagine at that moment what it might have been like to descend the rock-hewn steps into the pool of precious water to participate in the sacred ritual with the Sons of Light. Time stood still for me as I lingered there for a few moments after the shutter snapped, but as much as I wished to stay, I could not.

We went on to explore the other parts of the compound and to take a long look at Cave 4, located at the southern end of the mesa. There, located near the top of a sheer cliff, was a dark hole where many of the scrolls had been found. As I pondered the amazing discovery, my group turned back to the ruins, their curiosity easily sated. The gift shop and a hot meal beckoned to them. But I needed more time.

"You go along," I urged. "I'll meet you in a little while. I just need a few more minutes here."

"Okay," they said. "We'll be in the gift shop."

At last, I found myself alone with the few other tourists still milling about. I wandered aimlessly, taking it all in, stopping to peek into the numerous small rooms and to snap a photo of an Israeli woman archaeologist who was working diligently under a blue tarp—a reminder that many mysteries still remained to be unraveled here.

Soon, I worked my way to the edge of the community, the one facing the cliffs that rose sharply only a few hundred feet away. I stared up to the caves above me, so close, yet so far. There was no way to climb up there in the time I had, even if it was allowed. So I found a corner of an eroded wall to sit on, and I tried to still my mind and listen to my heart. I closed my eyes and took a deep breath "Thank you, Lord," I prayed, "for showing me the way." With those words, the feelings I had tried so hard to suppress came bursting forth. Tears once again streamed down my face and my chest began to heave in uncontrollable sobs of sadness and joy and guilt.

Guilt? Where had the guilt come from? I never realized until then that guilt was a part of it. In previous bouts with my emotion, I had identified the feelings of love and sadness and joy, but now I realized that guilt was there also—and in strong measure. And then it came to me, not as a distinct memory, but more of a knowing. Yes, of course! It was the guilt of not standing up for him. It was the guilt of not having the courage to try to help as he was dragged off to his death. It was the guilt of fleeing, along with the others, in fear of losing my own life. *We were all cowards,* I thought. *We ran. None of us believed in him enough to follow him to the cross. Instead, he died with thieves on either side of him, rather than with those who loved him so much.* Even now, as I write these words, it is painful to admit to such cowardice. The pain and sorrow well up once again, preventing me from typing for a while. I have to gather myself and try to find the words to describe what happened to me that day at Qumran. I guess it could best be described as a gift from God to help me in my quest for answers. So much of my life began to make sense for the first time—why I was driven to search for answers to the mystery behind the story of Jesus and to the secret teachings regarding the sons of God, which I somehow knew had been kept from the world for so many years. "Ask and ye shall receive," are the words that come to mind. If you are willing to learn, the truth will be shown to you.

But if I was given the knowledge of the origins of the guilt so that I might understand my feelings, it came with another "knowing" that it was okay. We were all forgiven and we had been forgiven, even from the beginning. In fact, over the passing weeks and months I came to understand that there was a grander process involved than I could ever have imagined only a short time before. I began to see that the scenario that played out at Golgotha that fateful day had its makings even before Jesus incarnated. In fact, it was part of a great plan that was made by a large group of souls to provide a lesson for the human race—a lesson about love and spirituality. In order for this lesson to have a lasting value, it would have to be punctuated by an event so dramatic that it could not go unnoticed or be forgotten for a long, long time.

## A Gathering of Souls

The plan was made and a number of souls volunteered to play roles in the drama so that the lesson could be taught. But, as it happens with human existence, once they entered their human bodies, the players were not able to remember what their exact roles would be or what the details of the plan were. If they knew it all, they would forfeit their own opportunity for spiritual growth and a chance to make their own choices. What made Jesus remarkable was that he, and he alone, overcame the amnesia and, with time, he came to realize the nature of the plan and the terrible death that lay in store for him. I began to see that his soul made the greatest commitment, took the greatest risk, and made the greatest sacrifice to be a player in the drama. Not because it was he who would be crucified, for many ultimately were murdered for the parts they played, but rather because his soul came from the highest level of ascension—that nearest the Source, God-force, or the Godhead, as it is sometimes called.

This was a difficult concept for me to understand at first, but with time I began to see that there are many dimensions or levels (some say seven) through which the soul must travel before it can be reunited with the Godhead. We are at the lowest level—no great surprise! The world of physical density in which we feel totally separated from God is the level farthest removed from the All. As the soul progresses, it moves through these other levels, each time learning more important lessons, until it can be reunited. Just getting out of this level may take thousands of lifetimes, and once a soul accomplishes this it seeks to move on rather than slip back. The souls who volunteered to come back and assist in this great plan were from different levels, but all knew that even though the mission would be difficult, the potential for growth would be worth it. The risk would be getting trapped once again in the amnesia of the dense physical world. Jesus, coming from the highest level, had the most to lose.

The problem with entering this dimension is that it is so easy to create bad karma that may have to be repaid in a future incarnation. Any act of unkindness, any act not motivated by love, any attraction to physical pleasures such as wealth or lust could lead to a downward spiral. So it was agreed that the souls would gather in a place that would be minimally susceptible to such backsliding. It would be a place where the purity of the souls could be more easily maintained and where fewer temptations would be found. It would be a place removed from the sinful ways of the big cities, yet at a place where the great cultures of the civilized world all converged—Greek, Roman, Jewish, and Arab. This spot—Qumran—was the chosen place.

All of this I began to realize as I sat alone on the rocks at Qumran. In the solitude of that moment a lifetime of emotions was released and I felt a tremendous comfort and peace, such as I had not felt before. I let the feeling flow over me and consume my every cell. Alone in the remote corner of the community of prophets, on a beautiful day in April, I sat and cried like I had never cried over events that happened a long, long time ago.

**The Essenes**

Hardly anyone, save Bible scholars, had ever heard of the Essenes prior to the 1947 discovery of the Dead Sea Scrolls. The word "Essenes" is not mentioned in the Bible. Neither is the Qumran community directly mentioned, nor is any place like Qumran even described. In fact, the word "Essene" is not even mentioned in the Dead Sea Scrolls. Bible scholars and historians had known about the Essenes, however, for many years because the Essenes are mentioned in the many history books that tell the history of the Jewish people. As for Qumran, archaeologists believed it to be the ruins of an old Roman fort, unworthy of serious excavation. Recently, some archaeologists have made the case for the notion that the ruins represent nothing but an old pottery factory. In fact, a kiln has been found there and the clay within it has been matched to the clay jars in which the scrolls were stored. There is no doubt there is a connection between Qumran and the scrolls. But during its two-hundred-year history, there is also no doubt that the site was used by different people for different things, including at one time a Roman outpost.

The little that was known about the Essenes prior to 1947 led historians to believe that the group was a small, irrelevant Jewish sect that disappeared shortly after the destruction of Jerusalem by the Romans in A.D. 70. All that began to change after a Bedouin goat herder stumbled upon a cave full of earthen jars stuffed with leather scrolls in 1947. Gradually it became clear that what had been discovered was an entire library of sacred texts belonging to a community of Essenes living on the shores of the Dead Sea. Quickly, scholars began to search for any information that could shed light on this amazing discovery.

Around A.D. 70, a naturalist known as Pliny the Elder, writing about his travels in Palestine, commented that he had come upon an Essene monastery on the western shore of the Dead Sea. Hebrew historian Josephus Flavius wrote shortly after the time of Jesus that the Essenes were known for taking in children and teaching them: "The Essenes would receive the children of other people when they were still young and capable of instruction and would care for them as their own and raise them according to their way of life." Josephus also tells of Essenes who were tortured (as early Christians were) and who "cheerfully resigned their souls, confident that they would receive them back again. For it is a fixed belief of theirs that the body is corruptible and its constituent matter impermanent, but that the soul is immortal and imperishable" (Vanderkam in Shanks 1992, 200).

The implications of these passages are important, for they represent the earliest known mentions of the Essenes. First, we see that there is a historical record of the Essenes living on the shores of the Dead Sea at time of Jesus. Secondly, we are told that they had the tradition of taking in young children and teaching them their ways. Thirdly, we get a glimpse into the beliefs of the Essenes with regard to the soul. They believed that their souls were immortal and that they were not afraid of death because they knew that they would "get them back again." Could this be a veiled description of a belief in reincarnation?

Certainly, the Essenes had a belief in the resurrection of the soul. The term "resurrection" is found in numerous places in their writings, but it is not always clear what they meant by that. It seems to refer to the resurrection of the soul, rather than the body. Some interpreters wish to believe that the Essene use of the word meant they believed in the resurrection of the body, as in orthodox Christianity, but that is not what is actually stated.

Hippolytus, an early Christian writer, who lived and wrote much later (A.D.170-236), claimed that the Essenes did believe in the resurrection of the body, but no convincing evidence has been found among the scrolls (Vanderkam, in Shanks, 201). For orthodox Christianity such issues are of paramount importance, for if, as we shall see, the Essene beliefs are at the foundation of early Christianity, and if Jesus himself was a member of this mysterious sect, then differences between the two must be accounted for. And if it turns out that Essenism is the true foundation of Christianity, then what is it that has been practiced by millions and millions of Christians for the last two millennia?

## The Scrolls

Recognized for their true value, the scrolls were sought out by collectors, governments and, of course, religious institutions. In the end, most of the scrolls fell into the control of a French Catholic institution known as the *Ecole Biblique et Archeologique* (the Bible School of Archaeology), controlled indirectly by the Vatican. Those first eight men (no women) chosen to study the decrepit leather parchments were predominately Catholics, and even though the documents were most pertinent to the history of the Hebrew people, there were no Jews either appointed to the committee or even allowed to examine the documents. An undertone of anti-Semitism was always a factor in the treatment of the scrolls. In fact, so much control was placed over the parchments that almost no other Bible scholar or historian was ever allowed to see them. (A few of the scrolls did end up in the control of the Israeli government and are on display in Jerusalem.)

For more than forty years, this small fraternity allowed only their chosen graduate students to join them in their pursuit. In fact, those who control the scrolls were chosen more for their loyalty and predisposition to protect Christianity than for their expertise as historians or for their knowledge of preservation of such delicate documents.

As a result, there quickly grew a suspicion and antagonism among other scholars, who believed that the cabal had no interest in science at all, but only in protecting their church's belief system. During the more than forty years they controlled the scrolls, only their translations, interpretations, and publications were made available to the public. Less than half of the material was published during this time.

There were about nine hundred different books or scrolls in the Qumran library. More may yet be found, and some are known to have been destroyed by the Bedouins who found them—used as tinder for their fires. Only twelve books were intact or almost intact, including the only one made of copper, and which mysteriously listed great treasures of gold and coins that had been hidden in numerous places in ancient Palestine. None have been recovered, as far as anyone knows.

The rest of the scrolls were broken into many thousands of tiny pieces, many smaller than a thumbnail. Once sorted out, they were categorized into four basic types of books: books of the Torah (the first five books of the Old Testament); books of commentary on the scriptures (written by unknown Essene authors); books written by the Essenes about their secret society (known as the sectarian texts); and books of secret occult wisdom, including the Books of Enoch, and some on astrology (quite an embarrassment to the Church). The Books of Enoch include information on the angelic hierarchy that oversees life on Earth, known variously as the Watchers, Archons, Archangels, or the sons of God, and with the history of the world before the great flood when angelic beings descended from the heavens and mated with humans, creating a hybrid race.

Of these, the latter two categories were the most exciting and potentially the most dangerous to modern-day Christian traditions. For in the sectarian texts were found ample evidence that the basic beliefs of Christianity originated at Qumran among the Essenes. And, more importantly, the Qumran documents predated any known copies of the Old and New Testaments by at least one hundred years in some cases, and hundreds of years in others.

Whereas the earliest Gospels of the New Testament were written in Greek (a language not spoken by Jesus or his disciples), the scrolls were written in ancient Hebrew and Aramaic, which were the languages of Jesus and his followers. What is more, the scrolls dated to the time of Christ, between 120 B.C. for the oldest and A.D. 68 for the most recent, although carbon dating is not precise enough to tell exactly when they were written. So the time frame fits in easily with the time when Jesus lived and died. Because the scrolls cannot be precisely dated, those who controlled the scrolls were able to use other, more subjective, means by which to guess the approximate date when each scroll was written. The most controversial of these is called "paleography," a method which attempts to categorize chronologically the way that letters were written in different time periods, as well as the handwriting styles of the times, in order to judge the approximate year in which the scroll was made. Many scholars complain that paleography is not a precise enough science to allow such narrow distinctions, and therefore, the controllers of the scrolls, whose religious beliefs might interfere with their scholarly objectivity, could justify dating the scrolls in such a way that distanced them from Christianity.

In short, the Dead Sea Scrolls, whatever they contained, had the potential for either supporting today's version of Christianity or exploding many myths that might have been created in the ensuing hundreds of years during which the o rthodox Church was haggling over who Jesus was, what he taught, and how he should be regarded. The scrolls provided a peek into the world of Jesus never before available. Now we could see the naked truth, free of the storytelling, fanaticism, and constant revision and editing carried out by well-intentioned zealots. The scrolls were like a time bomb for the Church if they fell into the wrong hands—the hands of true, objective scholars who were free from the centuries of dogma and religious doctrine created by committees of anonymous, bearded old men.

But then, in 1991, a series of events took place in which a group of outside scholars conspired to effectively steal, not the scrolls themselves, but photographic negatives of the documents. By 1992, historians and scholars were suddenly able to obtain their own copies and to begin their own translations, interpretations, and publications on the meaning and implications of the ancient texts.

## Jesus Was an Essene

It is far beyond the scope of this book to render a complete examination of the scrolls and the years of controversy surrounding them. At best it is my purpose to point out some amazing facts that we now know with certainty about the texts and the Essene sect that wrote, copied and maintained them in their fabulous library in the desert.

To begin with, the Essene community at Qumran defined its beliefs and its way of life in great detail, so we can easily see a remarkable resemblance between the Essenes and the story of Jesus in the New Testament. The Essenes believed that their mission was to remain pure, far removed from the corruption of the cities, particularly Jerusalem, so they could herald the arrival of the Messiah, sent by God to liberate them and to re-establish their rightful control over the Jerusalem Temple, which was then in the hands of the Pharisees. The Pharisees, they believed, were corrupted because they cooperated with the Roman authorities, who appointed them to be the high priests. This is very reminiscent of what Jesus and his followers believed.

The Essenes believed they were the true keepers of the covenant the Jews had made with God and that only they knew how Judaism should be kept. Only they were adhering to the laws of Moses and the prophets. All other Jews were corrupt. The Essenes were the righteous ones. They called themselves the Sons of Light and envisioned themselves fighting God's war on Earth, the same one the angelic forces were fighting in the heavens against the evil Watchers, whose mission it was to corrupt human souls. They believed in the pre-existence of the soul and in the resurrection of the soul after the death of the body. These beliefs also coincided with the story of Jesus and his disciples.

Amazingly, even though they lived in the desert, they practiced ritual bathing, during which their souls were cleansed of sin (baptism) in special bathing pools, which collected rainwater from the nearby mountains through channels carved in the rock.

They practiced communal meals, as did the early Christians, during which they passed the bread and wine, as in the Last Supper. They also took vows of poverty and gave all their belongings to the community, just as Jesus asked his followers to do. In fact, the first statute of the Community Rule (the rules of the sect) stated: "All...shall bring all their knowledge, powers, and possessions into the community."

Another statute stated: "The new member's property shall be merged and he shall offer his council and judgment to the community." Besides eating together, they prayed together, just as did the early Christians.

The New Testament describes the first Christians this way in the Acts of the Apostles: "The faithful all lived together and owned everything in common. They sold their goods and possessions and shared out the proceeds among themselves according to what each one needed. They went as a body to the Temple each day" (Acts 2:44-46).

Just as Jesus had twelve apostles, the Essene community was governed by a man they called the Teacher of Righteousness, who also had a council of twelve. This Messiah was considered divine (if not God incarnate) and gifted with the powers to understand and translate scriptures and other sacred texts.

More importantly, both the early Christians and the Essenes were dominated by a central figure whose teachings formed the foundation of their beliefs. In the New Testament, of course, it was Jesus, but in the Essene sect, it was the Teacher of Righteousness.

Many scroll fragments mention sayings, events, or phrases familiar to readers of the Gospels, such as "the healing of the sick," "announcing glad tidings to the poor," and "resurrection of the soul." Another Qumran scroll says, "Among the poor in spirit there is a power..." while in Matthew 5:3, Jesus says: "Blessed are the poor in spirit for theirs is the kingdom of heaven." Another scroll says, "All those who observe the law in the house of Judah...God will deliver because of their faith in the Teacher of

Righteousness." Similarly, in Romans 3:21–23, Paul says: "Deliverance comes to everyone…who believes in Jesus Christ." The similarities are so striking that anyone can see the connection clearly, yet how the Essene writings and beliefs made their way into the New Testament is still a mystery.

Frustratingly, the Essenes avoided using proper names or dates in their writings, probably because it would be dangerous to do so. Instead, they referred to their members by titles, so the names of Jesus and the apostles are not found in the texts. The Teacher of Righteousness is a title that could easily be applied to Jesus. His teachings, in some cases, were almost identical. An Essene rule said: "Anyone who transgresses one word of the Laws of Moses, on any point whatsoever, shall be expelled."

Jesus, in his sermon on the mount is quoted in Matthew (5:17–19) as saying: "Do not imagine that I have come to abolish the Law of the Prophets. I have not come to abolish, but to complete them….Therefore, the man who infringes even one of the least of these commandments and teaches others to do the same will be considered the least in the kingdom of heaven…"

Although no copies of New Testament Gospels have been found among the scrolls, the Messianic nature of the texts and their references to concepts such as "piety," "righteousness," "works," "the poor," and "mysteries" lead many to believe that the earliest form of Christianity was being practiced at Qumran, but not as a new religion. Rather they practiced what they believed was the true Judaism.

Those wishing to become members were put through a rigorous two-year apprenticeship before he or she could become a full-fledged member. It is quite possible that women were also Essenes, as archaeologists have uncovered the graves of men, women, and children near the community.

Some scholars, such as Robert Eisenman of California State University at Long Beach, have gone so far as to say that Jesus, John the Baptist (a close relative of Jesus), and even his parents, Joseph and Mary, were all Essenes. Such a conclusion would not raise any eyebrows if it were not for what the scrolls *do not* say about Christianity that today's Christians accept on faith:

There is no mention of the virgin birth.

There is no mention of the crucifixion, although some fragments imply the Essene leader was persecuted by the Pharisees and even murdered.

There is no mention of the resurrection of their leader in bodily form.

There is no mention of anyone walking on water or raising anyone from the dead.

There is no mention of an apostle who was given authority to carry on the mission of the Teacher of Righteousness.

In short, it is hard for today's Christians to equate The Teacher of Righteousness with the way that Jesus is portrayed in the New Testament. Christian writers have tried their best since the scrolls were discovered to point out all the reasons why Jesus could not have been connected with the Essenes. In his compilation of essays on the subject called *Jesus and the Dead Sea Scrolls: The Controversy Resolved*, James H. Charlesworth tries to make the case that Jesus could not have been an Essene. Besides the obvious differences pointed out above, Charlesworth and other writers argue that the Jesus of the New Testament differed significantly in his teachings and in his behavior from the Essene doctrines.

They point out that the Essene sect wanted more than anything to separate itself from the rest of humanity. They did so by isolating themselves. (There were, however, Essene communities nearby, such as the one on the outskirts of Jerusalem. There were probably Essenes who lived in communities populated primarily by non-Essenes.) Nevertheless, their documents indicate that to remain pure, they could not mingle with outsiders. Some of the scrolls even say they should love one another, but they should hate their enemies. On the other hand, Jesus taught his disciples to "love your enemies."

While the Essenes would not mingle with the impure, Jesus went out of his way to visit the lepers and the sick. He was kind to Roman soldiers and to Gentiles as well. Yet, it is certain that Jesus was intimately familiar with Essene beliefs and teachings because he quotes from them in the New Testament. In Matthew 5:44, Jesus says "You have heard that it used to be said, 'You shall love your neighbor and hate your enemy,' but I tell you love your enemies, and pray for those who persecute you, so that you may be sons of your heavenly father."

Nowhere in the Old Testament does it say you should hate your enemies. That phrase is only to be found in the writings of the Essenes. Beyond that, Jesus had a different view of purity—one that had nothing to do with an unclean body or with which foods one ate. Unlike the Essenes, Jesus preached in Mark 7:16, "There is nothing outside a person, which when entering can defile one; but the things which come out of a person are what defiles a person." While the Essenes were obsessed with the cleanliness and purity of all things they came in contact with, Jesus seemed to have no such concerns. His concerns were with a heavenly or other-dimensional world where material objects had no impact.

Finally, Jesus broke with the Essenes also in his relationship to women, whom he honored and treated as equals. There may have been women in the Essene community at Qumran and elsewhere, and they may have even married and had children, but there is nothing in the scrolls that permits a woman to have equal standing with men. As with the rest of Judaism at the time, as well as with orthodox Christianity of later years, women were second-class citizens.

But as a counterargument, I conclude that even though Jesus was unique and rose above the petty squabbles of the Essene sect, he was most likely born into, this does not mean that he was not an Essene to begin with, only that he ultimately outgrew the Essenes. No doubt many of them were shocked, and perhaps dismayed, by the mature Jesus who preached that we should love our enemies and we should treat women as equals, but then so were others. His ideas were radical for his times and not even his own disciples could accept his teachings. The problem with messiahs is that they don't always turn out the way they are imagined to be. The missing link between the Essene sect and the writings of the New Testament has not yet been found. But that should come as no surprise when we are reminded of the total improbability that the Essene library of sacred documents would ever be discovered in the first place.

Many scrolls were destroyed by time and by those who first found them. There may be many that have yet to be found. The Qumran library as it stands today is incomplete. Further pieces of the puzzle are yet to be revealed; some are lost forever. It is also possible that there was a parting of the ways between Jesus and the members of the Essene community and that he left to preach his own beliefs and to find his own unique way to salvation. His travels could have taken him to far-away places such as India, Egypt, and Persia, as some believe—the final chapters of his life not recorded by the Qumran scribes. There is also another possibility. It could be that Qumran was a spawning ground for prophets and messiahs, and that over a hundred years or so, a number of Jesus-like preachers (such as John the Baptist) left the sanctuary and gathered to themselves their own disciples to preach Essene beliefs, each in his own way. It may be that, through divine fate, it is the story of the man named Yeshua Ben Josef (as Jesus was known at the time) that has withstood the test of time and changed the world forever.

### John the Baptist

Among the many biblical scholars who see a connection between Christianity and the Essene sect is German scholar, Otto Betz. Betz concludes that John the Baptist was probably raised at Qumran and must have lived there during his early years:

"My own view is that the Baptist was raised in this community by the Dead Sea and was strongly influenced by it, but later left to preach directly to a wider community of Jews" (Shanks 1992, 206).

In the New Testament, John is portrayed as a key player in the transition from Judaism to Christianity. He is described as a prophet who came out of the wilderness to call for repentance and to cleanse the souls of sinners through submersion in water to prepare them for the Kingdom of God. He is portrayed as a forerunner to Jesus and was considered a true prophet by the people. The Baptist's life, like that of his relative Jesus, was dedicated to preaching the sins of the material world and the need to shun wealth and material possessions in order to devote oneself to living within the laws of God. In the New Testament, we are told in Luke (1:80): "And the child (John the Baptist) grew and became strong in the wilderness til the day of his manifestation to Israel."

Where else, we must ask, could a child grow up in the Judean wilderness and emerge from the experience with a strong conviction that baptism was a necessary ritual for salvation of the soul? The answer seems obvious. John the Baptist was raised at Qumran as a member of the Essene community. This conclusion also makes it highly likely that Jesus was similarly involved with the Essenes at an early age, and like John, left to begin his own ministry at some point.

1. The Madonna and St. Giovannino.

2. Closeup of UFO in painting at left.

3. Aerial vehicle in fourteenth-century fresco of Crucifixion.

4. Closeup of painting showing man looking up at UFO.

5. Australian aboriginal cave art depicting spirit-creator gods.

6. Medieval tapesty of life of the Virgin; note UFO upper left.

7. The caves of Qumran.

8. Fragment of Books of Enoch from Dead Sea Scrolls.

9. Jars in which the Dead Sea Scrolls were found.

10. The ossuary of the high priest, Caiaphas.

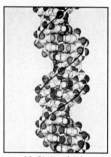

11. DNA molecule.

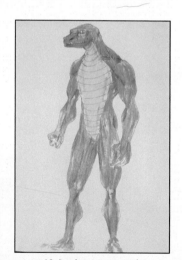

12. Reptilian extraterrestrial.

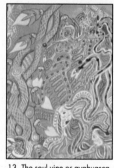

13. The soul vine or ayahuasca, containing DMT.

14. "Nordic" extraterrestrial.

15. Hooded nonhuman entity from UFO reports.

124

# Color Plates

**1.** *The Madonna and St. Giovannino* by fifteenth-century Italian artist Filippo Lippi (?) hangs in the permanent collection of the Palazzo Vecchio in Florence, Italy. The painting includes a number of anomalies, not easily explained. First, in the upper left corner, one can see what appears to be the sun. But below the sun are three anomalous, glowing objects. In the right corner, behind the Madonna, there is what appears to be a metallic object giving off luminescence. Below this object, standing on the shore, are a man and his dog peering up at the object.

**2.** Closeup of the unidentified object in *The Madonna and St. Giovannino.*

**3.** An aerial vehicle found in a small detail of a fourteenth-century fresco depicting the Crucifixion of Jesus.

**4.** Closeup of upper right-hand corner of *The Madonna and St. Giovannino,* showing a man and dog looking up at a UFO.

**5.** Australian aboriginal cave art, possibly 10,000 years old, depicts the spirit-creator gods called the *Wandjina.* Aborigines claim they encounter these beings during trance states. (From *Rock Paintings of Aboriginal Australia* by Elaine Godden and Jutta Malnic)

**6.** A medieval tapestry depicting the life of the Virgin Mary shows an object looking much like the flying saucers of today, floating in the sky in the upper left-hand corner.

**7.** The caves of Qumran can be seen in this photograph of the cliffs behind the ruins of the Qumran community, once home to the Essene sect.

**8.** A fragment of the Books of Enoch found among the Dead Sea Scrolls illustrates the poor condition of the great majority of the scrolls.

**9.** The jars in which the Dead Sea Scrolls were found are made from clay that came from the kiln found in the ruins of Qumran.

**10.** The ossuary of the High Priest Caiaphas, who is said in the Gospels to have condemned Jesus to death by turning him over to the Romans, is one of the few authenticated artifacts proving the accuracy of some portions of the New Testament. (*Bible Archaeology Review*)

**11.** The DNA molecule.

**12.** A reptilian being drawn by a UFO contact experiencer.

**13.** The "soul vine," called *ayahuasca* by Amazonian shamans, contains the DMT molecule which, when absorbed by the pineal gland, induces an out-of-body experience. In this altered state of consciousness, the shaman communes with other-dimensional beings who teach them the medicinal uses of plants. Note that the vine grows in the shape of a double helix reminiscent of the DNA molecule. (Drawing by Pablo Amaringo, Amazonian shaman, in *Ayahuasca Visions* by Luis E. Luna and Pablo Amarigo)

**14.** A drawing of a tall, blond, "Nordic-looking" being as reported frequently in UFO cases.

**15.** A drawing of a hooded nonhuman entity as reported in numerous UFO cases.

*"When the Most High apportioned the nations,*
*when he divided the sons of man, he established*
*the borders of the peoples according to the num-*
*bers of the* **sons of Israel.**" *(emphasis added)*

Deuteronomy 32:8

*"When the Most High apportioned the nations,*
*when he divided the sons of man, he established*
*the borders of the peoples according to the number*
*of the* **Sons of God.**" *(emphasis added)*

Dead Sea Scroll fragment of Deuteronomy 32:8

found at Qumran

## CHAPTER EIGHT

# The Sons of God

TAKE A CLOSE LOOK at the passages above. Do you see a contradiction? Did God divide mankind into nations (perhaps races) according to the "sons of Israel," as it says in the Bible, or according to the "sons of God," as it says in the earliest known version of Deuteronomy found in the Qumran caves?

Even Bible scholars have been puzzled by this Bible passage, which makes no sense. How could the sons of Israel have been used by God to apportion borders when he divided the sons of man into nations? After all, Israel didn't exist before the apportionment. The truth is, the passage was changed by unknown Jewish editors, who it seems did not care for the original version of the text.

Interestingly, the passage reads correctly in some Bibles. For example, the Revised Standard Versions, which are based on the Greek Septuagint (a third-century translation for Greek-speaking Jews), refers to "sons of God" just as does the Qumran fragment, which is dated to the time of Jesus (late first century B.C. to early first century A.D.). Since the scroll fragment predates by about two hundred years all other known versions of the text, experts now presume it to be the most authentic.

Southern Methodist University Bible scholar Ronald S. Hendel commented about this seemingly minor discrepancy as follows:

> Apparently, somewhere along the line in the transmission of the standard rabbinic Bible, someone felt the need to clean up the text by literally rewriting it and substituting "Sons of Israel" for the original "Sons of God." (Shanks 1992, 172)

But why was the change made? What was wrong with the term "sons of God"? And what is the difference between the Biblical term "sons of man" and the term "sons of God"? This distinction is important in our understanding of who Jesus was because he often referred to himself as the "son of man," knowing there was a difference.

This passage in Deuteronomy is taken from the "Song of Moses," which describes the events just before Moses died and presumably represents knowledge that Moses was given by God. According to this story, the sons of God are angelic beings who were present at the beginning of the world and who were assigned to rule over the peoples of the Earth. According to this apportionment, Yahweh was given authority over the people of Israel and this implies that each of the other deities was assigned his own "flock."

Hendel infers that "...the sons of God at one time played a far more important role in the early history of humanity than is generally remembered...." (Shanks, 174). Hendel found many references to these angelic beings in the Bible, but also in other non-Biblical sources such as the writings of the Mesopotamian cultures of Sumeria and Babylonia, as well as the pre-Israelite Canaanite traditions. In the case of the latter, Hendel found Canaanite texts written 1,400 years or so before Christ in cuneiform writing on clay tablets that contained many references to the sons of God. These were discovered in 1928 at the ruins of the city of Ugarit on the Syrian coast.

In the Canaanite traditions, the chief god was known as El, whose name literally means "God." This is identical to the Sumerian god known as Enlil, which was abbreviated as Il. The archangels, who would be considered sons of God, have names all ending in the suffix el, as in Mika-el, Rafa-el, Uri-el, Sara-el, etc. (In ancient Sumer, the world's oldest known civilization, these heavenly beings were known as the Annunaki). The Canaanite god El had a wife called Asherah and between them they bore children known as the sons of God. Such a pantheon of immortal gods can also be found in the Phoenician and Ammonite writings, dated several centuries later, as well as in the Gnostic writings discussed in a later chapter. For these other cultures, the sons of God were all of equal divinity, but for the Israelites, their god gained special stature, according to Hendel, who comments: "In Israelite worship, Yahweh had subsumed the essential function of the other gods" (Shanks, 174). Such deferential treatment is understandable considering the commandment given them by Yahweh, not to "worship any other god but me."

**Genesis**
Biblical references to the sons of God actually begin in the Book of Genesis:
> When mankind began to multiply on the face of the Earth, and daughters were born to them, the Sons of God saw that the daughters of men were beautiful, and they took wives of them from anywhere they chose. And Yahweh said, "My spirit will not be strong in man forever, for indeed he is but flesh. His lifetime will be 120 years." The Nephilim were on the Earth in those days, and also afterwards, when the sons of God mated with the daughters of men and they bore children for them: these were the heroes of old, the men of renown. (Genesis 6:1–4)

For those of us raised in the Judeo-Christian religions, the above passage seems bizarre and out of context with orthodox teachings. The first thing we notice is the mention of the term "sons of God" without any explanation.

The fact is that orthodox religion has found mention of the sons of God an embarrassment, to say the least, because it seems to fly in the face of the notion that there is only one God. For the most part, such passages have been ignored, brushed aside as "aberrations," or misinterpreted. Furthermore, the idea that the sons of God came to Earth and had sexual relations with human women, thereby creating a race of half man/half gods, is too incredible for most modern Christians or Jews to even contemplate as being grounded in fact.

Yet, the passage is there and, as will be seen, it represents only the tip of the iceberg when it comes to understanding the hierarchy of angelic beings. In fact, the many mentions of the sons of God in the Bible are based upon other, much more extensive sources that predate even the book of Genesis, some of which were found among the Dead Sea Scrolls. These include the Books of Enoch and the previously mentioned writings of the early Mesopotamian cultures.

**The Elohim**

Although one Jewish word for God is Elohim, which is generally used in the singular, the word is, in fact, the plural form of the word El, which we now know was the name for the male Mesopotamian and Canaanite god. In spite of the fact that the term "Elohim" is the plural form of El, it is used in the Bible as both plural and singular in meaning.

Examples of where the authors of the book of Genesis used the plural form are in the story of the creation of the human race (italics added):

The Elohim said, "Let *us* make man in our own image. (Genesis 1:26).

In the Garden of Eden when the serpent tempts Eve, he says:
"You are not going to die by eating the fruit. No, the Elohim will know that the moment you eat it, your eyes will be opened and you will be the same as the *gods* by telling good from bad (Genesis 3:4).
In the story of the Tower of Babel:

[The people said] "Come on; let us build ourselves a city and a tower whose top will reach the skies." And the Lord came down to see the tower and said, "Look, the people are united and they have one language… Now nothing will stop them from doing what they take in their minds to do. Come on, let *us* go down there and confuse their language so they cannot understand one another's speech" (Genesis 11:1–9).

In the story of Adam and Eve, after they ate from the fruit of the tree of knowledge:
Behold, the man has become as one of *us*, to know good and evil; and now, lest he put forth his hand and take also of the tree of life, and eat and live forever, he must be driven from the garden. (Genesis 3:22)

These references to plural gods in Genesis show a disturbing common theme. The gods, it seems, created the human species in their own image, yet wanted to keep humans in their place for fear that they too might achieve immortality and become gods. When men attempt to build a tower to reach the gods in the heavens, the Elohim thwart their efforts by confusing their language. Earlier, we learned that one of the duties of the gods was to divide mankind into nations, thereby creating differences and, consequently, conflict. By keeping the nations at war and the languages confused, the gods could be assured that man would be kept in place. This system seems to have worked quite well, even up to the present day.

## The Nephilim
In telling the history of the world and of the Hebrew people, Jewish writers were compelled to tell the story of the intermixing of the heavenly host (variously called sons of God, Archons, Aeons, angels, or Watchers) with the human race, and of the hybrid progeny of these sexual relationships. In so doing, they had to acknowledge that a host of gods existed, that these gods had physical bodies, and that they traveled regularly from their heavenly

abodes to Earth and even lived on Earth, side-by-side with humans, at some point in the distant past.

Hebrew writers called the hybrid children of the gods Nephilim, meaning "fallen ones." Historian Zecharia Sitchin, in his series of books called the *Earth Chronicles,* analyzes the ancient texts and translates the word to mean roughly "those who came down from the heavens to Earth." In some cases the Nephilim are referred to in the Bible as the "heroes" (men who had great powers and did great deeds) and in other places they are called giants.

For example, in the book of Numbers (13:33), as the Israelites are invading the land of Canaan, Moses' scouts report that "All the people whom we saw…were people of great size; there we saw the Nephilim…and we seemed in our own eyes like grasshoppers, and so we must have seemed in their eyes."

Sometimes the Bible uses the words "Anaqim" and "Rephaim," which seem to be terms for different types of Nephilim, but descriptions are lacking from the texts. Goliath, the giant who was said to have been slain by King David as a child, is described as one of the Rephaim (2 Samuel 21:19). By the time of David, few Nephilim remained on Earth, most having been destroyed by the great flood and the rest killed off by the Israelites as they advanced toward the Promised Land (Joshua 11:22).

So here we must make an important distinction between the true sons of God (those immortal, God-created beings that rule the Earth, and possibly many other worlds in the universe) and humans who were the product of unions between these gods and human mothers. Throughout history there have been many persons from almost every culture in the world who have been said to have been born of earthly women, but sired by a god. Jesus is by no means the first one of whom this has been said. Beginning with the ancient Sumerian kings, we find references to these demigods who ruled by divine birthright. The Pharaohs of Egypt, the Incan rulers of Peru, and the dynastic kings of China and Japan all had the same tradition: that long ago the gods interbred with humans to create special lineages of humans to serve as rulers of their nations. This, I believe, is actually true, in spite of the fact that many political rulers such as the Roman emperors, often proclaimed themselves to be gods for the purpose of maintaining political control over their gullible subjects. These half-gods are not the sons of God we refer to in this book. In this case, the term "sons of God" refers only to the higher, immortal, and all-powerful gods, said to have been created by the one true God to create and rule over the physical dimension.

## The Great Flood

The story of the great flood is one that appears in the writing and oral history of hundreds of cultures around the world. That which appears in the book of Genesis is merely one version that had its roots in the earlier cultures of Mesopotamia. There are, however, a few differences. The earliest written records of the flood, those of the Sumerians and Babylonians, which predate the Bible by nearly a thousand years, describe a world that is suffering from overpopulation. It seems that when the gods created the human race, they did not plan for their creation to suffer a natural death by disease. Humans who were not killed through accidents or murder would live for hundreds of years. (If this is so, then we can assume that the aging process is a factor of genetic engineering, an idea that has only recently been considered plausible by geneticists studying the human genome.)

As a result, the world became overpopulated, and the god Enlil (El) decreed that there would be a great flood to kill off the human race.

However, El's edict is thwarted by his brother Enki (who is depicted as a serpent-being in the Sumerian story.) Enki warns a wise and righteous man to build an ark in order that he and his family might survive the coming flood. To reconcile their differences after the flood, the gods arrive at a compromise. They agree that to avoid overpopulation, they will decree that in the future, humans will be subject to natural death and thus, death by disease was born. Another way of saying this is that the gods reprogrammed the genetic structure of man to incorporate disease and death.

This story is obviously related to the flood account in Genesis. In Genesis 6:1–4, God decrees that man will have a limited lifespan after the flood:

My spirit will not be strong in man forever, for indeed, he is but
flesh. His lifetime will be 120 years.

However, it is noted by Hendel that the conclusion of the story is altered in the Israelite version:
> The flood is no longer the result of the sons of God mating with
> the daughters of man…The motive in Genesis 6:5–8 is the increase
> of mankind's evil on the Earth, not the increase in population, nor
> the mixing of gods and mortals. (Shanks, 175)

The Genesis story, however, does carry a remnant of the older version
in its use of the word "multiply," as in Genesis 6:1–4:
> When mankind began to multiply on the face of the Earth…

And: Yahweh saw that the evil of mankind multiplied on Earth.

These passages indicate that the authors were aware of the overpopulation story, but altered it to suit their own perception of the human race
as inherently evil. But even the Genesis story has a major contradiction. In
one instance the cause of the flood is the mating between gods and humans
(Genesis 6:1–4), while in another it is human evil:
> Yahweh saw that the evil of mankind had multiplied on the Earth,
> and that all of the thoughts of his heart were only evil continually.
> And Yahweh repented that he had created mankind, and he was
> grieved in his heart. Yahweh said, "I will wipe out mankind, whom
> I created, from the face of the Earth…." (Genesis 6:5–7)

Interestingly, the Genesis authors leave the impression that God blamed
mankind for having beautiful daughters who "enticed" the sons of God to
mate with them! From this example we can see how Jewish writers changed
the creation story of earlier cultures to include the notion that mankind
was by nature sinful and flawed. This concept remains today as the basis
for modern-day Judeo-Christian theology.

Such editing on the part of the authors of the Bible was, in fact, quite common, as would be expected in a book that was written by many writers over thousands of years and translated and copied many times by unknown persons. Along the way, the cultural biases and morals of the men who wrote it were invariably etched into the book that is purported by some to be the exact, holy words of God.

The small fragment of the Book of Deuteronomy found at Qumran is but one example of an ancient text discovered in modern times that reveals how unknown persons altered the Bible over many years. In this case, a small fragment of a scroll serves as a clue that reveals a much larger and important picture—the strange relationship between the human race and a superior race of beings that was appointed by God to watch over the Earth since time immemorial. The existence of these beings became a point of contention within the Hebrew priesthood, which was divided about the nature of God and the sons of God.

## Who Wrote the Bible?

Richard Elliot Friedman, professor of Hebrew at the University of California, San Diego, in his excellent book, *Who Wrote the Bible?*, explains the confusion in the Old Testament about the various names used by the Hebrews to refer to God. In one place, he is called Yahweh (anglicized by the King James version translation as "Jehovah") and in other places he is called Elohim, as if it were singular in form. In other cases the term is used in the plural.

Friedman explains that Bible scholars have discovered that there were at least four major writers of the first five books of the Old Testament (contrary to the myth that they were penned by Moses himself.) Researchers have long been puzzled as to why many stories appear twice in the Bible, often with contradictory information. For example, in Genesis, there are two different versions of each of the following stories: The creation of the world and its life forms; the story of Noah and the ark; the covenant between God and Abraham; the naming of Abraham's son, Isaac; the story of

Abraham's claim to a foreign king that his wife, Sarah, is his sister; Isaac's journey to Mesopotamia; and many others.

A careful examination of the texts reveals that in most cases, one version of a story always referred to God as Yahweh and in the other story, God is referred to as El or Elohim. There were obviously two different groups involved in telling the stories, the "Yahwists" and the "Elohists." To discover this, you simply read the book of Genesis carefully and make note of the following facts: In one story, God first creates plants, then animals, then man and woman. But in the second version, God first creates man, then plants and animals and finally he creates woman. In the two versions of Noah and the flood, God gives contradictory instructions regarding how many of each animal to take aboard the ark. It is a good exercise to discover these differences for yourself, so rather than point out the differences, I refer the reader to the book of Genesis.

So how did the Bible get so confused if it is purported to be the inerrant word of God? The answer, according to Friedman, is that at one time there were two completely separate states, Judah and Israel, with two different kings, two different temples, and two different sets of high priests. This lasted for about two hundred years (from about 920 B.C. to 722 B.C.). When the northern state of Israel was eventually reunited with the southern state of Judah, and they came under one king, there was an obvious dilemma. During the intervening years, the two cultures had developed different versions of similar stories due to human nature, which causes men to interject their own preferences and biases into what should be sacred writings.

Wouldn't it have been interesting to have been present when the Elohist and the Yahwist priests were ordered by the king to agree on which stories were the more accurate? High priests are not the type of people who are prone to compromise. No one would admit that his version was inferior to the other. So, a compromise of sorts was reached. Both versions would be considered correct, in spite of the obvious contradictions. They would be placed side by side without comment or explanation. In other places, the different stories would be woven together, as if they were one. After all, the priests knew why this was being done (for political reasons), and most other people couldn't even read anyway. So, for millennia, we have been left with scriptures that are supposed to be the holy word of God, but with glaring contradictions that make it seem as if God couldn't remember the order in which he created the world, as well as numerous other details.

As Friedman states regarding the obvious dilemma: "But what were they to do with two documents, each purporting to recount sacred national traditions, but emphasizing different persons and events—occasionally contradicting each other? The solution, apparently, was to combine them" (Friedman 1987, 87).

This discovery also highlighted a major difference between the two forms of Judaism that developed during the period of separation. One culture, those who referred to God as Elohim, maintained their belief that there were numerous gods of which their god was one. The other culture had elevated their one god to a higher status and the other gods to minor players with little power. These they referred to as angels. In time, this is the view that prevailed and became the "orthodox" belief system, but the ancient truths can still be found in the Bible if you look hard enough.

### The Watchers

The secrets of the other gods are revealed in the documents hidden in the caves of Qumran by the Essenes at or around the time of Jesus. These documents were considered to be sacred texts by the Essenes and the secrets they held were among the most closely guarded, due to their controversial nature. I am quite certain that Jesus himself was well acquainted with these documents and with the existence of these heavenly sons of God. Their story is told in the ancient Books of Enoch, referred to in the Bible, but in a quite abbreviated form. In the Books of Enoch, these beings are known as the Watchers, because their purpose is to watch and rule over the Earth.

The story of the Watchers, as told in the Dead Sea Scrolls, was translated from their ancient Aramaic into modern English by one of the original scroll researchers, a Catholic priest named Joseph Milik. In his 1976 book, *The Books of Enoch*, Milik explains that Enoch was the first among the children of men born of the Earth who had learned writing, science, and wisdom directly from the angelic beings known as the Watchers. According to Genesis 5:21–24, Enoch was the father of Methuselah and great-grandfather of Noah. He lived to be 365 years old, but he did not die a normal human death: "When he was 365 and in constant touch with God, he disappeared, for God took him."

Enoch lived in the time before the great flood when the Watchers were intermingling with humans and creating hybrid children known as Nephilim. The Books of Enoch are called "apocalyptic," meaning that they contain hidden secrets. They fall into a category of ancient scripture labeled pseudepigrapha, which means that they were written by unknown authors in the name of another. (In truth, much of the Bible, including the New Testament books of Matthew, Mark, Luke, and John, was written by unknown hands, but are not classified as pseudepigrapha. So the classification does not mean that the documents are false.) In the case of the Enoch texts, historians were aware that they existed even before the Qumran find because portions of similar texts written in Slavonic had been found in Russia and Serbia. Another copy, believed to have been penned two hundred years before Christ, is written in Ethiopian. Undoubtedly, however, the stories upon which the documents are based have origins in antiquity.

### The Greatest Secret

In fact, the story of the Watchers originates in the culture of the world's first civilizations—the lands of Sumer and Babylonia. The word "Sumer" actually means "Land of the Watchers," and "Babylon" means "Gate of the Gods." In the Sumerian writings, the Sumerians depict themselves as being of non-human origin—the creations of superior beings who descended from the heavens and who instructed them in the sciences. These Sumerian/Babylonian gods were described as ruling over the Earth and making the great decisions regarding the fate of the human race.

So we can see that the Books of Enoch, because they carried forth knowledge from the most ancient of sources, were considered sacred scripture for centuries, until orthodoxy eventually rejected them because of the subject matter dealing with sexual activity between the Watchers and humans. Increasingly, the orthodox view turned away from the notion that beings from heaven could have physical bodies or could wield such power.

Yet the Books of Enoch make it clear that such was the case. For example, the story of Enoch's departure from the Earth reads much as a modern-day alien abduction case:

> I was in my house alone and was resting on my couch and slept. And when I was asleep, great distress came up into my ear…And there appeared to me two men, exceeding big….They were standing at the head of my couch and began to call me by name. And I arose from my sleep and saw clearly those two men standing in front of me…and was seized with fear…and those men said…do not fear…thou shalt today ascend with us into heaven…. They brought before my face the elders and rulers of the stellar orders.

This description is quite similar to that in the book of Daniel (4:13): "I saw in the visions of my head as I lay in bed, and behold, a Watcher, a holy one, came down from heaven…."

As the story is told, Enoch was chosen by the good Watchers to bring the evil ones a message:

> Then the Lord said to me: "Enoch, scribe of righteousness, go tell the Watchers of heaven, who have deserted the lofty sky…who have been polluted with women and have done as the sons of men do, by taking themselves wives…that on the Earth they shall never obtain peace and remission of sin" (Enoch 12:4–7).

From this we see that the Watchers are, in fact, the same sons of God mentioned in Deuteronomy and in other places in the Bible. But through the Books of Enoch we get a more complete telling of their story, and we begin to see that the Bible authors used these earlier texts as the basis for their narratives.

In 2 Peter 2:4, for example, it says: "For if God did not spare angels when they sinned....If he did not spare the ancient world, when he brought the flood...but protected Noah." The passage refers to the sins committed by the angels (Watchers) when they descended from the heavens to have intercourse with humans and their subsequent punishment by God. Again, in Jude 6, we find another reference to the Watchers: "And the angels who did not keep their position of authority but abandoned their home [in the heavens]."

It is obvious that the Bible authors used the Books of Enoch as a reference when they wrote their sacred texts, yet they chose to tell only a small portion of the entire story and they changed it to suit their needs. So it is little surprise that among the Dead Sea Scrolls were found not only the books of the Old Testament, but also the Books of Enoch, revered at the time as sacred, God-given documents that explained the history of the world.

We are also able to see that the term "angel" was, in fact, synonymous with the word "Watcher." This means that angels were known to be not merely ethereal beings without bodies, but also powerful, willful beings, who could, and often did, descend to Earth in physical form to interact with humans and to create hybrid offspring, just as we find today in the UFO/alien abduction phenomena. These were (are) the sons of God for whom God apportioned the nations when He "divided the sons of man," as it says in Deuteronomy.

This is perhaps the greatest secret ever kept from humankind, even though it is in plain sight in the Bible. Not many people today would believe that there is a race of beings far superior to humans that has coexisted with and interacted with humankind since the beginning of the world. Even for those who believe in angels today, few would see them as physical beings that, in fact, have authority over the Earth and all its life forms. Few would see them as our controllers—our masters. Even at the time of Jesus, such knowledge was guarded and preserved as secret doctrine. The fact that the verse quoted at the beginning of this chapter (Deuteronomy 32:8) was edited by orthodox Jewish writers to delete the reference to the sons of God shows how this knowledge was being systematically eradicated more than two thousand years ago.

*Perhaps we are under some sort of discreet surveil-
lance by higher beings on a planet of a nearby star.
It is not clear exactly how these cosmic game wardens would do this without our detecting them,
but with a higher technology such supervision may
be relatively easy.*

—Francis Crick, *Life Itself,* 1981, 158
Nobel Laureate for his co-discovery of the
double-helix nature of DNA, explaining his
theory that extraterrestrials seeded life on Earth.

CHAPTER NINE

# Science Discovers the Secret Rulers

## DNA from Outer Space

IN AUGUST 2004, the National Aeronautics and Space Administration (NASA) made two announcements that could change the world. On August 30 a team of NASA astrobiologists revealed that they had found a meteorite (known as the Orgueil meteorite), which fell to Earth 140 years ago and which they believe holds definitive proof that life exists in outer space. They found extraterrestrial microfossils in a type of space rock known as carbonaceous chondrite, and presented their extraordinary findings at the International Symposium on Optical Science and Technology.

As reported on MSNBC.com, the team's presentation showed detailed photographs of fossils, which were referred to as "stunning" by some in attendance. The close-up photos, in high definition, showed fossilized traces of cynobacteria (aquatic and photosynthetic bacteria, which are able to manufacture their own food). Such bacteria are found in Earth rock and are the oldest known Earth fossils, dating to 3.5 billion years ago. (Amazingly, this type of bacteria is still found living on Earth today.)

However, the bacteria found in the Orgueil meteorite spent millions of years traveling through outer space before arriving on planet Earth. It is not known where in the universe the meteorite might have originated, but wherever it came from, the bacteria must have been created by the same source that all life on Earth depends on: deoxyribonucleic acid, the DNA molecule. The exciting conclusion is that DNA, as we know it here on Earth, exists in the same form in outer space.

Responding to concerns that the meteorite might have been contaminated with the bacteria when it plunged into the Earth, NASA astrobiologist Richard Hoover said that the composition of the fossils argues strongly against that possibility: "The organic matter…contains isotopes that absolutely could not be from terrestrial contamination. We are seeing things that are unbelievably detailed in content and morphology."

This remarkable discovery, unlike the famous but controversial Mars meteorite known as ALH 84001, which was inconclusive in the minds of many scientists, could put the matter to rest once and for all. There is life in outer space and it is strikingly similar to life on Earth.

**New Worlds Discovered**

Only one day later, on August 31, a team of NASA astronomers, working from the Keck Observatory in Hawaii, announced that they had found two new planets outside the solar system unlike any others found before. The hundred or so extra-solar planets previously discovered have all been giant gaseous planets like Jupiter. The new planets, believed by NASA to be made of rock and ice, are about the size of Neptune—only about fourteen times the size of Earth.

Simultaneously, in Europe, astronomers announced a similar discovery of a planet circling a different star. With new technology and methods for searching for distant planets, scientists now believe it is only a matter of time before Earth-like planets are found, and with that, the possibility that they might bear life—even intelligent life.

Given the size of the universe, the potential abundance of DNA in outer space, and the potential for millions or billions of Earth-like planets, the odds have increased dramatically that highly-developed alien civilizations exist and that many of them might be hundreds, thousands, or even millions of years more advanced than our own. Some might have conquered the barriers to intergalactic space travel and they might have been exploring other worlds for millennia. Such beings would appear to more primitive cultures like our own to be godlike in their abilities.

The implications for these remarkable findings may not be obvious to everyone, but as early as 1996 *Time* magazine warned its readers about the implications of such a discovery in a cover story titled "The Harmony of the Spheres," which described the excitement in scientific circles when the first extra-solar planet was discovered. The author, Paul Davies, states:

> The discovery of life beyond Earth would transform not only our science but also our religions, our belief systems, and our entire world view. For in a sense, the search for extraterrestrial life is really a search for ourselves—who we are and what our place is in the grand sweep of the cosmos (Davies 1996, p 58).

This description of a psychological tsunami that could someday engulf the world is more pertinent now than ever before. There is a tsunami coming, and like a giant wave that suddenly transforms an unsuspecting shore, the coming psychological tsunami will cause humanity to accept the unthinkable: we are not alone in the universe and we have never been alone. The science fiction of yesterday will become the fact of the new day.

The evidence that this shift in human thinking is upon us can be found almost daily in new discoveries in science that, little by little, change our paradigm, chipping away at our egocentricity and our arrogance. When it arrives, we humans will be forced to see ourselves, not merely as citizens of a country or even of a planet, but of an entire galaxy. It will herald a new age of thinking in every field of science and philosophy and religion. But we won't be able to say we weren't warned.

## DNA Is Not from Here

Some of our best scientific thinkers have been trying to tell us there is something very strange about the molecule known as DNA. The more we know about it, the more alien it appears.

To begin with, the DNA molecule is an extraordinarily complex, microscopic, self-replicating "machine," which morphs itself into every life form on Earth, from bacteria to oak trees to human beings. From the moment it was discovered, it was clear that something about DNA didn't make sense. The uniformity of the DNA found in every cell of every living thing was shocking. (This is even more shocking if bacteria from outer space are identical to those on Earth.) This one molecule, by simply rearranging the letters in its mysterious code, is responsible for the diversity of all life on Earth. At the molecular level, there is virtually no difference between a leaf and a human.

For a species that prides itself on its superiority and its individuality, this finding was not welcome. It just didn't compute. This enigma led its discoverers to begin asking a series of important questions: Where did DNA come from? How did it get here? How did it evolve into such a complex, powerful entity? Surprisingly, these questions have already been answered to the satisfaction of some of our best scientists: DNA is an alien.

According to Francis Crick, who won the Nobel Prize along with James Watson for the discovery of the double-helix shape of the molecule and its importance as the source of all life on Earth, DNA could not possibly have originated on Earth. In his 1981 book *Life Itself*, Crick speculates on the origins of this incredibly complex molecule. Expanding on a theory he first developed in the 1970s together with Leslie Orgel, a pioneer in prebiotic chemistry, Crick writes that DNA was either brought here by spacefaring extraterrestrials, or that it was seeded here through the use of robotic spacecraft by some distant, advanced civilization. Crick and Orgel call their theory "directed panspermia."

The notion that DNA arrived here from outer space was originally proposed by a Swedish chemist and Nobel laureate, Svante Arrhenius, at the turn of the century, but the theory he called "panspermia" proposed that it arrived here in meteorites. Crick and Orgel do not believe DNA could survive the plunge through the Earth's atmosphere riding on the back of a rock. Directed panspermia indicates that someone directed DNA towards Earth intentionally. (Unfortunately, Crick did not live to know about the latest find of fossilized bacteria from outer space. He died in July 2004, a month before the NASA announcement at the age of 88.)

Crick arrived at his conclusions after conducting a sophisticated computer analysis to calculate the odds that a complex molecule could have been formed by accident, such as a chemical reaction caused by a lightning bolt striking a primordial ocean. He discovered that the odds were so outrageously against such an occurrence that he ruled it impossible.

### Did Someone Make DNA?

Given that information, Darwinists might argue that DNA must have evolved, just as any living organism, through trial and error, over millions of years. But that argument doesn't work either. DNA, in its present form, appears to have been present in the first bacteria found in fossilized form dating to 3.5 billion years ago. Such bacteria, just like the ones from outer space, are identical to those found on Earth today. There is absolutely no evidence for an evolutionary process for the molecule. Crick discards the evolutionary hypothesis along with the accidental hypothesis, and is left with few alternatives. Either DNA was sent here or brought here by a super-race of extraterrestrials, or it appeared here as an act of God. Of course, God could have created DNA and seeded it throughout the universe, but it is doubtful a reputable scientist would pitch his camp with creationists who dispute the whole idea of evolution.

In any case, Crick and Orgel must have been in an uncomfortable position, as noted scientists, when they discovered the truth about DNA. It is much to their credit that they were willing to go public with their discovery and their highly controversial theory. To defend against the inevitable ridicule from the scientific world, Crick fought vigorously to disavow any perceived connection between his theory and any modern-day UFO theories that might be similar. In *Life Itself,* Crick writes:

> The whole idea stinks of UFOs or the Chariots of the Gods or other common forms of contemporary silliness. Against this I can only claim that whereas the idea has indeed many of the stigmata of science fiction, its body is a lot more solid. It does not really have the major features of most science fiction, which is a great leap of the imagination.... Each of the details which contribute to the required scenario are based on a fairly solid foundation of contemporary science. (Crick 1981, 149)

It seems as if Crick was quite sure of his discovery and was trying to tell us something. As far as he was concerned, DNA is not from here, and that means life exists in outer space. But in spite of the explosive nature of his conclusions, Crick's book did not have a big impact. It was not a bestseller, it had very little public impact, and the silence from the scientific community was quite remarkable. James Watson, who shared the Nobel Prize with Crick, wrote a book titled *DNA the Secrets of Life* in 2003. Watson does not even mention Crick's notion of directed panspermia, nor does he present any opposing theory. The entire topic of the origins of DNA is simply ignored.

Watson can hardly be blamed for not wanting to get caught in the nasty war between hardcore Darwinists who espouse the view that the DNA mystery can be simply reduced to spontaneous chemical reactions, and a new breed of "creationists," who find the hand of God in Crick's discovery that DNA is not accidental. This new form of creationism, labeled in recent years "intelligent design" (or simply ID), has given new life to old arguments that the theory of evolution does not explain the origins of life or even the origin of man.

**Intelligent Design**

To understand this argument fully, one must understand just how complex the DNA molecule actually is. First, it uses a four-character "alphabet" to create 64 different three-letter "words," including "start" and "stop" to separate "sentences." Ultimately, depending on how the letters and sentences are strung together, this one molecule creates all living things. But that is just the beginning. Before it can morph itself into a living creature, it must communicate this language to proteins, made up of the twenty amino acids. Proteins have their own twenty-letter alphabet, one letter for each amino acid. These letters combine to create hundreds of "words." The problem is that the two languages are mutually exclusive. They cannot understand each other. What is necessary for life to exist is a translator. Somehow (no one can explain how it happened) a translation mechanism was put in place. These translators are called enzymes, and once in place, the business of creating life could begin.

Crick compares a protein to a paragraph made up of two hundred letters lined up in the correct order. The chance of this happening over a period of billions of years by accident, he says, is equivalent to a number greater than all the atoms in the universe! So, the odds against the existence of two completely different alphabets and a translating mechanism is a number so great it is beyond our imagination.

When microbiologists speak of DNA they speak like codebreakers, using such words as "text," "code," and "language" to describe the molecule. Proteins and enzymes are referred to as "robots" and cells are referred to as "factories." The existence of these factories full of robots, speaking to each other in complex languages requiring translators is so incredible it seems like science fiction. If this did not happen by accident, and if it is not the product of evolution, the door is left wide open for others to speculate that a sublime, supernatural intelligence designed it all and put it together. This is just the door needed by many in the creationist camp to prove their point that it is God who created life on Earth, not an accident of nature. It could also mean that it was the sons of God: godlike beings capable of manipulating energy to create matter and powerful enough to create the intricate, self-replicating, intelligent, microscopic machine known as DNA.

This dilemma is one facing not only evolutionary science today, but also all fields of science. The further science sees into the nature of reality, the closer it gets to the mystical and the sacred. There are few scientists who want to be caught in the middle, much less caught crossing the line and embracing the notion that it might, in fact, be God, or His representatives, who created DNA, rather than extraterrestrials. In any case, it is becoming increasingly clear to open-minded scientists that someone or something designed and created the DNA molecule and then used it to seed life in the universe. In fact, some scientists, such as professor Paul Davies of the Australian Centre for Astrobiology in Sydney, believe that coded messages might yet be discovered in what is now called "junk" DNA. Writing in *New Scientist* magazine in the summer of 2004, Davies proposes that extraterrestrials might have encoded secret messages in the portion of DNA that seems to have no useful function. He and other computer scientists and cryptographers are already actively searching for patterns in the DNA code that could help us understand who created it and why.

But the evidence for outside intervention in Earth's evolutionary process, be it God or extraterrestrials, doesn't stop with the mysterious origins of DNA. According to the fossil record, there is further evidence that something has tampered with the normal evolutionary process of natural selection. First, there is what is termed the mystery of the "big bang" in evolution that occurred at the beginning of the Cambrian period, about 600 million years ago. (The whole idea of associating the term "big bang" with evolution is a bit of an embarrassment to science, yet it is a fact that cannot be easily swept under the rug.) In a sudden burst of creativity, the Earth's oceans, which (with the exception of bacteria) had been barren of life for billions of years, spawned an astounding array of multi-celled creatures. *Time* magazine reported in December 1995:

> Scientists used to think that the evolution of phyla took place over
> a period of 75 million years, and even that seemed impossibly short.
> Then, two years ago, a group of researchers…took this long-standing problem and escalated it into a crisis. First, they recalibrated

the geological time clock to about half its former length, then they announced that the interval of major evolutionary innovation did not span the entire 30 million years, but rather was concentrated in the first third. "Fast," observed a Harvard biologist "is now a lot faster than we thought, and that's extraordinarily interesting" (*Time* 1995, 70).

The article describes biological science in a state of crisis as its notions of how we got here crumble in the face of new scientific discoveries. The same is true for anthropology, which is grappling with the fact that there is another big bang to be dealt with in the origins of the human species.

The fossil record indicates that upright, bipedal, apelike beings, known as Australopithecines, developed about five million years ago. By three million years ago, a creature named *Homo habilis* appeared, who, with a larger brain, was able to fashion crude stone implements to aid in his struggle to survive. About one and a half million years ago, *Homo erectus*, considered to be the first human, appeared, followed closely by Cro-Magnon and modern *Homo sapiens sapiens*.

However, there is a problem with this timeline. As the late astronomer Carl Sagan notes in his book *The Dragons of Eden*, "If man had evolved naturally from reptiles, it would have taken 200 million years...." But, in fact, the extinction of the dinosaurs was only 65 million years ago, so there is a disturbing leap in human evolution that doesn't make sense. Sagan puzzled over the scientific dilemma created when anthropology discovered that man-made stone tools from around the world occur in enormous abundance all at once, rather than gradually. If evolution occurs gradually, as Darwin believed, then stone implements should be scarce in more ancient Earth strata, becoming more abundant in the more recent layers. But such is not the case.

Sagan also described the confirming evidence found in the fossilized remains of human skulls, indicating that the change in the size of the human skull was spectacularly fast. He quotes American anatomist C. Judson

Herrick, who exclaimed on the evidence for the sudden growth of the human skull: "Its explosive growth late in phylogeny is one of the most dramatic cases of evolutionary transformation known to comparative anatomy" (Sagan 1977, 97).

This evidence supports Crick's theory of extraterrestrial intervention in Earth's affairs. Crick speculated that whoever brought or sent DNA here might view life on Earth as an experiment, returning from time to time to see how things are going. He suggested that planet Earth might be a giant wildlife preserve, presided over by "cosmic game wardens." His theory is supported by the fossil record, and is also supported by the human record—the writings of our ancient ancestors.

### Genetic Engineering

Increasingly, scientists are asking: "What does it mean to be human? Can we see ourselves objectively? Are we a genetically engineered species, programmed to have limited senses so that we will not rise to the status of the gods?" Jesus told his unbelieving disciples: "Ye are gods." But they could not conceive of such a thing. He promised immortality to those who would follow his teachings, just as other mystics from many cultures have taught. Spiritual teachers say that we humans can be more than what we now are. If we work at it, we can train ourselves to see the truth about ourselves and the nature of reality. We are capable of reaching immortality.

Consider for a moment just how limited our senses are. Our eyesight is limited within a very small portion of the light spectrum. We have trouble seeing at night, we cannot see in X-ray vision or in the infrared, we can't see very well at a distance, and our peripheral vision is very limited. We can't see a tree grow and we can't see a speeding bullet. We are oblivious to much of what is happening in the world around us. Our sense of hearing is just as bad; we can only hear sounds in a tight range of frequencies. Many species in the animal world have better sight, hearing, and smell. As for the senses of touch and taste, they are virtually useless in helping us discern what the universe is like. We humans are like blind animals left to grope and probe around on an isolated island floating in an endless universe.

Furthermore, we could say that our bodies were engineered by someone to give souls the perfect instrument to experience a three-dimensional reality, where everything appears to be separate from everything else. We were given bicameral minds, bifocal vision, and binaural hearing. Most importantly, we are born into a body that is half of what our soul has been used to experiencing. In the dimensionless world from which souls come, there is no gender. Yet humans are born into a body that is either male or female, thereby splitting the soul in half, so to speak. Having a gender is not our normal state of existence; it is something we have to adjust to, but it is essential if we are to experience the state of separation. Here on Earth, the soul is isolated from its true self and grows to believe all things are separate. This is the development of the ego, which is constantly telling us: "Fend for yourself, you are all alone, look after yourself first, because no one else cares about you." It is the development and growth of the ego that is the greatest barrier between us and the true, multidimensional reality, and it is the main reason souls get caught up in the material world and the cycle or reincarnation. Is this an accident, or did someone plan it this way?

Based on our meager sensory perception, we humans believed for millennia that we lived on a flat Earth and that the sun and the stars revolved around us. It was with disdain and disbelief that the public first reacted to the news that scientists had discovered a microscopic world of creatures that lived on our food, on our skin, and in our bodies. The discovery of bacteria and viruses was a great shock to our view of reality, but it opened the way for a new age of reason and exploration that revolutionized the way we think and immeasurably improved the human condition. But it wouldn't have happened had someone not invented the microscope.

If we are to believe the ancient writings of our ancestors who described the origins of the human species and the role played by higher beings in our development, then we must consider the possibility that our limited senses are not an accidental product of evolution, but the result of an intentional act of genetic engineering by someone with far greater intelligence than ourselves. Recent discoveries by genetic researchers have stunned scientists and added a new perspective to this theory. In the process of mapping the genomes of humans and chimpanzees (our nearest living relatives), scientists at the University of California, San Diego, discovered that humans have an altered form of a molecule called sialic acid on the surface of our cells. This variation is coded for by a single gene in our DNA code. Sialic acids act as a docking site for many pathogens, like malaria and influenza. This may explain why we are more susceptible to such diseases than our closest living relatives, the chimps, which do not have this variant gene. (*Time*, 10-9-06, 46). This is particularly interesting due to the complexity of the human DNA code, which consists of three billion base pairs, but which differs by only 1.23 percent from the code for chimps. One might conclude that "someone" doesn't want humans to overpopulate the Earth—again.

## Psychic Humans

Today, with new discoveries in quantum physics, we humans are on the brink of another sweeping change in how we think about our universe. Subatomic particles, such as photons and electrons, defy everything we think we know about how the universe is structured. We can now see the possibility of a multi-dimensional universe in which space travel might be possible at near the speed of light or even instantaneously, by bridging time and space. Quantum particles display apparent extra sensory perception (ESP) and seem to move between our dimension and other unknown dimensions. They violate all the previously known laws of physics, yet they are the basic building block of matter. Quantum physics has discovered that at the root of the material world is a bizarre dimension that we cannot as yet comprehend. Michael Talbot expressed the astounding potential of quantum physics in his excellent book *The Holographic Universe*:

> There is evidence to suggest that our world and everything in it—from snowflakes to maple trees to falling stars and spinning electrons—are also only ghostly images, projections from a level of reality so beyond our own it is literally beyond time and space. (Talbot 1998, 1)

Quantum physicists are at the leading edge of this sweeping paradigm change which establishes in a scientific way that psychic phenomena, such as ESP, mind over matter, clairvoyance, and such things are part of the reality we live in. If, in fact, we live in a web of intelligent quantum particles that connect us to the rest of the universe through time and space, then we all should have psychic abilities. Many brave scientists are now studying and publishing on such previously taboo topics as the evidence that psychic phenomena are real and that intelligence can be found everywhere in nature, from plants to animals and insects.

Dean Radin, Ph.D., is the author of *Entangled Minds: Extrasensory Experiences in a Quantum Reality* and the bestselling *The Conscious Universe,* in which he makes the case for the reality of psychic phenomena, ranging from psychic dreams to psychokinesis and ESP. Radin is the laboratory director at the Institute of Noetic Sciences and has worked at AT&T's Bell Laboratories and GTE laboratories on advanced telecommunications systems. He conducted research on psychic phenomena at Princeton University, the University of Edinburgh, the University of Nevada, and in three Silicon Valley think tanks. He also worked at the Stanford Research Institute (SRI) as a scientist on a highly classified government program investigating psi phenomena. This research ultimately evolved into a secret program in which U.S. intelligence agencies used psychics to spy on America's enemies.

Radin concludes that there is so much scientific evidence for psychic phenomena that: "Someday psi research will be taught in universities with the same aplomb as today's elementary economics and biology. It will no longer be considered controversial, but just another facet of Nature one learns as part of a well-rounded education. In that future, no one will remember that psi was once considered the far fringe of science."

Is the human race ready to deal with this view of reality? Are we ready to consider the possibility that we live in an illusory world and that the real universe is both physical and nonphysical at the same time, just as mystics have told us for thousands of years? We can't go on forever denying the truth. Soon, it seems, we will have to give in to the paradigm shift brought on by these amazing scientific discoveries. Scientists will become mystics and theologians will become scientists. Ironically, it will be those who are most entrenched in their specialized fields who will have the hardest time adjusting. But regardless of how prepared we are, the human race is on the brink of a great transformation that will allow it to break free of its limited sensory perceptions and see the universe for what it really is. In so doing, we will have to come to terms with the fact that there are supernatural beings whose abilities go far beyond our own. That knowledge could create widespread fear and consternation among our egocentric race, and could cause severe repercussions in every area of human endeavor, from science, to religion, economics, philosophy, and particularly psychology. Such a paradigm shift could be chaotic, to say the least. But the Earth is being prepared for such a change. Those having contact with what we call aliens today are finding their psyches ripped open, their psychic awareness heightened. In *The God Hypothesis* I call these persons the shamans of the modern age. It is they and their remarkable children who will lead the human race into this amazing and bizarre future that lies before us.

### Communing with the Rulers of the Earth

In the meantime, scientists from different fields continue to be amazed by their discoveries that beings of a higher order than man may have been involved in Earth's affairs for millennia. Invariably, such discoveries are met, at first, with skepticism and fear, but finally with bewildered acceptance. In the *God Hypothesis*, I reported on the work done by highly respected psychiatrists and psychologists (such as Harvard professor Dr. John E. Mack), who with great skepticism began researching cases of alien abductions, only to find that their subjects showed no signs of mental illness. These many researchers gradually came to see that ordinary people (many with advanced degrees and in positions of authority in business and science) were indeed having real experiences with nonhuman entities.

Suffice it to say that the so-called alien abduction phenomenon has yielded an abundance of information regarding the nature and agenda of the variety of beings who are interacting with perhaps millions of people around the Earth. No one knows how many people have had contact experiences because there is no central database that holds all the well-documented cases that have come to light in the last thirty years or so. But I have spoken to researchers from many countries and have done research in the U.S., Mexico, and Australia. I have lectured at conferences throughout the United States and I have met hundreds of persons who have been touched by this phenomenon. I can say without hesitation that the phenomenon is universal and it has great consistency. Yes, it is characterized by fear and trauma, but also by expanded consciousness and awareness, and as we have already noted, by increased psychic abilities. Oftentimes these abilities are unwelcome because the visions of future events that people receive can be disturbing, and also because having enhanced psychic abilities makes people feel different and out of step with the mainstream.

But whether they like it or not, UFO experiencers are at the leading edge of human evolution. They are being prepared for the day when their abilities and programmed knowledge will lead the human race in an exciting new direction.

### Rediscovering Reincarnation

Other psychiatrists, such as Dr. Brian Weiss, author of *Many Lives, Many Masters* as well as other books on the subject of past-life regression therapy, have discovered that many of their patients are able to recover past-life memories and in the process are healed from numerous mental and physical afflictions. But even more amazing is the fact that in many cases, the individual also remembers existing in a nonphysical state during those periods between lifetimes, and being in the presence of powerful beings (that Weiss calls the "masters") who supervise and control the destiny of the soul.

The use of past-life regression therapy is growing quietly within the psychiatric community, and the use of hypnosis to help people with their addictions to smoking and alcohol is becoming a big business. In the course of using hypnosis on their patients, many therapists have encountered the masters discussed by Dr. Weiss. The consistency of these out-of-body experiences, as well as those reported by persons who have had near-death experiences (NDEs), is so great that we can come to some tentative conclusions about what happens when we die. (What a concept!)

I have found in my research, just as Dr. Weiss discovered in his, that human consciousness continues to exist after death, but without the need for a physical body. The soul travels to another dimension where it encounters not only familiar personalities of those who preceded it in bodily death, but also nonhuman entities who are in control of that environment. These masters or guardians of the soul's evolution greet the individual with feelings of great love that people describe as a feeling of "going home." This, they believe, is where they came from before they incarnated into the flesh. Then they are shown the life they have just left behind in great detail, the good and the bad. They get to not only see what they did, but also feel what others felt at the time. If they hurt someone, they get to feel the hurt and see how their act reverberated through the web of consciousness that we call the universe. They are also shown the good things they did and how love also affects the universe. It is explained to them where they succeeded in achieving spiritual growth and also where they failed.

Although time does not exist in this dimension, there still comes a time when they are involved with the masters in the planning of their next incarnation. The purpose is always to carry out a mission that will provide them with opportunities to learn those lessons they have not yet mastered, or to atone for past errors. The goal is to learn all that there is to know about unconditional love. That is the only way out of the cycle of reincarnation.

**Anthropology**
Anthropologists have also discovered the rulers of the Earth, specifically those anthropologists who have studied the shamans of the primitive cultures around the world. For thousands of years, native peoples have used trance-like states and hallucinogenic drugs to commune with non-physical entities they describe as gods. The shamans, who are medicine men or

women, claim that while in the trance state they are able to explore non-physical dimensions and commune with the spirits that reside there. These scientifically unsophisticated people have amassed a huge body of information, totally unknown to modern science, regarding other dimensions and secret knowledge. It is knowledge given to them by nonhuman entities of a higher order, who, they say, have always coexisted with humankind.

In his excellent book *The Cosmic Serpent*, Stanford-educated anthropologist, Jeremy Narby, Ph.D., describes his experience living with the shamans of the Amazon and his efforts to learn how they came to know which plants are useful for healing. The answer he kept getting was that they received the information from nonhuman entities they communed with under the influence of a hallucinogenic brew they call *ayahuasca*. They told him that the drug allowed their souls or minds to leave their bodies and to enter another dimension where these powerful beings exist. Naturally, as an anthropologist, he could not accept such an explanation. He believed the shamans were hiding the truth from him. That is, until he decided to actually consume the beverage himself. What happened next was almost more than he could take:

> I found myself surrounded by two gigantic boa constrictors (in another reality) that seemed fifty feet long. I was terrified.

Then, the snakes began speaking to him telepathically:
> They explain to me that I am just a human being. I feel my mind crack, and in the fissures, I see the bottomless arrogance of my pre-suppositions. It is profoundly true that I am just a human being and, most of the time, I have the impression of understanding everything, whereas here, I find myself in a more powerful reality that I do not understand at all and that, in my arrogance, I did not even suspect existed...my last link to reality had been severed...I never felt so completely humble. (Narby 1998, 7)

As he later studied Amazonian shamanism, energized by his newfound knowledge, Narby found "astonishing similarities in the practices and concepts of shamans the world over…Wherever they operate…they specialize in a trance, during which their soul is believed to leave the body and ascend to the sky or descend into the underworld. They all speak a secret language which they learn directly from the spirits…they consider these spirits to have come from the sky to have created life on Earth" (Narby, 17).

He concludes that modern science's discovery of the double-helix shaped DNA molecule, and its basic role as life's creative force, is, in fact, knowledge acquired by shamans thousands of years ago. He believes that shamanic practices around the world, going back to the most ancient civilizations, not only discovered how DNA works, but have actually communicated with the DNA consciousness, which represents itself as twin serpents, reminiscent of the double-helix shape of the molecule—two serpents, entwined around each other.

Narby's examination of the DNA molecule forced him to conclude that it is "an ancient, high biotechnology containing over a hundred trillion times as much information by volume as our most sophisticated information-storage devices. Could one still speak of a technology in these circumstances? Yes, because there is no other word to qualify this duplicable, information storing module. DNA is only ten atoms wide and as such constitutes a sort of ultimate technology. It is organic and so miniaturized that it approaches the limits of material existence." (Narby, 103-104)

**Who Rules the World?**

In *The Way of the Shaman*, anthropologist Michael Harner, Ph.D., describes a bone-chilling confrontation he had with beings from another world during his study of shamanic practices in the forests of Ecuador in the early 1950s. His primary objective was to study the religions of the Amazon people by interviewing the religious leaders of indigenous tribes. However, they explained to him that there was only one way to learn about their beliefs, and that was to participate with them in their ceremonial trance states which occurred when they imbibed *ayahuasca*. They explained that the drink was made from a special vine they called the "soul vine."

Harner describes a most disturbing experience that occurred after he drank the brew. After going numb, he seemed to go into what he called a "celestial cavern" where he found himself in a huge "fun house, a supernatural carnival of demons. Presiding over the activities, and looking directly at me, was a gigantic, grinning, crocodilian head." Then he found himself in an ocean and he saw a giant galley with hundreds of oars coming towards him. On board were bird-headed beings with human bodies, much like images found in Egyptian religious paintings. Although he considered himself an atheist at the time, he was certain that they were coming for his soul. He felt he was dying. His body felt as if it had turned into concrete.

Then Harner began receiving communication telepathically from non-human entities. They told him that secrets would be revealed to him because he was about to die and the information was not meant for the living. The beings, he said, "were giant reptilian creatures, reposing in the lowermost depths of my brain." They projected a vision for him of the Earth as it existed eons ago, before there was any life on it. "Then black specks dropped from the sky by the hundreds and landed right in front of me....They were actually large, shiny, black creatures with pterodactyl-like wings. They flopped down, utterly exhausted from their trip, resting for eons. They explained they were fleeing from something out in space. They had come here to Earth to escape their enemy. The creatures showed me how they had created life on the planet in order to hide within the multitudinous forms and thus disguise their presence." He was shown how over hundreds of millions of years they transformed themselves into every plant and animal species "The dragon-like creatures were thus inside of all forms of life, including man. *They were the masters of humanity and the entire planet...We humans were but receptacles and servants of these creatures*" (italics added).

When he was revived from this near-death experience by his shaman friends, who administered an antidote when they saw he was dying, he related his experience to them. They were not surprised. They had all experienced the creator beings. It was from them that they received their secret knowledge.

**DMT: the Spirit Molecule**

Another scientist who discovered the existence of such beings by accident is Richard Strassman, M.D., author of *DMT: the Spirit Molecule*. Strassman conducted a five-year research study at the University of New Mexico under the auspices of the U.S. Food and Drug Administration and with funding from the National Institute on Drug Abuse and the U.S. National Institutes on Health. Between 1990 and 1995, he administered more than four hundred doses of the drug N.N. Dimethyltriptamine (known as DMT) to sixty volunteers through injections.

Interestingly, this very molecule is the active ingredient in *ayahuasca*. DMT is actually produced in small quantities in the human body by the mysterious pineal gland, which is found in the center of the brain. This gland has been identified by mystics as the location of the soul or the mind and the point of entrance and departure of the soul from the body during out-of-body experiences and during death and birth.

Dr. Strassman set out to test his hypothesis that excessive production of DMT by the pineal gland might account for near-death experiences and other mystical states. But early in his research project, Strassman was shocked and perplexed as his subjects began reporting out-of-body experiences that took them to other realities. There, they encountered strange, nonhuman beings whose appearances were often described as reptilian or insectoid. In some cases, the subjects found themselves on operating tables in futuristic, high-technological settings, while the nonhuman entities conducted experiments on them, implanted tiny objects in their bodies, and even raped them. In short, they were reporting the same kind of experiences reported by those who have had what we call alien abductions.

Strassman says: "Only later, when the study was well underway, did I also begin considering DMT's role in the alien abduction phenomenon." (Strassman 2001, p 322.) It was at that point that Strassman turned to Dr. John E. Mack, whose two books on his work with persons experiencing nonhuman contact are considered classics in their field: *Abduction: Human Encounters with Aliens* (1995) and *Passport to the Cosmos* (1999).

In a telephone interview, Mack told me that Strassman had turned to him for advice because he had no idea how to handle the highly traumatic experiences his volunteers were having during their sessions. Ultimately, Dr. Mack wrote an endorsement for Strassman's book because he felt the research had broken new ground in the search for answers about the alien abduction phenomenon. He and I agreed that many UFO experiencers report that they are taken out of their bodies in some of their abduction experiences. Sometimes they can't be sure if the experience was in or out of body. We also agreed that the beings might be able to induce out-of-body experiences in humans by remotely stimulating the pineal gland (by unknown means) whenever they want contact.

We both agreed that Dr. Strassman's findings supported the research done in the area of alien abductions by showing that there is a connection between the pineal gland, DMT, and out-of-body experiences during which persons report nearly identical experiences.

"Just because the experience takes place in another dimension or reality doesn't make it less real," John explained. "It just means we have a lot to learn about other realities."

Other realities, controlled by nonhuman entities, which have total power over the bodies and spirits of humans, is a concept we have discussed at great length in this book. Until now, such discussions have been limited to the fields of mythology, theology, and alien abductions. But now, we find anthropologists, medical doctors, psychologists, and even microbiologists having to wrestle with the same, bothersome questions: "Who are these beings who have such power over us?" And, more importantly, "*Who are we?*"

(Author's note: The reader should understand that in cases of what is called alien abduction, there is plentiful physical evidence to support the fact that at least part of the experience has physical effects. Researchers regularly find unusual needlemarks, bruises, scars, incisions, scoop marks, and even tiny objects under the skin. Additionally, there is often supporting witness testimony by those who shared the experience or were aware that the experiencer was missing during the time of the abduction. Furthermore, nonhuman contact often affects entire families and extended family members of all ages, genders, races, and religions. Such evidence precludes those knowledgable about the phenomenon from concluding that it is merely the product of a chemical reaction in the brain.)

## PART THREE

# The Secret Teachings

*"(The Kingdom of God) is inside of you, and it is outside of you. When you come to know yourselves, then you will be known, and you will realize that you are the sons of the living Father."*

The words of Jesus
according to the Gospel of Thomas
The Nag Hammadi Texts

## CHAPTER TEN

# The Secret Gospels and the Sons of God

IN DECEMBER 1945, two years before the discovery of the Dead Sea Scrolls, an Egyptian peasant made an amazing find while digging around a boulder in the mountains near his home. He unearthed a red earthenware jar containing thirteen papyrus books bound in leather. The books contained fifty-two different texts buried nearly 1,600 years before, presumably by early Christians. Some of the texts were clearly copies of much older documents dating back to A.D. 140, and some scholars believe that some of the writings may even be older than the Gospels of the New Testament, which date back to A.D. 60–110. Because the discovery was made near the Egyptian town of Nag Hammadi, these important books have become known as the Nag Hammadi texts.

Shortly after their discovery and before they were translated, Bible scholars announced excitedly that the find would mark a new epoch in the study of the origins of Christianity. After all, they seemed to contain books of the Bible never before seen and references to earlier, possibly more authentic versions of both the Old and New Testaments. Since all biblical scholars are aware of the extensive editing process that the Bible has suffered, they realized that the Nag Hammadi texts could shed new light on the origins of Christianity and on the life of Christ. But the enthusiasm soon turned to shock and disbelief as these scholars began to realize that the God they thought they knew was not the same one described in these documents. After a brief spate of publicity, the texts were buried once again. This time, though, they were buried in the vaults of museums and academic institutions that were seemingly unwilling to make the potentially earth-shaking information available to the general public. It wasn't until 1977 that a complete English edition of the texts was published, and by then few members of the public remembered or even cared that they existed.

## A Different Christianity

According to Elaine Pagels, author of *The Gnostic Gospels* (1975), Professor Gilles Quispel of the Netherlands was one of the first reputable scholars to read and translate the fragile documents. The mind reels at the shock he must have experienced when he deciphered the first line of text: "These are the secret words which the living Jesus spoke, and which the twin, Judas Thomas, wrote down." The title of the document was the *Gospel According to Thomas*. But unlike the other Gospels of the Bible, this one was a secret gospel. It introduced the incredible notion that Jesus had a twin brother, although some scholars believe that the term "twin" was used loosely at the time to refer to individuals who looked alike and thus could refer to one of Jesus' brothers, Thomas, who bore a resemblance to him.

That there was a Gospel of Thomas was already a known fact. As early as 1890, fragments of a Greek document with that title had been discovered. But here was the entire text along with other unknown texts, such as the *Gospel of Philip*, the *Secret Book of John* (known as the Apocryphon), the *Secret Book of James*, the *Gospel of Truth*, the *Gospel to the Egyptians*, the *Apocalypse of Paul*, the *Gospel of Mary Magdalene*, and the *Apocalypse of Peter*. Although the books contained many of the sayings known from the New Testament, there were also those that were completely new and offered a totally different view of Jesus and his teachings. In other words, here was an entire treasure trove of priceless texts that spoke in intimate detail about the life of Jesus in ways not revealed by the New Testament Gospels.

In *Thomas* for example, Jesus says:
If you bring forth what is within you, what you bring forth will save you. If you do not bring forth what is within you, what you do not bring forth will destroy you.

Passages such as these, which sound something like what a psychotherapist would say today, differentiate the belief system of these early Christians from those of modern-day Christians, as well as from their Jewish contemporaries. Both orthodox Jews and Christians teach that God and man are separated by a great void and that only a few chosen ones have the ability to receive His revelations. But the authors of these texts believed differently. They believed that self-knowledge is knowledge of God and that the flame of God burns within each and every one. Each person, without the aid of a priest or religious institution, has the ability to receive revelation from God by discovering his own soul connection to the divine. Because of their belief that the path to God was through knowledge, these early Christians were known as Gnostics—from the Greek word *gnosis*, meaning knowledge.

## The Trap of Reincarnation

Further setting the Gnostics apart from the prevailing orthodox teaching was their belief that Jesus did not come to save us from sin (they did not believe in original sin), but rather to serve as a guide to spiritual knowledge. Those who attain enlightenment through knowledge, they believed, become like Jesus—free of the bonds of the physical world. They believed that Jesus wanted us all to become like him and that, once we did, we would become his equals. This notion is even borne out in the words of Jesus himself in the New Testament when he tells his disciples, "Anything I can do, you can do also." By teaching his disciples the mysteries of spiritual healing and the secrets of the soul, Jesus was constantly urging his followers to follow in his path, known as the Way, and to become more like him. "Ye are gods!" he told them, prodding them to recognize their own inner divinity.

The idea that humans are unaware of their own divinity is a frequent theme in the Gnostic Gospels. Their understanding of the cosmos was quite different from that of the orthodox. For Gnostic Christians, God was not a being, but the essence of all things physical and not physical in the universe—the All. This, they believed was the true Father of Jesus. This most high God was not the creator of the universe, but merely provided the essence from which matter is constructed. The actual construction was and is accomplished by intermediary beings, led by one who, in his ignorance, believes himself to be the true God. This flawed, conscious being, known as the Archon or Demiurge, unaware of his true origins, fashioned the material world in his own flawed image and is served by an army of beings called variously Archons, Aeons, Watchers or sons of God. It is their task to rule over the physical world and to prevent its inhabitants (humankind) from learning about their true nature. For if humans understood that they had the divine spark of the All within them, then they would know that they, themselves, were gods and that their ultimate destiny was to reunite with the true God.

Thus the idea of salvation was quite different for Gnostics. They believed that it was not to save man from his sins that Jesus came to Earth, but rather to save man from his *ignorance*. Through knowledge of his divine nature, man could escape the physical realm, which continues to entrap the soul in its cycle through life, death, resurrection of the spirit and being returned again, through reincarnation, to physical form. In this context, the term "resurrection" refers to reincarnation—the cycle and evolution of the soul.

This concept was made clear to the Apostle John during a vision he had of the resurrected spirit of Jesus. In *The Secret Book of John*, Jesus explains the cycle of life and the entrapment of the human soul. John asks Jesus, "Christ, the souls,…when they come out of the flesh, whither will they go"? Jesus answers: "To a place for the soul… [The righteous soul] escapes from the works of wickedness and…will be saved and raised up to the rest of the Aeons."

John asks another question: "Those who have not known the All, …whither will they go?"

Jesus answers: "[The souls are delivered] to the powers, which are under the Archon. The souls will once more be cast into fetters and led about until they are saved from lack of perception, attain knowledge, and so will be perfected and saved…. It [the soul] no longer goes into another flesh [after it is perfected]."

So here we have a striking difference between the Gnostic and the orthodox Christian's perception of what happens in the afterlife. As Jesus explained to John, when a righteous man dies his soul is "raised up to the rest of the Aeons (angels)." But when one who has not led a righteous life and who has not attained knowledge dies, *his soul is delivered to those beings, which control the cycle of life. Those souls are once more "cast into fetters" of the flesh until they learn to become righteous.* Life on Earth, then, is considered a punishment for unrighteous souls and a trap for those who do not attain gnosis. Salvation comes from overcoming the cycle and being released to a higher level of existence. Jesus explains to John that there is a hierarchy of godlike beings who are given power over the souls of humans and who enforce the law of karma by causing souls to reincarnate until they get it right.

In the Gnostic texts, Jesus sounds more like the living Buddha, leading some scholars to suggest that there might be a connection between Gnosticism and Hindu or Buddhist tradition. Edward Conze, a British scholar of Buddhism, points out that Buddhists were in contact with early Christians because of flourishing trade routes that existed at the time. In the second century, the Greek Christian writer Hippolytus commented on Buddhist practices, which he saw as heretical:

There is…among the Indians a heresy of those who philosophize among the Brahmins, who live a self-sufficient life, abstaining from eating living creatures and all cooked food. They say that God is light—to them God is discourse, not that which finds expression in articulate sounds, but that of knowledge (gnosis) through which the secret mysteries of nature are perceived by the wise.

It seems that at the time of Christ in what is now known as the Middle East, there was an intermingling of religious and philosophical thinking that influenced early Christians. Could it be that Jesus himself practiced and taught spirituality similar to that taught by Buddha? Were such things as vegetarianism and reincarnation part of the lost teachings of Christ? There are those who believe that there is evidence that Jesus traveled widely during years of exile from Palestine between the ages of twelve and thirty, the gap that is unaccounted for in the Bible. Holger Kersten makes a convincing argument in *Jesus Lived in India* (2001) that in India there is a long tradition that someone very like Jesus traveled, studied, and taught there at about the time of Christ. Could it be that Buddhist teachings influenced Jesus and that much of what Christ stood for and taught was actually edited out of the Bible as it passed through the hands of zealots and committees formed by the Roman Empire and the Catholic Church? What if the Gnostic texts more closely reveal the truth about Christ than do the Gospels of the New Testament? What if Christianity was never meant by Jesus to become an institution sanctioned by empires and used as an excuse to launch wars and to massacre the pagan peoples of the world? If all of this is true, then the form that Christianity takes today is an adulterated one that prevailed because orthodox Christians had the power of the Roman Empire to enforce their beliefs, while Gnostic Christians lacked the power to protect their writings from the censors.

But today, this alternative Bible allows us to decide for ourselves if the Christianity that exists today is better or worse than that of those who were branded as heretics and whose writings were systematically destroyed over the centuries.

To be sure, some Gnostic texts cast doubt on the most sacred Christian beliefs such as the virgin birth and the bodily resurrection of Christ, while others tell a different version of the origin of the human race. In the *Testimony of Truth,* for example, the story of the Garden of Eden depicts the serpent as the bearer of divine wisdom, rather than a wicked and sly deceiver, as in the book of Genesis. Here the serpent offers Adam and Eve knowledge and wisdom while the Lord (the Demiurge) tries to prevent them from attaining spiritual knowledge with threats of death.

## The Resurrection

Gnostic Christians reject the literal interpretation of the resurrection of the body and explain it in various ways. Some argue that those who claimed to have seen the resurrected Christ really experienced Jesus on a spiritual level during dreams or visions seen during ecstatic trances. Such visions, they argue, are no less valid or real than having seen him in the flesh and, in fact, were meant to demonstrate the immortality of the human spirit. Such a view is a direct contradiction of some passages in the New Testament, which indicate that some of the apostles experienced a flesh- and-blood Jesus after the crucifixion.

For example, in the book of Luke, the apostles at first assumed they were seeing a ghost, but they were challenged by Jesus who said, "Handle me and see, for a spirit does not have flesh and bones, as you see that I have" (Luke 24:36–43). To prove his point, Jesus asks for something to eat. As they watched in amazement, he ate a piece of broiled fish. Yet other stories in the Bible are not clear on this point and scholars are suspicious that some of the events in the Bible are the fabrications of religious partisans, eager to preserve their version of truth. Luke and Mark both relate that Jesus appeared to them in another form, not his earthly form, as they walked on the road to Emmaus. Luke says that they talked with a stranger for several hours and invited him to dinner. When he sat down with them to bless the bread, they suddenly recognized him as Jesus. Then, "he vanished out of their sight" (Luke 24:15–31). In the book of John, Mary Magdalene is described as having seen a man near the grave of Jesus whom she took to be a gardener, but when he spoke to her, she suddenly recognized him as Jesus. Strangely, he ordered her not to touch him (John 20:17).

John also tells the story of how Thomas (one of Jesus' brothers) refused to believe in the resurrection until he had actually seen him for himself. When Jesus does appear, he tells Thomas, "Put your finger here, and see my hands; and put out your hand, and place it in my side; do not be faithless, but believing" (John 20:26–31).

So it is that the issue of the resurrection of Jesus in the flesh became one of the early controversies in the Christian religion. To Gnostics, it didn't matter whether the resurrection was physical or not, or whether Jesus's spirit took on a new semi-physical form after death. The important thing was that Jesus was still alive in spirit, just as we all will be after the death of the physical body. But to orthodox Christians, who took the stories literally, this view was heretical. To them, it was absolutely necessary for a true Christian to believe in the physical resurrection of Christ and subsequently in their own physical resurrection at the Second Coming.

## Mary Magdalene

Why was this so important to orthodox Christians? According to biblical scholar Elaine Pagels, the belief in physical resurrection served a political convenience. It allowed orthodox Christians to claim legitimate authority as successors of the apostle Peter, because he claimed to have seen Jesus in the flesh after he died.

"From the second century," she says, "the doctrine has served to validate the apostolic succession of bishops, the basis of papal authority to this day."

After the Crucifixion, according to Luke and John, Jesus appeared to Peter and named him as his successor. Orthodox Christians have claimed that this alone makes Peter the successor to Jesus because Peter was the first to see the resurrected Christ. But are these facts powerful enough to allow orthodox Christians today to claim their heritage as the primary keepers of the faith? The claim is, at best, a tenuous one.

First, the resurrection of Christ might not have been completely physical as some accounts in the Bible suggest. Secondly, the assertion that Peter was the first to see the resurrected Christ is contradicted by the gospels of Mark and John, who both name Mary Magdalene as the first witness of the resurrection. We might ask why Mary Magdalene was never considered the new leader of the Christian movement. The answer to this seems quite clear today.

The apostles were Jewish men who lived by Jewish rules. In their society, notwithstanding the teachings of Jesus, women were treated as second-class citizens and could not serve as leaders, particularly religious leaders. So it is that the official Church developed over the following two hundred years the rigid structure of a three-tiered hierarchy of bishops, priests, and deacons— all men. Gnostic Christians rejected this notion and called it "the faith of fools."

Worse yet, as if it were not enough to steal the right to lead the Jesus movement from Mary of Magdala, the leaders of the orthodox Church also sought to portray her as minor figure among the disciples and also as a prostitute, so that she could never be remembered as she truly was—the apostle most beloved by Jesus and the one who understood, better than all the rest, the deeper meaning of his teaching.

In the lost *Gospel of Philip*, the early dissension among the disciples over Mary's role is described. He portrays Mary as Jesus' most intimate companion and as the wisest:

...(He loved) her more than the disciples and used to kiss her [often] on the [mouth]. The rest of the disciples were offended by it.... They said to him, "Why do you love her more than all of us?" The Savior answered and said to them, "Why do I not love you as [I love] her?'"

(Words placed in brackets indicate where the parchment was worn, torn, or missing. The translators must make educated guesses, given the context of the passage, as to what words to include. In the above case, for example, one might argue that Jesus did not kiss Mary Magdalene on the mouth. It could have been somewhere else on her body, such as her cheek or forehead. However, the offense taken by the other disciples indicates that wherever Jesus kissed her often was not an innocent location. Translators are left with having to decide which other body locations are most appropriate in this case. In the end, it must be the reader's imagination that fills in the blanks. The word mouth seems the best choice, when one considers all the other alternatives.)

This, along with other clues in the Gospels, has led some to speculate that Mary was, in fact, the wife of Jesus and that they may have had children whose existence would have been seen as a threat to the Church and who therefore had to be hidden. (See Laurence Gardner's *Bloodline of the Holy Grail* [1996] and *Genesis of the Grail Kings* [2000].)

In the *Gospel of Mary Magdalene*, it is Mary who takes the leadership role after the Crucifixion, rather than Peter. Terrified and depressed, the disciples ask her to tell them what Jesus taught her secretly, and she agrees. But Peter objects to the teachings, asking angrily: "Did he really speak privately with a woman and not openly to us? Did he prefer her to us?"

Levi comes to Mary's defense by saying, "…if the Savior made her worthy, who are you… to reject her? Surely the Lord knew her very well. That is why he loved her more than us."

In another text, the *Pistis Sophia*, Peter again complains that Mary is dominating the conversation with Jesus and he asks Jesus to stop her from speaking, but Jesus refuses. Mary tells Jesus that she is intimidated by Peter because "He hates the female race." Jesus sides with Mary and assures her that whoever is inspired by the Spirit, whether man or woman, is divinely ordained to speak.

Another of the books found at Nag Hammadi, *The Dialogue of the Savior*, portrays Mary Magdalene as one of three disciples who received special teachings from Jesus. Of the three, which included Thomas and Matthew, Mary was said to have been the prize student: "…she spoke as a woman who knew the All."

In the lost *Gospel of Mary Magdalene*, we get to hear her side of the story. She describes the appearances that Jesus made to her as visions received in dreams or ecstatic trances. When she sees Jesus in such a vision, she asks him: "How does he who sees the vision see it?" Jesus answers: "…the visionary perceives it through the mind." Yet when she ran to tell the other disciples what had happened, she says that Andrew and Peter did not believe her. According to this text, there was tension between her and some of the other apostles. In this case, Peter was suspicious, not only of the testimony of a woman, but also of the notion that one could see the Lord in visions.

## Gnosticism and Women

Contrary to the orthodox beliefs, Gnosticism was so favorable toward women (as a result of how Jesus treated them and the status of Mary Magdalene among his disciples), that women were given places of authority and respect. According to Kurt Rudolph in his book *Gnosis* (1987):

> The percentage of women was evidently very high and reveals that Gnosis held out the prospects otherwise barred to them, especially in the official Church. They frequently occupied leading positions either as teachers, prophetesses, missionaries, or played a leading role in the cultic ceremonies (baptism, eucharist) and magical practices, exorcisms.

Furthermore, the concept of chastity was not one that most Gnostic Christians adhered to since they did not believe that Jesus or his disciples were celibate. A second-century Gnostic teacher named Valentinus taught that sexual intercourse was good for a person's spiritual development because it takes male and female to form a whole, a concept essential to Gnosticism.

As for the tradition that developed in the orthodox Church, which required priests to be strictly celibate males, it would be sad indeed if their centuries of celibacy (or attempts at it) were based on a falsehood promoted by a group of men who held women in low regard and who particularly despised Mary Magdalene for the great threat she posed to their claim to power.

Since it was common for rabbis to be married in the first century, it should come as no surprise to learn of the legend that Jesus and Mary Magdalene were not only married but that they also had children whose lineage was claimed by a long line of French kings known as the Merovingians. French legends tell the story of how Mary, her children, her sister Martha, and her brother Lazarus fled Palestine by boat a dozen years after the Crucifixion for the shores of France to the area of Provence. There she continued the teachings she had learned from her husband and was considered a high priestess, a prophetess, and a healer. While Paul and his followers went to Rome, preaching their concept of Christianity, which ultimately excluded women from positions of authority, the Gnostic teachings survived and thrived in France for hundreds of years.

According to researcher Margaret Starbird, who has made an intense study of the subject, "French legends confirmed the missionary endeavors of Mary Magdalene in southern France and her grave was fortuitously rediscovered near Marseilles in 1279…"

To this day churches throughout this region of France are dedicated to Mary Magdalene. Starbird continues:

> The Gnostic Christians extolled wisdom as the "beloved of Christ" incarnate in Mary Magdalene…. Wisdom was one of the significant attributes often associated with Mary Magdalene from the very earliest days of the church, when exegetes of Scripture often equated her with the Holy Sophia as well as the beloved sister-bride from the Song of Solomon. Among the Gnostics…(she) was known as 'the woman who knew the ALL, who received secret teachings from Jesus that were not imparted to the apostles….Mary Magdalene was the pre-eminent disciple and teacher of Christ's Gospel, the 'Apostle of the Apostles.'" (Starbird 2003, p 25)

### Finding God Within

This early break among the disciples of Jesus eventually led to two distinct branches: those who believed Peter to be the rightful heir to the teachings because of his claim to have seen the resurrected Jesus in physical form, and those who believed that anyone who saw the Lord through inner visions had equal authority to the original twelve apostles. This idea, of course, would negate the authority of priests, bishops, and the entire orthodox Church since anyone could claim to have seen Jesus in a vision and, therefore, claim equality with the apostles. It seems that those who followed Peter, and later Paul, relied on the public teachings which Jesus offered to the masses, while another group challenged Peter's authority and adhered to the secret teachings known and understood by only a few.

Valentinus wrote that Jesus shared certain mysteries with his closest followers, but these were kept secret from outsiders. According to Mark, Jesus told his disciples: "...to you has been given the secret of the Kingdom of God, but for those outside, everything is in parables; so they may indeed see, but not perceive and...hear, but not understand...."

It was this secret teaching which separated Gnostic Christians from the orthodox Church. And, just as Jesus would not reveal the secrets to just anyone, they also would not share them with those who had not proven themselves to be spiritually mature. As a result, Gnosticism was limited to the few who could understand the secret teachings, while orthodoxy grew large in numbers due to its appeal to the masses. It was this difference that eventually almost obliterated Gnostic beliefs. As the Church grew more powerful, it was able to search out and destroy Gnostic writings and put to death those who practiced or preached Gnosticism. By about the year 200 or so, virtually all Gnostic teachings had been excised from the new Christian religion, all their writings were censored or destroyed, and eventually, every one of the Gnostic texts was omitted from the New Testament.

Ironically, the eventual leader of the Christian movement, Paul, claimed his right as an Apostle by virtue of the Gnostic notion that he received a revelation through a vision of the resurrected Jesus. Paul states in 2 Corinthians 12:2 that the revelation he received had hidden mysteries and secret wisdom which he shared only with the mature. He said that he received the knowledge while in a state of ecstasy when he was *"caught up to the third heaven, whether in the body or out of the body, I do not know."*(Italics added)

We can only imagine how Peter might have reacted when he heard this story coming from Paul, a man who only a few days earlier had been pursuing the followers of Jesus to bring them to justice before a Roman court. His revelation had come to him as he traveled on the road to Damascus to seek out the remaining disciples. A bright light suddenly appeared in the sky and blinded Paul and his companions. Then, Paul claimed, he heard the voice of Jesus and he became converted. (Amazingly, this notion of finding Jesus or God through divine revelation (gnosis) was a Gnostic belief and leads us to believe that Paul, himself, was a Gnostic. That this did not prevent him from becoming the leader of the orthodox Church is something of a mystery.)

## Receiving Gnosis

The type of ecstatic experience described by Paul is exactly what every Christian Gnostic sought. However, they believed that such a state could only be achieved by having worked hard to attain a high level of understanding of the secret teachings. Paul, who was a Pharisee, had not been schooled in such matters, nor had he gone through the requisite training period. For that reason, Peter doubted Paul's miraculous conversion and required him to enter the ranks of the apostles as an initiate and to remain with them for two years. (This is precisely what the Essene community at Qumran required of its new members. In all likelihood, Paul was on his way to Qumran at the time of his vision, as the code name for the hidden sanctuary of Qumran was "Damascus," and it was there that Paul most likely became an Essene initiate. However, it seems Paul did not complete his initiation satisfactorily, for a conflict with the leaders, probably James, brother of Jesus, sent him on a mission to preach far from Palestine, into what is today Turkey, Greece, and finally, Rome. Because he was absent when the Roman's destroyed Qumran and then Jerusalem in about A.D. 68, his writings and influence outlasted those who stayed only to be murdered.

In the Gospel of Philip, it is pointed out that not every initiate was able to reach this high level of understanding. Mere participation in the rituals and beliefs did not make a person a true Christian: "…many people go down into the water [during baptism] and come up without having received anything." Referring to such rituals as professing the creed, belonging to the Church, or even martyrdom, he said: "Anyone can do these things." These, he said, are not what counted. Then he quotes Jesus as saying "By their fruits you shall know them." In other words, a person's actions—his works during his lifetime were what identified him as a true Christian.

So how did an initiate arrive at the point of spiritual maturity needed to become a full member? He had to live in a righteous manner, as did Jesus, and ultimately learn to receive his own revelation from God by entering into the highest altered state. One of the longest of the Nag Hammadi texts is one called *Zostrianos*, in which a spiritual master describes the procedure for attaining enlightenment. First, one had to remove from himself physical desires. (Sex for procreation, however, was acceptable for most Gnostics.) This had an important practical purpose. By practicing an ascetic life, the initiate cleansed his mind and spirit for the purpose of making his connection with God. Secondly, he had to eliminate the "chaos in the mind." In this quiet, meditative state, the initiate could receive visions and revelations from God.

Other Gnostic documents propose that there are levels of insight that the initiate must reach before achieving gnosis. They recommend using chants made of sacred words and vowels, similar to the tones used in what we would call transcendental meditation today.

One of the effects of reaching the highest altered state was to achieve an out-of-body experience. In a text called *Allogenes*, the author reports achieving an out-of-body state during which he saw "holy powers" that gave him knowledge (Pagels 1979, 136.) The author reveals that "I knew myself as I am.... [I was filled with] revelation... I received power.... I knew The One who exists in me."

Pagels notes that "such a program of discipline, like the higher levels of Buddhist teaching, would appeal only to the few.... The methods of Gnosticism did not lend themselves to mass religion. In this respect, it was no match for the highly effective system of organization of the Catholic Church...which offered a creed requiring the initiate to confess only the simplest essentials of faith...." (Pagels, 140-141).

Catholicism won out over Gnosticism because it was so easy for anyone to become a Catholic and so difficult to become a Gnostic. Pagels points out: "It is the winners who write the history...their way" (Pagels, 142).

To be sure, the Gnostic texts are full of warnings about the difficulty of

receiving gnosis. The Gospel of Thomas warns that the road to enlightenment through self- knowledge is not easy. It quotes Jesus as saying: "Let him
who seeks continue seeking until he finds. When he finds, he will be trou-
bled, he will be astonished, and he will rule over all things." Further it quotes
Jesus explaining that the kingdom of God: "is inside of you, and it is outside of you. When you come to know yourselves, then you will be known
and you will realize that you are the sons of the living Father."

In this sense, the coming of the "kingdom of God" is symbolic for a
state of transformed consciousness. According to Thomas, anyone can become Christ-like through knowledge. Jesus came to Earth to set an example and to show humanity the Way to become like him. Jesus is quoted saying:

"Whosoever will drink from my mouth will become as I am, and I, myself will become that person, and the things that are hidden will be revealed
to him."

In the Gospel of Philip, it said that whoever achieves Gnosis becomes
"no longer a Christian, but a Christ."

This idea would be repugnant to the orthodox view, which holds that
God and man are separate.


**The Essene Connection**

The resemblance of Gnostic Christianity to the philosophy and beliefs of
the Essene community at Qumran should be by now evident. Gnostic Christian beliefs and organization have a high correlation to those described in
the Dead Sea Scrolls' sectarian documents. Both groups separated themselves from mainstream religious thinking and believed they were the true
keepers of God's mysteries. They both shunned material goods and espoused
an ascetic lifestyle. Both the Essene library and the Nag Hammadi texts relate detailed descriptions of a hierarchy of angelic beings whose task it is to
watch over humans and their souls. They both felt persecuted by those who
lived in ignorance of the truth and they both believed that they alone possessed secrets pertaining to the true nature of reality and of the soul

Both groups had a system of initiation for new members that rigorously prepared them to achieve an enlightened state in which they could make their own connection to God. They both sought to teach their members how to attain a level of perfection that would enhance their ability to prophesy and heal.

It should go without saying that all of the above characteristics also applied to Jesus and his disciples as described in the New Testament.

Importantly, Gnostic Christians also believed in an eternal struggle between the forces of darkness (ignorance) and the forces of light (gnosis). As the Essenes before them, they believed that outsiders were living in ignorance, unaware of their true selves and in opposition to God's true laws. Such an existence, they believed, is like a nightmare because the human psyche is easily tricked by the many illusions created by the forces of darkness (the Demiurge) that lure them into the physical pleasures.

One of the most important connections between the two groups is found in the Gnostic text called *The Second Treatise of the Great Seth*. Here the author declares that the Gnostic Church is the true Church because Gnostics are the "Sons of Light," the exact same term used by the Essenes to describe themselves. The author explains the persecution Gnostics endured in a way similar to the way in which the Essenes depicted their torment by the Pharisees: "We were hated and persecuted not only by those who are ignorant, but also by those who think they are advancing the name of Christ, since they are unknowingly empty, not knowing who they are, like dumb animals."

The Sons of Light, on the other hand, had achieved liberation through secret knowledge and they alone practiced the true Christianity. While orthodox Christians abdicated all direct contact with God to the clergy, the Gnostics shunned a strict hierarchical system, preferring to share the opportunity to lead the congregation or to prophesy with other members, sometimes on a rotational basis—including women. Such a practice would be heretical to the mainstream Christians.

While Gnostic Christians maintained a strict and lengthy period of training for their initiates, just as did the Essenes, the Church that Paul built was making it easy for anyone to call himself a Christian. By the end of the second century, the criteria for belonging to the Catholic Church included a four-step process that is still in use today. New members had to confess the creed, accept the ritual of baptism, participate in worship, and obey the clergy. Anyone who agreed to do this could be a member. The trade-off, from the Gnostic point of view, was that the individual had to give up his own direct connection to God and accept the idea that the Holy Spirit (God) was present only in the clergy and that it was only through the Church that one could hope to reach God.

Ignatius, the bishop of Antioch, defined the power of the bishop this way:

> Let no one do anything pertaining to the Church without the bishop…Wherever the bishop offers [the eucharist] let the congregation be present, just as wherever Jesus Christ is, there is the Catholic Church. It is not legitimate either to baptize or to hold an agape [ritual meal] without the bishop…To join with the bishop is to join the Church; to separate oneself from the bishop is to separate oneself from God….” (Pagels 1979, 105).

The Gnostic response was to call orthodox bishops “waterless canals, because they profess knowledge, but they have not been enlightened.” Contrary to the bishop’s declaration, Gnostics believed that the true Church of Christ was not a physical place, but a purely spiritual state, and that they had been chosen before the foundation of the world to be representatives of the powers of light on Earth and had been given by God the power to teach, heal, and prophecy.

## Gnosticism Survives

The Gnostic form of Christianity, which taught the karmic concept of reincarnation, was carried on far beyond the early days after the crucifixion, in spite of the fact that Gnostics were hunted down and murdered by adherents of the other Christianity. By the middle ages, in the eleventh and twelfth centuries, such beliefs were still taught in an area of France then known as the *Languedoc* because of the strange language spoken there called Occitan (thus the name *langue d'Oc*, meaning "language of Occitan"). In this area, somewhat removed from the seat of the Church of Rome, women were respected as equals in a sect known as Catharism. Among the Cathars it was believed that being a Christian meant striving to become perfect, like Jesus. Those who reached that state, whether man or woman, were called *parfaite*, or perfect. The attainment of perfection came through a ritual baptism by the laying on of hands by other perfected ones.

Just as the Gnostics of the earliest days of Christianity had taught, the Cathars believed that it was their duty to teach others the secret knowledge of the human condition: how we got here, where we came from, where we were, who put us here, and how to escape (redeem ourselves).

The Cathars taught that humans are really angelic beings who have been kidnapped by the forces of darkness (the secret rulers of the Earth) and put into the bodies of men, which they made in their own likenes. (Churton 1997, 74). This, they believed, accounts for the fact that we yearn (on some level) to return to the dimension from which we came, the realm of pure spirit, which we enjoyed prior to our arrival on Earth. Through the Cathars' rite of spiritual baptism, the person was released from the hell of further incarnations or embodiments. For the Cathars and the Gnostics before them, hell was not some deep pit in the bowels of the Earth, but rather the Earth itself. The dark entities, they believed, created the physical dimension in an effort to trap beings of light (angels) into an existence separate from God and light.

*"Brief were my days among you, and briefer still the words I have spoken. But should my voice fade in your ears, and my love vanish in your memory, then I will come again, and with a richer heart and lips more yielding to the spirit will I speak. Yes, I shall return with the time, and though death may hide me and the greater silence enfold me, yet again will I seek your understanding....Know, therefore, that from the greater silence I shall return....Forget not that I shall come back to you....A little while, a moment of rest upon the wind, and another woman shall bear me."*
—Kahlil Gibran, *The Prophet*

## CHAPTER ELEVEN

# Jesus and Reincarnation

THE WORDS OF THE POET Kahlil Gibran are like an echo of the lost teachings of Jesus. The New Testament tells us clearly that much of Jesus's teachings were kept secret, revealed only to his closest associates. Much of what he said in public was said in riddles and parables, difficult to comprehend. Even his closest disciples had difficulty understanding the meaning of these stories. Often, he would have to explain what he meant in plainer words when the crowds had gone. His most secret teachings were so controversial and dangerous that they were preserved through an oral tradition, or written only in secret texts, passed hand-to-hand among the spiritually mature. We have learned that those who carried on these secret traditions were known as Christian Gnostics who believed that the path to salvation lay in spiritual knowledge, rather than in blind faith.

Sadly, those who possessed such documents or taught such beliefs were systematically searched out and killed, the documents destroyed, after Jesus was gone. At first the quest to destroy Jesus's teachings was carried out by the Roman authorities in cooperation with the Pharisees, the Jewish sect appointed by the Romans to control the Jerusalem temple. Later, a dozen or more Christian sects turned against each other in a struggle to determine which would carry on Jesus's teachings. As a result, what came to be called orthodox Christianity represents the beliefs of a powerful majority sect, which had the power to impose its views by force. Among the early Christian sects, there was the faction led by James, the brother of Jesus, who was of the opinion that Jesus did not intend to form a new religion, but simply to define the true form of Judaism. Christianity under James' leadership would have been an ascetic Jewish sect, practicing the difficult life of self-sacrifice, service to others, and eschewing the material world. Mary Magdalene, Jesus' favorite and best student, and other disciples are said to have fled to live out their lives in semi-obscurity in distant countries, such as France, Greece, or what is now Turkey. Their views were thought to have been lost forever.

As a result, Christianity took a radical turn after the death of Jesus. Some might say that Christianity was hijacked and transformed into something it was never meant to be. A faction led partly by Peter, one of Jesus's disciples, but mostly by Paul and his followers, who never knew Jesus personally, prevailed and became the purveyor of the form of Christianity we know today. They turned their church away from the secret teachings and from Judaism, which Jesus practiced, and toward a form of religion that would appeal to the masses. Instead of the rigorous path of self-sacrifice and mystical learning required of Jesus' followers, Peter and Paul espoused a Christianity that was easy for the masses to understand and accept. It offered an easier path to salvation.

This resulted in the distillation of a complex set of principles into a simple formula that appealed to a wide audience of mostly illiterate and simple-minded followers. The deeper mystery of the migration of the soul was stricken from the record, not because it was false, but because it was too frightening to contemplate and, later, because it was politically unacceptable to the Roman authorities, who made Christianity the official religion of the State. Consider, for example, the argument against reincarnation made by St. Augustine, Bishop of Hippo (A.D. 353–430), whose beliefs had a formidable impact on the molding of modern Christianity (italics added):

> Of the impiety of those who assert that the souls which enjoy true and perfect blessedness, must yet again and again in these periodic revolutions return to labour and misery. What pious ears could bear to hear that after a life spent in so many and severe distresses…that this will happen endlessly again and again, recurring at fixed intervals, and in regularly returning periods?…Who, I say, can listen to such things? Who can accept or suffer them to be spoken? *Were they true, it were not only more prudent to keep silence regarding them, but even, to express myself as best I can, it were the part of wisdom not to know them.* For if in the future world we shall not remember these things and by this oblivion be blessed, why should we now increase our misery, already burdensome enough, by the knowledge of them? If, on the other hand, the knowledge of them will be forced upon us hereafter, *now at least let us remain in ignorance,* that in the present expectation we may enjoy the blessedness which in the future reality is not to bestow; since in this life we are expecting to obtain life everlasting, but in the world to come are to discover it to be blessed, but not everlasting.
>
> —St. Augustine, *The City of God*

The words of St. Augustine are clear enough. He does not deny reincarnation, but rather, he argues that ignorance of it is bliss. He simply could not stand the notion that he might have to come back to Earth at a future time and endure such "labour and misery." He would rather not know such things, and his views on the subject were made the law of the Church, and stood in stark contrast to those who denounced ignorance in favor of knowledge. As a result of such thinking, the teaching of reincarnation, one of Jesus's most important lessons, was declared heretical. Once this was done, anyone caught teaching it or in possession of documents describing it was put to death and the documents destroyed.

So what is reincarnation? Why is it so hard to accept and why was its knowledge so dangerous to possess? The concept is really not so difficult to understand. It has been referred to by many names: the Law of One, the Law of Cause and Effect, the Law of Karma (in Eastern philosophy), metempsychosis (by certain mystery schools), or the transmigration of the soul. The concept can be found in the ancient writings of Eastern philosophy, in the lost books of the Gospels, and even in the Bible itself, if you know where to look.

### The Law of One

The Law of One, a concept that was already ancient in Jesus's time, has a relatively simple premise. It states that there is no separation in the universe. Any apparent separation that we humans perceive is but an illusion created by god-like beings (Archons in Gnostic writings) who control the physical dimension. In reality, everything is connected because the One True God is, in fact, a conscious, living universe, and everything in it is a part of it and is made up of the same material. This One True God, in Gnostic teachings, is the God of Light, the true Father of Jesus. In such a universe, man and God are not separated, as it may seem to those in the physical world, but are actually always directly and intimately connected to the whole (God) through the soul, which exists in the nonmaterial reality underlying the material world. In such a perfectly balanced universe, every action of any part of the whole is felt throughout the whole, just as a pebble thrown into a pond creates ripples that travel to every part of the pond. If a person does something good to others or to the Earth or its creatures, that positive energy reverberates throughout the whole and creates wellness. And if a person does something negative, that also reverberates and causes others to do bad things as well, magnifying the original bad deed.

What goes around, comes around, and doing harm to others has the effect of harming oneself. The effect of one's actions may not be immediately apparent, but wrongs must be righted and atonement must be made in future existences. Beings of a higher order than man act as shepherds of the soul to ensure that karma is fulfilled. In such a universe, there is only one logical form of behavior: to love all and to treat everyone and everything as one would treat oneself. There you have it: the Golden Rule, the central teaching of not only Jesus, but many spiritual masters throughout the ages.

Knowing this, we can see in the teachings of Jesus numerous ways in which He enunciated the Law of One and the principle of cause and effect:

"As ye sow, so shall ye reap."

"Judge not, lest ye be judged."

"Love thy neighbor as thyself."

"He who killeth by the sword, must be killed by the sword."

"He who leadeth into captivity, must also be led into captivity."

Do not be vengeful, but "forgive those who trespass against you."

"Love your enemies."

These are but a few examples of where Jesus taught the Law of One to the public, without having to explain the intricacies of how the universe works. In each case, the teaching describes a universe that is ruled by cause and effect. But as we all know, the seeds we sow don't always mature in our lifetime. One might kill by the sword and yet die of a heart attack. We might die before we forgive our enemies or those who have trespassed against us. These sayings only make sense when we aware that we live many lifetimes and that what we failed to accomplish in this life we will have to accomplish in another. For those who want more literal evidence, there are actually specific references to reincarnation in the Bible, and in the Lost Gospels.

### The Gnostic Gospels

As we have learned in the previous chapter, the discovery of the Nag Hammadi Texts (or he Lost Gospels of the New Testament) gave modern-day scholars and Christians an opportunity to decide for themselves if the documents deserved to be excised from the New Testament, or if they contain information that is relevant to the life story, and teachings of Jesus.

Their legitimacy has been the subject of debate for two millennia, but until their discovery, it was commonly believed that all such documents had been destroyed, and their owners murdered. But it seems that the monks living in the nearby monastery, perhaps fearing they would be caught with the texts, carefully preserved them and hid them from the authorities. As with the Dead Sea Scrolls, the owners never had the chance to return to retrieve them. Amazingly, within a two-year period, 1945–1947, a treasure trove of information about the ancient world of first and second century Palestine was made available to archaeologists (and ultimately the public). Now we don't have to accept the arguments of those opposed to Gnosticism. We can read the texts for ourselves and make up our own minds.

When the Gnostic texts found at Nag Hammadi were translated, it was the first time Christians were able to read the books that didn't make it into the New Testament, but which were known to have existed, because the founders of the orthodox Church regularly lambasted the heretical writing in their own books. Of course, this presented a rather one-sided and slightly biased perspective, as we have seen in the writings of Augustine. Since the texts were translated into English in 1977, we Westerners have been able to see and read for ourselves what the Church founders were willing to murder for to keep us from seeing. What was so terrible about the beliefs and writings of these early Christians?

First there was the Gnostic cosmology that denied that the Hebrew God, Yahweh/Jehovah, was the true God. They believed that Jesus was not his son, but rather the son of the one true God of Light, the God of highest authority. In fact, they believed that the Hebrew God, and his band of Archons had created the physical world to entrap the souls of humans in a vicious cycle of reincarnation. Jesus, in their view, was sent to Earth by the true God to teach humankind the reality of its entrapment and to reveal the Law of One so that souls could escape the physical world.

Perhaps even more abhorrent to the Church was the Gnostic notion that Jesus did not want a Church built on a hierarchy of priests claiming a special connection to God. Rather, they said Jesus taught that every person had the ability to connect directly to God by seeking spiritual revelation through meditation and ecstatic states. Priests, they believed, were empty channels, through which God's spirit did not flow, and were unnecessary and even counter to God's will.

One of the more controversial books of the Nag Hammadi Library is the *Secret Book of John*, which was well known to the orthodox leaders in the first centuries A.D. Iranaeus, in his book, *Against Heresies* (A.D. 185), attacks the book for John's belief that Yahweh is a jealous God "because he knows that he is not the sole divine power." John characterizes Yahweh as a "monstrous abortion of darkness," who has trapped the light-spirit of man in darkness and matter. John reverses the basic assumptions of the Judeo-Christian theologies by asserting that Adam and Eve did not sin when they ate of the fruit of the tree of knowledge (gnosis), but rather they began the process of redemption through their disobedience to the creator God. In fact, it was the creator-God (whom they called Ialdabaoth) who they believe committed the first sin by creating the physical world.

John describes a vivid vision during which the law of karma is revealed, and how the unrighteous must come back to the physical world time and time again until they become enlightened. Jesus uses the term "cast into fetters" to describe the imprisonment of the soul in the physical dimension.

The term, "cast into fetters," was often used by Gnostics to describe the way the soul is forced to reenter the physical world to correct previous misdeeds and to learn completely what it means to love unconditionally. It is the sons of God, who rule humankind, who ensure that the Law of One is carried out and that each soul corrects the errors it made in its previous incarnations. Ultimately, the soul passes the final exam by living a life of unconditional love. This kind of love can be described as a love for all persons and living things, without strings attached and without conditions that, if not met, will break the bond of love, mercy, and understanding.

## Reincarnation in the Bible

As we can see, a determined effort to rid the Bible of reincarnation was carried out by those who called themselves orthodox shortly after the death of Jesus. A more systematic effort came in A.D. 325 when Roman emperor Constantine the Great legalized Christianity. Constantine, with the help of his mother Helena, deleted as many specific references to reincarnation as they could find in both the Old and the New Testaments. Their concern was a political one. If the people believed in reincarnation, Constantine thought, they would not obey the laws, thinking they could simply make up for their wrongs in another life. (Actually, when one truly understands that the physical world is a trap for souls, the opposite is more likely to happen. But Constantine was not a spiritual person; he did not actually become a Christian until he was on his deathbed. His motives were purely political.)

In A.D. 553, the Second Council of Constantinople reconfirmed Constantine's decision and declared the belief in reincarnation a heresy against church and state. Anyone still left alive who taught reincarnation was doomed. But, amazingly and thankfully, Constantine's purge of the Bible was not complete for two reasons. First, the Church fathers could not envision a time when common men would be able to read the Bible. That knowledge and privilege was believed to be reserved only for the priesthood, and the priesthood believed what it was told. Secondly, it was impossible to delete the concept of reincarnation completely from the Bible because it is the central part of Jesus's teachings and the cornerstone of true spiritual knowledge. Trying to hide it is akin to insisting that the Earth is flat. Such falsehoods can only prevail temporarily. Spiritual laws are truths that always win out in the end, because they are available to anyone who searches within himself.

An easy way to find the teaching of reincarnation in the Bible is to turn to the last book of the Old Testament—the book of Malachi. Malachi was one of many ancient Hebrew prophets who recorded their visions and prophecies for posterity. In chapter 4, verses 5 and 6, Malachi says that the

Lord revealed to him: "Behold, I will send you Elijah the prophet before the coming of the great and dreadful day of the Lord. And he shall turn the heart of the fathers to the children, and the heart of the children to their fathers, lest I come and smite the Earth with a curse."

Elijah, of course, was one of the Hebrews' greatest prophets remembered as the one who was carried into heaven in God's chariot of fire (2Kings 2:1). While walking with his successor, Elisha, it is said that: "And as they went on and talked, behold, a chariot of fire and horses of fire separated the two of them. And Elijah went up by a whirlwind into heaven."

Elijah was also well known for being an overzealous follower of Jehovah. During a confrontation with Canaanite priests over whether Jehovah was stronger than their god Baal, Elijah had 450 of their prophets put to death by the sword (1 Kings 18:17–40).

Now, skipping forward to the New Testament, in chapter 11 of the book of Matthew, verses 9–16, we find these interesting words of Jesus as he speaks to his disciples about his relative John the Baptist.

Yea, I say unto you, [he is] more than a prophet. For this is he, of whom it is written, 'Behold, I send my messenger before thy face, which shall prepare thy way before thee.' Verily, I say unto you, among them that are born of women there hath not risen a greater than John the Baptist....*And if ye will receive it, this is Elijah, which was for to come. He that hath ears to hear, let him hear* (italics added).

In this passage, Jesus is clearly telling his disciples that John the Baptist is the reincarnated Elijah, who was prophesied to return to Earth. The lesson is so difficult for His disciples to accept and understand that Jesus concludes His lesson by saying, "He that hath ears to hear, let him hear." Why was that necessary? It seems as if Jesus knew only too well that some would reject this information because they were not ready to hear it. They were not yet spiritually mature enough to understand.

But lest there be doubt that this was Jesus's true meaning, we can read in Luke 1:17 the words attributed to the angel Gabriel, who appeared to the priest Zechariah to tell him that his elderly and barren wife Elizabeth (relative of the Virgin Mary) would soon bear him a son: "And he shall go before Him in the spirit of Elijah, to turn the hearts of the fathers to the children, and the disobedient to the wisdom of the just; to make ready a people prepared for the Lord." That son, of course, was John the Baptist.

Another place in scripture in which reincarnation is explicitly discussed is in Matthew 16: 13–14. Jesus asks of His disciples: "Whom do men say that I, the son of man am? And they said, 'Some say that thou art John the Baptist, some say Elijah and others Jeremiah or one of the prophets.'" This conversation took place after the death of John the Baptist, who was beheaded by King Herod Antipas. It makes it clear that Jesus, his disciples, and the people in general were all aware of the concept of reincarnation. Additionally, the story illustrates how even a great prophet such as Elijah is subject to the law of karma. When John is beheaded, he fulfills his own karmic need to right the wrong he committed as Elijah in a previous life when he had the priests of Baal put to death by the sword. He had killed by the sword and now he had to be killed by the sword. The lesson is clear. If the law of karma applies to great prophets, then how can it not apply to ordinary men and women? The answer, of course, is that it applies to everyone. It is an immutable law of the universe and understanding it is essential to the salvation of the soul.

*"Because of the divisions that had arisen among
the people into sects, as the Pharisee, the Sadducee
and their divisions, there had arisen the Essenes
that had...kept the records of the periods when individuals had been visited with the supernatural
or out of the ordinary experiences, whether in
dreams, visions, voice or what-not, that had been
and were felt by these students of the customs of
the law...the promises and the many ways these
had been interpreted by those to whom the preservation of same had been committed."*
—Edgar Cayce on the Dead Sea Scrolls 1970, 125
Channeled on November 18, 1937

CHAPTER TWELVE

# Edgar Cayce on Jesus and the Essenes

### Other Ways of Knowing

NO DISCUSSION OF THE CONNECTION between Jesus, the Essenes, and the Dead Sea Scrolls or reincarnation would be complete without including the vast literature regarding the late and quite remarkable Edgar Cayce, known as America's Sleeping Prophet. In order to compress this information into one chapter, I must assume that the reader has some knowledge of who Edgar Cayce was and the amazing legacy he left the human race in the form of thousands of psychic readings he performed during his life, between 1901 (when he first began giving medical diagnoses while in a deep trance) and January 3, 1945, when he died. (For readers who would like to find out more, there are several books regarding Cayce's works cited in the reference section in this book.)

Because Cayce's readings were written down by a stenographer, there exists to this day a tremendous volume of material at the Association for Research and Enlightenment, Inc. (A.R.E.), located in Virginia Beach, Virginia, and available to the members of that organization. The materials in those files have been used by scholars to write numerous books regarding different topics that Cayce discussed during his trance states, including the Dead Sea Scrolls, the mysteries of reincarnation, Jesus and the Essenes, and even the lost continent of Atlantis. All this, in spite of the fact that Cayce was a devout Christian and even a Sunday school teacher in a Presbyterian church! Because he had no memory of what he said while in a trance, he was quite often aghast at the words he had spoken (when they were later read back to him), for his readings often contradicted his beliefs and the doctrine of his church. Today, Cayce would have been called a trance channeler, using New Age terminology, because the words and information that came from him during his sessions did not come from his conscious mind, nor even his subconscious mind, but rather from a disincarnate source. After lying on a couch and relaxing, he would experience a blinding flash of light. Then, according to his testimony, he would then find himself in a vast library, which he referred to as the Hall of Records. When asked a question by those in the room where he was lying, a being, who Cayce referred to as the Keeper of the Records, would guide him, in this other dimension, to a particular volume, which Cayce could read telepathically. Cayce believed that he was merely a conduit used by God to communicate important information that the human race needed to know. Additionally, his readings made it clear that every action of every person in every lifetime was recorded and maintained in the ethereal Hall of Records. The information is accessible to highly enlightened persons during periods of ecstasy, or what we call today altered states.

### The Qumran Community

The Dead Sea Scrolls were discovered in 1947, but their true significance was not recognized for several years. Thus, their connection to the Essene sect was unknown for some time after their discovery and the ruins of Qumran remained a mystery until excavations began several years later. Only a very few historians had ever heard of the Essenes, who are barely mentioned in the history books of the time. Because the word Essene is not mentioned in either the New Testament or the Old Testament, it was assumed by historians that the sect was a minor Jewish group that played no important role in the religious life of the Hebrew people, much less the origins of Christianity. (According to Cayce, the word "Essene" meant "expectancy." In other words, the Essenes were those who were expecting the Messiah to be born into their midst. This concept was found to be true when the texts were interpreted, as we have seen in chapter six.)

It is a mystery that Edgar Cayce, while in a deep, self-induced trance, made the connection between the Essenes and the origins of Christianity almost two decades before the discovery of the Dead Sea Scrolls. Once the Scrolls were interpreted, scholars were shocked to find in them the basic ingredients of Christianity. Only then did they become interested in that little-known and misunderstood sect. Because Cayce died in 1945, and the scrolls were found in 1947, he did not live to experience the satisfaction of knowing his psychic readings had been accurate. In the introduction to his book, *Edgar Cayce on the Dead Sea Scrolls*, Glenn Kittler, under the editorship of Cayce's son, Hugh Lynn Cayce, says:

> Before the discovery of the Dead Sea Scrolls, no acknowledged expert in history or religion ever put forth the possibility that Jesus, Mary, Joseph, John the Baptist, and other leading figures in the Gospels were associated in any way with the Essenes. Yet for over twenty years, the Life Readings given by Edgar Cayce had been producing information regarding the association.

Born on March 18, 1877, on a farm in Kentucky, Cayce displayed psychic abilities from the age of about six years old, telling his family about visions he had regarding such things as the communication he experienced with relatives who had recently died. In later years, he would lie on a couch and put himself into a deep, somnambulistic trance and answer questions put to him regarding diagnoses and cures for persons hundreds of miles away. Many of these were documented and shown to have actually worked. Doctors began referring hopelessly ill patients to him from all over the world. The documented accuracy of Cayce's medical miracles serve as an important benchmark for the material he later channeled regarding topics that he, as a Christian, did not believe in, such as the concepts of karma and reincarnation, as well as the existence of Atlantis. It is reasonable to expect that if his medical readings were verifiable, then there is a good chance his other readings were accurate as well. This is not to say that channeled information is one hundred percent accurate, for even the best psychic channelers (and there have been many) must convert the information they receive into the language they are familiar with and filter it through their own strongly-held belief systems. Nevertheless, in Cayces' readings we find uncanny accuracy regarding information he could not possibly have known beforehand.

### Cayce's Readings on the Essenes

One of Cayce's early mentions of the Essenes came in a reading on a hot June afternoon in Virginia Beach when a woman came to him for a spiritual reading. In trance, Cayce told her that she had lived during the time of Christ and was among the "holy women and those in close acquaintanceship with many who were the teachers or the apostles, or the disciples— many of those women, as Mary, Martha, and Elizabeth." He said that she was one of those who "dedicated their lives…[to assisting] those of the Essenes." Her name then was Eloise and it was her job to run a school on the "way that goes down towards Jericho to the northernmost coast from Jerusalem." She had been trained, Cayce said, "in the schools of those that were of the prophets and prophetesses," and she was "indeed a prophetess" in that lifetime. She had known Jesus and his family. By choosing to serve as an Essene and to assist Jesus Christ in the preparation for this Messianic purpose, she had moved her soul closer to God.

The reader may note that the route described by Cayce would have taken a traveler directly to where Qumran is located, on the northernmost coast of the Dead Sea, near Jerusalem. The route described is also in the area where John the Baptist baptized Jesus in the Jordan River. Qumran is in the wilderness, where it is said Jesus went after his baptism, and, of course, the wilderness is where the Gospels tell us John the Baptist was raised. Most scholars today believe that it is highly likely that John the Baptist was raised by the Essenes at Qumran, after his elderly mother and father (Elizabeth and Zechariah) died. (Elizabeth, we are told in the New Testament, was a relative of Mary, the mother of Jesus, so John the Baptist was also related to Jesus in some way. This makes the probability high that Jesus knew of and had spent time at Qumran.)

Even though Cayce was a Christian and an avid Bible reader, he was not likely to have had knowledge of Qumran or the Essenes, because, mysteriously, neither the sect nor the community is mentioned in the Bible. This fact presents a paradox for historians who clearly see Christian origins in the Essene writings and in the community at Qumran. Theories abound as to why this is so. But two are foremost in the minds of many: First, the Essenes were exceedingly secretive (some might say paranoid, with good reason) due to the fact that their criticism of the Jewish authorities and the Roman rulers made them targets for assassination. (This is what happened to Jesus when he went public with his teachings.)

It has been mentioned that the Essenes did not refer to their members by proper name, nor did they refer to their community other than by the code name, Damascus" and to themselves as the Sons of Light or the Keepers of the Covenant. So, these early followers of the Teacher of Righteousness, during his life and afterward, would have shared in the Essene desire to keep their secrets. In fact, they would have been sworn to secrecy. Secondly, it is possible that the authors of the New Testament, writing many years after the death of Jesus and the destruction of the Qumran community, did not want to give credit to the Essenes because the Scrolls make it clear that their form of Christianity was a Jewish form that required its members to be Jewish and follow the laws of Moses in the strictest sense.

Their beliefs would never have allowed men to join the sect without being circumcised, for example. Yet, for Peter and Paul, who founded the orthodox Church, circumcision and following the strict laws of Moses became secondary to the belief that Jesus was God. They found their converts among the Gentiles, for whom circumcision and Jewish laws were not attractive.

However, both in the Gospels and the Lost Gospels, we learn that some of the disciples of Jesus continued to believe as the Essenes did, even after Jesus' death on the cross. One in particular was James, one of Jesus' brothers, who is seen today by Bible scholars as the true keeper of the teachings of Jesus and the leader of the Jerusalem church. These beliefs created a split among those followers of Jesus who survived the weeks and months after the Crucifixion. James and his followers were in direct conflict with the self-appointed apostle Paul, whose writings and teachings dominate the Gospels we know today. It was he and his followers who broke away from the Jewish faith and went on missions, during which they converted Jews and Gentiles alike to the notion that salvation could be theirs if they only believed that Jesus was God.

This concept relieved the converts of having to follow a strict discipline and of having to give up their wealth, as Jesus taught. After all, the fact that Paul was himself a Roman citizen from a well-to-do family protected him from persecution for years, until even he met his own death in Rome (it is believed) at the hands of the Roman authorities.

### Essenes and Gnosticism

Interestingly, Cayce's readings made specific mention of the complex role of women in the Essene sect, which he said was widespread at the time of Jesus and existed not only at Qumran, but also throughout Palestine and the Middle East. (Cayce placed the Essene headquarters at Mount Carmel, on the shores of the Mediterranean Sea, even though archaeological evidence has not yet verified that claim. It could be that Cayce's conscious mind could simply not accept the notion that anyone could live on the Dead Sea, and it merely misconstrued the information he was receiving.)

In any case, women, Cayce said, played a vital role in Essene life and were involved in the birth, training, and public ministry of Jesus. This is supported not only by the fact that female remains were found at Qumran but also in the texts discovered at Nag Hammadi, which describe how the early Gnostic Christians permitted women to prophesy and lead services. Cayce's readings also coincide with the Gospels, which make it clear that Jesus honored women and treated them as equals, sometimes to the dismay of his male disciples.

Cayce's teachings describe the universe as being guided by a universal consciousness (God), rather than being ruled by a male deity. Cayce describes a living, conscious, and intelligent universe, in which everything that exists is linked by a web of consciousness. He called this immutable fact the Law of One, and its corollary the Law of Karma.

In Cayce's visions, he saw that souls are extensions of this genderless universal consciousness and are made of the same essence as God. "A soul knows it is of God," Cayce said, "but also of itself and also of every other soul." This condition of unity with God, yet (because of free will) separateness from Source gives the soul its consciousness. "A soul," he said, "is both masculine and feminine, both positive and negative, both aggressive and responsive" (Kittler 1970, 53). The downfall of the human race was in the fact that some souls enjoyed the experience of human incarnation so much that they tried to be like God. This caused the birth of the ego, which causes humans to see themselves as separate from and better than others, including the plants and animals.

This was also the birth of guilt and the creation of negative karma. Earthlike planets elsewhere in the universe, Cayce said, are places for souls to go to experience what it feels like to be separate from God. Evolution, he continued, proceeds differently on each planet. (This could account for why aliens from other planets might look quite different from Earth's humans.)

The experience of incarnation can be exhilarating and ego expanding, as well as frightening and depressing, leaving the soul with the feeling that it has been abandoned. Even though evolution proceeds differently on other planets, the outcome is the same. Once released from the physical body, the soul resumes its journey, attempting to return to the Source of all creation. Cayce's readings confirm the Gnostic belief in reincarnation and Jesus's teaching of the recycling of the soul. Just as Jesus states in the *Secret Book of John*, Cayce's readings support the fact that souls which succeed in refusing to be obsessed by the temptations of the physical world get promoted and are then allowed to proceed to higher realms reserved for the spiritually mature. Those souls, which have become enamored of the physical pleasures and material goods, must try again by reincarnating into the flesh in a new body.

Much to my relief and possibly to the reader's, however, Cayce points out that a soul receives "certain credits, which could be accumulated in each incarnation and eventually result in success." These karmic brownie points if you will, could be any thought, word or deed, which God could accept as good in terms of morality, justice, or the betterment of mankind."

A soul's ability to progress in its next life depends on its sensitivity to subconscious memories of lessons learned in the past. This requires the person to know himself, by learning to tap into his soul memories through the use of meditative or other altered states. An enlightened soul, Cayce reports, "at the threshold of God, would have in its consciousness much, even all, of the knowledge and wisdom of the subconsciousness…" Such a person "could do marvelous things—heal, raise the dead, read minds, reveal the past, disclose the future." One who developed such elevated psychic powers, Cayce said, was one who had been "Christed." The notion that such perfection is available to all of us was also one central to the Gnostic Christian traditions.

According to Cayce, Jesus himself had reincarnated many times in the past. In one life, he was the mysterious Enoch, a great patriarch who lived before the Deluge. In another, he was the high priest of the Hebrews, Melchizedek, and in another, Joshua, who succeeded Moses. Each time, his message was the same. He wanted people to learn that to be saved from the vicious cycle of reincarnation they must lead simple lives in service to their fellow humans. This, he said, was the Way to salvation from reincarnation. It was by setting the example for others as to how to live a life without creating negative karma that he hoped to save the human race. Cayce summarizes the lesson to be learned by following the Way of Jesus:

How can ye do his bidding? Not in mighty deeds of valor, not in exaltation of thy knowledge or power, but in the gentleness of the things of the spirit: love, kindness, longsuffering, patience. These, thy elder brother, the Christ has shown thee, that thou, applying them in thy associations with thy fellow man, day by day, here a little, there a little, may become one with Him as he has destined that thou shouldst be....Let thyself, then become...a channel through which His manifestations in the Earth may arise (Kittler 1970, 58-59).

No better description could there be of the Essenes and their efforts to achieve Christedness, than that described by the Jewish philosopher, Philo of Alexandria, who wrote of them in about A.D. 20:

They were a sect of the Jews, and lived in Syria Palestine, over 4,000 in number, and called Essaie, because of their saintliness....Worshipers of God, they yet did not sacrifice animals, regarding a reverent mind as the only true sacrifice. At first they lived in villages and avoided the contagion of the evils rife therein. They pursued agriculture and other peaceful arts; but accumulated not gold or silver, nor owned mines. No maker of warlike weapons, no huckster or trader, by land or sea was to be found among them; for they saw in slavery a violation of the law of nature, which made all men free brethren, one of the other.

## Astrology and Out-of-Body Experiences

The reader will remember that among the Dead Sea Scrolls were those dedicated to the science of astrology. This was a particular embarrassment to the Dead Sea Scroll scholars, whose belief system did not include the concept that the movement of the planets and stars could have an impact on life on Earth. Yet, today, Scroll scholars are ready to admit that astrology was a sacred teaching of the Essenes and in most of the civilized world of the time. In fact, they are even convinced that the famous three kings who visited Jesus at his birthplace by following the Star of Bethlehem were not kings at all, but astrologers from distant lands, whose astrological knowledge guided them to find the Jewish Messiah.

This concept is also verified by readings Cayce did for a woman who had lived at the time of Jesus and was one of his teachers. Her name at that time was Judy.

"Tell about Judy teaching Jesus, where and what subjects she taught him, and what subjects she planned to have him study," Cayce was asked.

"The Prophecies!" Cayce responded. "Where? In her home. When? During those periods from his twelfth to his fifteenth to sixteenth years, when He went to Persia and then to India. In Persia, when His 'father' died. In India when John (the Baptist) went first to Egypt, where Jesus joined him and both became the initiates in the pyramid or temple there."

"What subjects did Judy plan to have Him study abroad?" Cayce was asked.

"What you would today call astrology."

"Was Judy present at any of the healings or the feeding of the multitudes?

"Those where she chose to," answered Cayce.

"Was she present at the Crucifixion?"

"No," answered Cayce, "that is, in mind (she was) present. For remember, Judy's experience at that time was such that she might be present in many places without the physical body being there."

In numerous readings, Cayce said that Jesus and the Essenes studied astrology and other mystical teachings, such as those mentioned in the Books of Enoch, regarding the angelic realms and their influence on life on Earth. In 1938 Cayce described the type of records studied at that time: "Those same records of which the men of the East (the Magi) said ... 'by those records we have seen His star.' These pertained then, to what you would call today astrological forecasts, as well as those records which had been compiled and gathered by all of those of that period pertaining to the coming of the Messiah."

Another Scroll scholar, Professor John Allegro, wrote:

We have a number of (Essene) works referring to the movements of the heavenly bodies, and not all their study was of purely academic interest. For them, the stars and their positions could affect men's lives, and amongst their esoteric documents we have one describing the influence of the heavenly bodies on the physical and spiritual characteristics of those born in certain sections of the Zodiac(Kittler 1970, 203).

Cayce's readings make it clear that today's Bible, both the Old Testament and the New Testament, were heavily tampered with by committees and well-meaning zealots who did not understand or did not want to believe the historical truths. Those who believe that the Bible is infallible simply do not know the facts. They have not read the Dead Sea Scrolls, nor are they familiar with the Lost Gospels. Most people simply do not understand how easy and how common it was for translators to interject their own opinions by merely changing a word. Although Bible scholars have always known that some editing and literary license was inherent during the compilation of the scriptures, we now see that the problem is much more serious. Entire aspects of the mystical teachings were excluded, edited, or rewritten entirely. Astrology, reincarnation, Jesus's training by the Essenes, his travel and study in India, Persia, and Egypt as a young man, and the important role of women in the ministry of Jesus were all left out. Additionally, the Qumran writings held sacred the mysterious Books of Enoch, as did first- and second-century Christians. But in the third century, the orthodox Church decided they should not be included in the Bible, and even though Enoch and the story of the angelic Watchers who rule over humankind are mentioned in the Bible, the actual Books of Enoch (which contain a vast amount of information about other dimensions and the angelic realms) were not seen again until 1773 when a copy was found in an

Ethiopian version.

Also banned were the *Secret* Books of Enoch, copies of which were eventually found in Russia and Serbia. These writings tell of Enoch's visit to the seven heavens and the revelation he received from God about the creation of the world. They describe the story of the fallen angels who mated with humans to create a hybrid race, and they explain the rudiments of astrology. Historians now know that these documents, once considered sacred and even studied by Jesus, were removed from the Bible because they were so mystical that the average person would not be able to understand them.

The Christianity of today, then, is simplified and sanitized in such a way that the average person might enjoy the comfort of believing one's soul is safe because he faithfully obeys the Church, goes to worship services on Sunday, gives money to the church, and swears his belief that Jesus is God. But according to Cayce, what is lacking in today's Christian life is adherence to the basic laws required for salvation: self-sacrifice, the need to search for spiritual self-knowledge, thereby receiving direct revelation from God, and (too often) the awareness that greed and the quest for material possessions are wrong. Absent also is an awareness that the religion they follow has a long legacy of using tainted doctrine to wage war on those who dared to challenge Church authority, placing women in a subservient role below God and man, destroying critical documents, slandering the names of those in opposition, and finally murdering anyone who stood it its way. In this regard, Catholics and Protestants are no different. Both have the same origins, share the same tenets of faith, and teach more or less the same doctrine. Neither has been willing to re-examine its basic belief system in light of the archaeological finds of the Lost Gospels at Nag Hammadi, or of the Essene scrolls found on the shores of the Dead Sea.

*...to you has been given the secret knowledge of*
*the kingdom of God, but for those outside, every-*
*thing is in parables, so they may indeed see, but*
*not perceive, and...hear, but not understand....*
The words of Jesus
from the Gospel of Mark


*And I saw the dead, small and great, stand before*
*God; and the books were opened: and another*
*book was opened, which is the book of life: and the*
*dead were judged out of those things which were*
*written in the books, according to their works.*
Revelations 20:12–13

CHAPTER THIRTEEN
# The Matrix Revealed

I N THE 1999 MOVIE *The Matrix*, a group of humans make the astounding discovery that the human race is living in an illusory reality, created by an advanced but malevolent computer intelligence for the purpose of controlling humankind. While human bodies lie in a vegetative
state, energy is sapped from them to provide fuel for the cybernetic entity,
which exists in the real world.

In the fake world, everything that humans see, hear, feel, smell, and
touch is created by a clever computer simulation and is being transmitted
into the brains of the unconscious humans via a computer hookup, directly
into their nervous systems.

A computer hacker named Neo (Keanu Reaves) is contacted by a group
of resistance fighters who reveal to him the great secret—the real Earth has
been laid waste and has been taken over by machines with artificial intelli-

gence. The machines have enslaved mankind and created a false version of 20th-century life—called the Matrix—to keep humans pacified and unsuspecting.

Once Neo accepts this amazing truth, he joins the resistance and learns that his destiny is to save the human race. He is the Chosen One, whose life mission is to overthrow the machines and restore humanity to its rightful place.

Of course you and I can see that the movie plot is merely a retelling of the story of Jesus, the Jewish Messiah, who was sent to Earth to warn humans that they are living in an illusory word, created for the purpose of entrapping their souls by tempting them with material things. He came to free humanity from those who created the false world we live in and who record all the evil things people do and use the information to keep the soul from leaving the three-dimensional world.

But at this point in the movie, unlike the story of Jesus, the Chosen One returns to the Matrix, not to preach love and forgiveness, but to do battle with the agents of the machine intelligence, making copious use of automatic weapons, powerful handguns and, of course, martial arts. Well, you can't expect Hollywood to get it exactly right, can you?

### The Real Matrix

In the Gnostic Gospels, Jesus tells his disciples that they are like orphans, not knowing where they came from, how they got here, what they are to do while they are here, where they are going when they leave, and what will happen to them when they get there. Two thousand years later, we humans still haven't learned the answers to these questions. We are still orphans and most are still prisoners in this amazing 3-D world created for souls who want to experience what it is like to be separate from God—the One—the All. The illusion is so clever that most people swear not only that it is real, but that it is the only reality. Those who believe so intensely in the material world live their lives accumulating material things, living self-centered, ego-driven lives, not realizing their every thought and action is being recorded in what has been called the Akashic record. These are the books that record our lives and which are used by the Rulers of the real matrix to judge the evolutionary progress of our souls.

Jesus tried in every way he could to make his disciples see that there was a real world just beyond this one, the one they were convinced was the only world. He explained to them that their souls came from this other heavenly realm and they would return to their real home after they died. He explained that death is an illusion—that it is like walking through a doorway into another dimension. There, they will be judged by their actions in this lifetime. There are higher beings there who will separate the wheat from the chaff. Those souls who have matured and learned to walk the paths of unconditional love and forgiveness are allowed to move forward in their journey back toward the light, the One, from which they originated. But those who have not are turned over to the dark Rulers and forced to return to the hellish place called Earth, to be born again of a woman and to live yet another life full of pain and suffering for the purpose of righting the wrongs done in previous incarnations and learning that a life in service to others is their only salvation.

## Know Thyself

The good news is that the Akashic record—the book of life—is open to us, if we wish to read it. And we have helpers, unseen guides that constantly try to push us in the right direction, so that we might reach a state of enlightenment. The books exist in another dimension in what is called the Hall of Records, cataloged for us by these mysterious rulers in another dimension. It is our task in life to access our own personal record and make contact with the divine. All we have to do is to *know ourselves.*

Edgar Cayce is quoted in *Edgar Cayce's Story of Jesus,* edited by Jeffrey Furst, (1976, 68) saying that "The study from the human standpoint of subconscious mind, subliminal, psychic, soul forces, is and should be the great study for the human family—for through [studying] oneself man will understand [his] maker….And that understanding is the knowledge as is given in this state [of consciousness]."(italics added) Altered states, in other words, are necessary to achieve self-discovery and the study of this should be humankind's top priority. Cayce himself stands as an example of the Way that Jesus and other spiritual masters throughout the ages tried to teach those who would listen about how to become enlightened—how to become Christed. Cayce, by knowing himself and his past lives (in Atlantis, Egypt, and during the time of Jesus) understood who he was, why he was here on Earth, what his purpose was, where he was going, how he would get there, and what would happen when he got there. Most importantly, he devoted his life to good works by using his psychic gift to help the human race.

Gnostic Christians taught that we do not necessarily need a religious institution to find the Way, nor do we require the assistance of priests, bishops, ministers, or mullahs. But we might need a teacher, a spiritual guide, or a good hypnotherapist to get us on our way. Yes, it is true that both Jesus and Edgar Cayce were gifted psychics and clairvoyants, even as children, but these are abilities that lie latent in all humans. We can work on them and improve upon them, but the first thing we must do is recognize them. It begins by realizing that we live in an intelligent, conscious, and meaningful universe and that everything is connected at the soul level. When we truly accept that concept, we begin to see how our thoughts, beliefs, intentions, and prayers shape the reality we live in. Pretty soon we begin to realize that unusual coincidences regarding the people we meet, the books we find, the movies we see, and the television shows we watch are not coincidences at all. Neither are the joys and the tragedies we all experience in our lives coincidences.

We realize there is a guiding force behind the scenes arranging our lives, sometimes blocking our way from directions we shouldn't take, and other times opening doors (or holes in clouds) that we are beckoned to pass through, we become acutely aware that there are choices to be made. It is those choices that ultimately determine our fate in the afterlife, or in future lives. I have learned that the Earth is a school for souls. It is a place where we must learn how to love unconditionally, but the lessons of unconditional love do not come easily. The greatest heartbreak, the greatest burdens, the most terrible tragedies are the events that provide us with the greatest leaps in spiritual growth and maturity.

For me, the great turning point in my spiritual life—the one that taught me the most about the true meaning of love—was also the most tragic and heartbreaking event a person can experience. I have already explained to the reader that I had lived a charmed life, and there wasn't a day that passed that I didn't thank God for the life of comfort, love, and joy I had been blessed with. Doors always opened for me at the times of greatest need—tragedy was only something I understood from a distance, as misfortune struck others, but none too close to me. Then, on a cold January night in 2003, my wife and I were awakened just after midnight by a persistent knocking at our door. There were two police officers on the porch, standing patiently, with grim expressions on their faces.

"What is it?" we asked anxiously.

"May we come in?" they asked.

"Yes, of course."

"Do you mind if we sit down?" one asked, after passing into the living room.

"What has happened?" I asked anxiously, ignoring the question.

"Do you know a Nicholas Lewels?" an officer asked.

"Yes, of course, he's our son," we answered.

"Well," the policeman said, "we are sorry to tell you that Nicholas died tonight."

"Oh, no!" my wife screamed out as she crumbled to the floor in disbelief and sheer, tortured anguish.

"What happened?" I asked, still in disbelief that such a thing could be true.

"He took his life a few hours ago. He shot himself with a handgun."

"Oh my God," I cried, as I knelt on the floor, embracing my wife who was caught in the throes of the purest heartbreak imaginable.

Nicholas was the oldest of our three children. He was 27 years old, a college graduate, a talented filmmaker and videographer, and a gentle, loving young man with everything to live for. Yet, in a deep depression, triggered by his discovery that the woman he loved had betrayed him with another man, he lost all hope and faith in the future and ended his life. The lessons he failed to learn in this life, although we spoke of them many times, were the lessons of forgiveness and that true love is not a jealous or possessive love, but unconditional.

The days, weeks, and months that followed that horrible night brought with them a pain so deep and a loss so great that our entire family reeled in disbelief that such a thing could happen to us. We were all so close. We shared so much love for one another and we were always there to support each other in times of need. We couldn't understand how such a thing could happen. Yet, it had.

As time passed, I began to see that our love for our son and for each other had never been so acutely felt as it was after he was gone. We didn't appreciate how much we loved him and how much he meant to us until he was no longer there to embrace, to share his laughter, his successes, or his disappointments. Tragedies such as these are lessons from God about the true meaning of love, and Nicholas's death brought forth an outpouring of love from literally hundreds of people, many whom we had never met, but who knew and loved Nicholas in their own way. The months after his death turned into a love-fest in our home, the likes of which we had never experienced.

Learning about love, real unconditional love, we found, is the hardest lesson in life, for part of the lesson is in being able to forgive those who caused so much heartache. Tragic events, we discovered, are opportunities sent to us by God to learn how to love and how to forgive. Our reactions and those of all involved, I am certain, are duly recorded in those mysterious books of life.

### Finding Meaning and Purpose

We may not believe in the books of life, or in angelic Watchers who record our every thought, or even in other dimensions unperceivable by our five senses. We may be absolutely certain we have no psychic abilities (just as I believed for most of my life), but, regardless, our connection to God and the universe is an absolute law of nature and cannot be eliminated or denied, without dire repercussions to our souls. In the Lost Gospels, Jesus says, "When you bring forth what is within you, it will save you. When you do not bring forth what is within you, it will destroy you." It is our choice whether or not to peer deeply within our souls, and to discover the totality of who we are, but it is a choice we will be given many times, in many lifetimes. Eventually, I believe, we will all get it right.

There is no greater satisfaction and excitement in my life than to be able to help others find purpose in their lives. Through my work as a hypnotherapist, as an author, as a public speaker, and as a guest speaker on radio programs all over the United States and in other countries, I have had such an opportunity. Particularly satisfying are those moments when individuals have come to me in distress, due to the strange occurrences in their lives that have left them confused, fearful, and even questioning their sanity. Through gentle understanding and through the use of altered states of consciousness, I have guided them to relax and to let their subconscious minds speak through them, allowing amazing miracles to become common occurrences.

Once, a woman with a successful practice as a psychotherapist and life-coach, came to me for help. She was puzzled and afraid because she suffered from terrible claustrophobia. It was so bad that once, while returning to America on a trans-Atlantic flight, she had suffered a sudden panic attack and actually rushed the exit door, believing she had to get out of the airplane. Thankfully, flight attendants were able to calm her down.

One can only imagine how frightening such an event would be. Although she is very spiritual and has helped her many clients with spiritual problems, she felt no connection to organized religion, especially the Christianity of her childhood. She explained to me that this was in part because of the overly self-righteous and judgmental nature of so many persons she had met who believed they were good Christians. She also blamed religious differences and religious intolerance for many of the world's problems. Another interesting facet of this highly successful woman was what she told me about her spiritual guide.

"I have always been guided by a voice that directs my life," she confided. "Ever since I was a little girl, I have occasionally heard this voice. When it speaks to me it always guides me in the right direction. I have learned to pay attention and heed what it says."

"Who is it that is speaking to you?" I asked.

"I don't know. I think of it as God, but I have never seen who it is," she answered with a bit of sadness in her voice. In the case of her claustrophobia, the voice had been silent, but due to a synchronous set of events, a mutual friend of ours had given her my book as a birthday present. She was fascinated, in part, because as a young woman she had had a close encounter with a UFO while driving in Mexico with some friends. When we met, we found we had an instant rapport, as if we had known each other before. This was helpful at the time, because it is often difficult for psychotherapists to ask for help. They often have no one to turn to. As a result, I was honored that she would trust me to help with her problem.

I suggested a light hypnotic trance to help her find out where such a strong fear might have originated. She could only think of one thing in her life that might be the cause. As a little girl, she and her brother had accidentally locked themselves in a small linen closet. The experience was traumatizing, but did not last for a long time, so it was not so distressing that it could cause such a severe reaction later in life.

She also explained to me during the interview that she was not good at visualizing while under hypnosis, but that she was better at feeling and hearing. This was a valuable clue to me as to how to engage her subconscious mind.

Because she was so naturally psychic, it wasn't long before she fell into a deeply relaxed state. I then suggested that she go back to the very first time she ever felt claustrophobic. She immediately began coughing and choking. Because she couldn't speak, I suggested she move beyond that experience to a point where she felt better. Her breathing became relaxed as she took in a great gulp of air. "I'm out of my body now," she said. "They were burying me alive!"

"Well, you're okay now," I said to calm her down. "Where are you now?"

"I'm back home. [The afterlife.] All my friends are here. They're all greeting me. They're laughing and smiling. It's great to see them again. I've left that life behind now."

"Good," I suggested. "But let's go back to see what was happening and what there was to learn from that lifetime." ("Home," in cases like this, always means the place where souls come from before incarnating into the flesh and where they plan their next lifetime.)

Although she didn't visualize the scene as some can, she somehow knew what happened, and afterward explained the horror of the experience she suffered in that lifetime. "I had been chained to a wall, with my hands up high, in a tiny space, along with one other person. We were being buried alive as heretics. This was in northern Spain during the years of the Inquisition. It was a tiny space and they were making a brick wall to encase us. I could smell the mustiness of the place and I could see them putting in the last brick. There was no air to breathe. It was a place like a monastery. We had been tortured and murdered in this cruel way because we did not accept the beliefs of the Catholic Church. The rage I felt was incredible."

Needless to say, such an experience could be the cause of her current problem with claustrophobia, just as it could be part of the cause of her problem with organized religion, particularly Christianity.

Nevertheless, I asked her if she could forgive those who had done this to her, and she agreed that she could because they were simply insecure and immature souls. She was able to see that her burial in that lifetime was a burden her soul had carried into this life, and that it was causing her problems. She agreed to let go of that fear and not to let it bother her anymore.

A few weeks later, she had to attend a professional meeting in another city, and she had no trouble on her round-trip flight. Her problem was solved. But something even more remarkable came out of that session. When she was in trance, I suggested she ask her guide to reveal him- or herself (you never know quite what will happen when you ask this question, because guides can take on many forms). In this case, the answer came as a great surprise to her and to me as well.

"It's Jesus," she whispered. "He has always been with me. And I was there with him when he lived on Earth and when he was Crucified," she explained now with great emotion and tears beginning to well in her eyes.

"Then how do you explain your feelings about Christianity?" I asked.

"He says (receiving information directly from Jesus at this point) not to judge him by the shadow he left behind."

"What does that mean?"

"He isn't responsible for what people have done in his name. They will have to answer for those things individually. Christianity has taken a wrong turn. It's not what he wanted to happen, but what others have done, using his name."

"How do you feel now that you know who your guide has been all this time?"

"Ashamed. I should have known. I loved him with all my heart then, and I still do."

This brief session made a huge difference in this woman's life in so many ways. Besides alleviating her phobia, it taught her a great deal about who she is and her purpose in life. Most importantly, she made a direct connection to God and to the Christ consciousness that guides her in her daily life. She still doesn't go to church, but she has made peace with her mentor and guide, Jesus, and understands that loving him and honoring him does not require her allegiance to a religious institution.

### Another Lady in Distress

A woman in her early forties came to me under unusual circumstances, to which I have now become accustomed. As she was driving down the street one Saturday morning, she had a strong feeling that she should turn into the parking lot of a Barnes & Noble bookstore and to go into the store. Although she had experienced a lifetime of UFO and paranormal experiences, she had successfully pushed that part of her life into a dark corner of her psyche in an effort to live a normal life as a housewife and mother. She had no idea that on this Saturday morning, the bookstore was holding a book signing event for Dr. John E. Mack. He was sitting at a table near the entrance, autographing copies of *Abduction: Human Encounters with Aliens*. I had arranged for his visit to El Paso.

She came directly to where John was signing books and asked what it was all about. Then she quickly made a U-turn and walked quickly to the back of the store. She wasn't at all ready to deal with the subject of UFOs. But her guiding inner voice kept urging her to go back, and she eventually bought John's book and also my book, *The God Hypothesis*. I took her name and number and a few weeks later we met again so that I could interview her at length. She explained how distressed she was when she discovered the reason she was guided to the Barnes & Noble bookstore that particular day. She was frightened about the whole UFO thing and the many related experiences since childhood. She had internalized the fears and they had manifested in numerous phobias.

In fact, she was absolutely certain that the beings who had been taking her all her life, and erasing most of her memories, were demonic or Satanic, and that she was being punished for her sins.

She felt she had been abandoned and that her religion, Christianity, had let her down. So when she finally decided to face her fears and undergo hypnosis, it was with great trepidation and anxiety.

"I'm so scared," she said, "I'm not sure I can be hypnotized."

"It's okay," I reassured her, "the worst that can happen is that you will relax for a while. After all, that's all hypnosis is about—relaxation." To further help her relax, I said a short prayer asking that all negative energies or entities be forbidden to interfere with the session. With that assurance, she began the inner journey of getting to know her inner self. Gradually, as her muscles relaxed, she gently slipped into that sleeplike state that allows the conscious mind to step aside and allow her soul self to take over. Contrary to what many persons believe about hypnosis, the subject, although in a deeply relaxed state, is usually aware of everything happening around him or her, and is able to remember what happened during the session once it is over. However, because an average session lasts between one and a half to two hours, the sessions are recorded so that the person and the researcher or therapist can refer to it at a later time.

In this case, as in many such cases, the woman eventually remembered being aboard a spaceship, or at least in a strange, round room, furnished only with an operating table in the middle. She found herself lying on the table and under the intense scrutiny of a group of small beings with big heads, gray skin, and big, black, almond-shaped eyes. She was beginning to panic.

"Just float above the scene," I suggested. "Look at the scene from above, as if you were out of your body, looking down." Immediately her breathing became relaxed, her expression changed from one of extreme alarm to one of calm. "What do you see?" I asked. "Can you describe the scene below you?"

"Yes," she said calmly. "I am lying on an operating table. There is a big light above me and there are four small people standing around the table."

"Can you describe them?"

"They have gray skin. They're short, maybe four feet tall, and they have big black eyes that wrap around the sides of their heads. They have no noses and just slits where their mouths should be. No ears, either. They're not human."

"What are they doing?"

"One is standing at the end of the table. I'm naked. He's spreading my legs apart," she said, starting to become anxious again.

"Go ahead and see what happens, but remember you made it through this okay and you can look at the scene from above without reliving the fear and anxiety of that time."

"Oh my! He just pulled something out of me! It's a tiny baby." She began to weep.

"Look at it carefully. What does it look like?"

"This isn't right! They are taking the baby. It looks like them, but part human."

"Okay," I said, "Now you know what happened to you when they took you. I want you to look at the scene from above and get away from the emotion, the fear. It's as if you have a videotape that you can pause and look at objectively."

"Okay," she agreed.

"Now that you have paused the picture and you can see it all objectively and without fear, I want you to deduce the intentions of these creatures. First, I want you to ask yourself if their intent is to harm you."

"No," she said without hesitation. "They aren't trying to hurt me."

"That's good to know," I suggested. "Now ask yourself if their intention is to frighten you."

Once again she responded without hesitation, "No, they aren't trying to frighten me."

"Good, that's really good to know. Now ask yourself if they are evil."

"No, I can't believe I'm saying this, but they're not evil. They're not evil! I was so sure they would be evil! I wasn't prepared for this. They're just doing their jobs. They are doing something important, for the greater good. It's is very important for them and for us, the human race."

"What do you mean by that?" I queried.

"We humans are destroying this planet. We are polluting everything. It's going to cause terrible problems for us. They [the beings] see us as primitive and violent. These babies they're making are more aware, more connected with the universe, with nature. They are part us and part them. They have the best of both species. So this is a very important project. I can't believe I'm saying this, but I actually feel honored that they are using my DNA to create this new species. Part of me will someday help create a better world."

"That's good," I said. "That means you aren't really the victim of some evil plot. So, now I want you to ask them to explain to you why they selected you for this project. Why is it that you, out of all the people on the planet, are the one lying on the table?"

"I see myself on a spaceship, far out in space, looking down on the Earth. I am wearing a white robe and I am standing next to a man who is wearing a similar robe. I know him," she said, beginning to weep once again. "This is before I came into this life and we are talking about what I am supposed to do in my next life. I am happy to be with him and I am happy to take on this mission. I'm supposed to be a part of this project to create a new species. I have known this man for many lifetimes."

"Does he have a name?"

"Yes, he has had many names. Here, on the ship, he is known as…as, well it's something like Sandanda. Something like that. No, it's Sananda. That's it, he is called Sananda here. But people today would call him Jesus," she said with tears streaming down her cheeks. (Unbeknownst to her, there are a number of psychics who claim to channel the disincarnate soul of Sananda, who they also say is Jesus, but by another name. There have been several books written about this subject.)

"But I thought he had abandoned you," I prodded.

"No, he has always been with me. I just didn't realize it. I blamed him for my misery and for allowing these bad things to happen to me. I was wrong."

"Why would he ask you to do such a thing in this lifetime and why would you agree? It's a traumatic life you chose."

"He is teaching me about karma and how we all live many lives, and in each life we make promises. There is an agreement that we make before we incarnate into a body, and then we have to fulfill our contract if we are going to progress to a higher level."

In a similar case, another woman's spirit guide explained that by choosing to enter the breeding program she would be getting karmic brownie points for her karmic book. She asked her guide (a tall, Native American) for clarification, and he explained to her that she could have had a normal life, but she chose this one with the understanding that it would count for the equivalent of five ordinary lives. This would be recorded in her book of karma, which is a record of her every action in every lifetime, of which there were hundreds. She also experienced a great relief and sense of purpose in her life, which until then had been confusing and frightening.

"It's like everything has fallen into place—all those strange experiences in my life since I was a child. It all makes sense now, even my fears—my fear of the dark, my fear that I had not locked all the doors and windows before going to bed, my fear of dentists (because of the similarity of the large light just above the head to the light used by the extraterrestrials during operative procedures), and even my fear of dolls and infants. It all makes sense now. I feel like for the first time in my life I can get grounded, have normal relationships, and get on with life."

Needless to say, these seemingly ordinary women had life-altering experiences during their nearly two-hour sessions. They learned their purpose in life, strange as it might be; they learned God had not abandoned them; and that they were not the victims they previously had believed themselves to be. All the crazy and mysterious events in their lives suddenly fell into place, and for the first time it all made sense. Their fears were greatly relieved and mysterious phobias melted away. In the months that follow each case study I keep in touch with my subjects to see how they are processing what they learned under hypnosis. The positive results seem always to be lasting, but sometimes other problems arise as they try to balance the two very different realities they live in.

In the case of the woman who lived in the mountains of New Mexico, her fears had not returned and her new joy for life had not diminished. Her biggest problem was that, in her joy, she shared her secrets with members of the small Christian church she and her family attended. She was shocked and stunned by their reaction.

"You are possessed by demons!" they accused. "This is something evil!"

Shortly thereafter, she and her family were asked to leave the congregation. This caused her husband embarrassment and consternation. He was having problems accepting her story. But as for her, she was content with her new understanding of the universe around her and the role she was playing in it. She would find new friends, and her husband gradually came to her support. Life is never easy, but it is a lot easier when you understand who you are, why you are here, and what you're supposed to do.

The cases in this book of persons who have had UFO/Jesus-related experiences are but a few. There are many more in my files too lengthy to include here, but these are fairly representative of those many cases in which ordinary people have had extraordinary experiences and discovered their true purpose in life.

*And ...while they beheld, He was taken up; and a
cloud received Him out of their sight. And while
they looked up steadfastly, toward the heaven as
He went up, behold, two men stood by them in
white apparel; which also said, "Ye men of Galilee,
why stand ye gazing up into the heaven? This
same Jesus which is taken up from you into
heaven, shall so come in like manner as ye have
seen Him go into heaven.'*

Acts of the Apostles 1:9–11

## CHAPTER FOURTEEN

# The Apocalypse

### The Second Coming

OW CAN WE DISCUSS the Jesus mystery without addressing the issue of the apocalypse, the end of times when many Christians believe Jesus will return to the Earth?

For those who take the Bible literally, then, according the above verse in the Acts of the Apostles, Jesus will come to Earth this time not as a baby born of a virgin but on or in a mysterious cloud, the same way he was seen leaving by his disciples. In other words, Jesus will return in a vehicle of some sort, traveling in the sky.

The Rev. Barry Downing, Ph.D., a Presbyterian minister and the author of *The Bible and Flying Saucers*, points out that the term "cloud," when used to describe an aerial phenomenon associated with God or angels in the Bible, is most likely a code word or metaphor for a flying saucer or spacecraft of some sort. After all, we all know that clouds are insubstantial and incapable of carrying any weight. In any case, Christians have been awaiting the return of Jesus for nearly 2,000 years, and hopes are running high today, given the state of world turmoil, particularly in the Middle East. The Book of Revelation's horrible descriptions of the war-torn end days as envisioned by the Apostle John weigh heavily on all good Christian minds. Yet the inclusion of the book in the Canon of the New Testament was heavily debated. Many in the Church were against it. It was too confusing and full of vindictiveness and anger toward all those who persecuted the early Christians, primarily the Romans. Even so, in the end, it was selected and others rejected.

As a result, it has become, for those seeking to see the future in ancient texts, a primary reference for what will happen if the course of human events does not change soon. Had I been on the committee that made that decision, I would have voted an emphatic "No!" I really wish the Book of Revelation had been left out. I can think of numerous others that would have made a better choice. But alas, here we are in the midst of a Holy War with fundamentalist Christians quoting from that dreadful book as if it were a blueprint for days ahead, and using it as justification for the United States to enter into all-out war against the forces of Islam. I find it far more educational to read instead what Edgar Cayce had to say about the future.

In *Edgar Cayce's Story of Jesus*, Cayce says that the second coming of Jesus will be linked to vast Earth changes and remarkable discoveries: the reemergence of the continent of Poseidia; the discovery of the Hall of Records left by the Atlanteans, buried deep beneath the Sphinx in Egypt (underground tunnels have already been found there); a shifting of the Earth's poles; and the beginning of a new cycle for humanity. Included in this scenario is "the beginning of a new sub-race of humans and a great influx of souls from Atlantis, Lemuria and other ancient civilizations." (Furst 1976, 101). Incredibly, UFO research in the past twenty or so years has confirmed Cayce's prediction that a new species of humans is emerging; perhaps a major jump in the evolutionary process is currently underway.

Additionally, Cayce predicted "great upheavals in the Arctic and the Antarctic, triggering volcanic eruptions," and a period "when His light will be seen again in the clouds." He said "many souls will incarnate at this time to help prepare the way for His day on Earth" (Furst 1976, 101). We have already seen the polar caps begin to break up and melt at a startling rate, and the tremendous numbers of UFO sightings over the past fifty years could be thought of as the "lights in the sky" referred to by Cayce. My own work has taught me that there are many souls incarnating today who are here to take part in some great plan. Souls are gathering again, just as during the time that Jesus came before, to help prepare the people.

These dire predictions of Earth changes are similar to the warnings given by UFO beings to those persons with whom they have had contact. In some cases, those contacted by UFO beings have been told that a great extinction of animal species has already begun and that the human race itself is in danger of becoming extinct due to the levels of pollution in our food chain . Certainly, world climate change is an issue that has become a matter of utmost importance today and is being debated heatedly by world organizations and governments. Among those many hundreds of UFO experiencers I have had the pleasure and honor to know and interview, ecological concern is universally considered greatly important. Somehow, they have been imbued with the knowledge that the Earth is facing an ecological disaster of biblical proportions. This is true of those who have had UFO contact in all parts of the world. Many describe having been taught, through visions or through holographic projections, the dire consequences the Earth will face if humankind cannot change its ways.

The years 2004 and 2005 brought with them calamitous events never before dreamed of by the public or even by scientists. The tidal wave of biblical proportions that killed nearly 300,000 people in south Asia was caused by one of the most powerful earthquakes ever recorded. That was a wake-up call to the entire world that upheavals in the Earth's crust could cause devastation and destruction unlike anything ever witnessed. Then the state of Florida was hit by four major hurricanes, one right after another, leaving behind them a huge path of destruction and setting new records for property losses. Then in early September 2005, hurricane Katrina, a cate-

gory 5 hurricane the size of the state of Texas, scored almost a direct hit on
the city of New Orleans and the Mississippi coast, leaving the area virtually
uninhabitable for months. Parts of it are still a wasteland. It was the country's greatest natural disaster ever, so far. Such destructive events were fore-
told by the UFO beings. Even so, many political leaders in the U.S. and some
scientists insist that global warming is not a top priority issue and certainly
not one caused by the actions of humankind. Governments continue to
drag their feet when it comes to creating laws and policies that would curb
the emission of dangerous greenhouse gases and that would provide funding for the discovery of alternative energy sources.

In spite of the fact that world events seem to be confirming Cayce's
prophecies, we must remind ourselves that Christianity as it exists in the
Gospels, in the Gnostic Gospels and even in the writings of the Essenes in
the Dead Sea Scrolls has always been about an imminent apocalypse. For
the ancient Hebrews, the world was always about to end. After being held
in bondage by the Egyptians, Israel suffered conquests and invasions from
the Assyrians, Babylonians, Greeks, and Romans, to name but a few. There
was always a dream of and a need for a great Messiah to deliver them from
whomever was their nemesis at the moment. The Essene library at Qumran is full of references to the final battle between good and evil that will
rid the Earth and the heavens of the Sons of Darkness. Roman rule was the
harshest punishment they could imagine that God could visit upon them.
The pagan rulers did not respect the Jewish laws and their prophets. Their
ruthlessness in punishing their opponents was without mercy—a crush-
ing, humiliating, and public death. The end of the world had to be near.

In the Gospels we find that the disciples of Jesus believed the end was
near and that Jesus would be back soon (even during their own lifetimes)
to right the wrongs inflicted upon them by the Romans and the Pharisees
who controlled the Jerusalem temple. Various religious sects and cults ever
since then have predicted that the end of the world was just around the corner and that a new age would begin with the return of Jesus. The end of the
first millennium seemed the perfect time for this to happen, but life went

on as usual. Then came the end of the second millennium, and again predictions were made about the Second Coming. Time and again, would-be prophets have been embarrassed by their lack of ability to predict the moment when the great apocalypse will occur. In recent times, there were many who saw the beginning of the end in the Y-2K computer problem.

Of course, nothing of the sort happened. Some people believed the alignment of the planets on May 5, 2000, would cause a pole shift, which would wreak havoc on the Earth. Many believed that when we reached the date June 6, 2006 (6-6-06), which is close to being the sign of devil, 666 that the great Day of Judgment would arrive. It didn't. Much is being written and said about the end of the Mayan calendar in 2012. Why did the Mayan people, who kept track of the movement of the stars and planets with astounding accuracy, decide that the calendar should end in that year? Will this be the end of the world? I am not betting on it and I believe such talk just creates fear in people's minds without good cause.

I am not about to make any predictions regarding when the so-called, end times might occur. I can only report what I know and what I have discovered through my research. No doubt there is much in my findings that point to an era in the not-so-distant future when the Earth will suffer great upheavals. I believe this is due to the worldwide ecological damage done through ignorance and lack of spiritual maturity by humans, who have lost touch with their innate connection to the One. But the future is not cast in stone. Quantum physics teaches us that the future is made up of probabilities that are determined by the decisions we make each moment of our lives. We have it in our power to create a different outcome, but do we have the will to do it? That is a question that only time can answer. If the human race is able to focus its intent on saving the Earth and its creatures, great change will occur almost overnight. I am still hoping and praying that this will happen.

### Agenda of the Rulers

Let us suppose for a moment that what is proposed in this book is true: we live in a special dimension created by superior beings for the purpose of allowing spirit beings (us) an opportunity to feel what it is like to be separated from God—the Oneness which is at the core of the universe or of the many universes. Let's assume that these beings were so clever in their ability to manipulate energy and matter that they were able to create this matrix and create bodies for souls to wear while they explore their creation. Let us also assume that once souls experience this amazing amusement park ride, they get caught up in the intense feelings provided by the five physical senses and forget who they are and where they came from. We forget that we are really part of the Whole and not independent creatures, alone and abandoned on a tiny grain of sand on the edge of a great galaxy of stars.

If this is true, then we must also assume that these entities of a higher order than humankind have always watched over us and tinkered with their construct for their own mysterious purposes. They, of course, exist in a different dimension where time and space are not relevant. They would seem to us to be immortal and all-powerful. It would be logical to assume that they can take on physical form at their pleasure and interact with humans for whatever purpose they choose, at any time they choose.

These Watchers or Rulers would no doubt have a far keener ability to see into our past and into our future than we do. They would have known for a long time that the human race was heading for disaster. After all, those persons having UFO experiences have been warning us of ecological and nuclear disaster since at least the 1950s when the modern-day wave of UFO sightings began. UFO researchers have known about this early warning system for a long time, but many were skeptical. Because UFO occupants behave in surreptitious ways, researchers have assumed they are not all to be trusted. As a result, the dire warnings of global ecological disaster have not been taken seriously nor communicated properly to the public.

In any case, the fact that there were warnings at all is an important clue in the solving of this great puzzle. Some of the beings are trying to help us avoid disaster. This means we have friends among the Rulers. They are not all indifferent to our fate. In fact, I believe there are those whose mission it is to confuse and divide the human race for the purpose of creating strife and dissension, while others are trying desperately to help us understand that we live in an artificial matrix and that there is a way out. If such is the case, then we can understand how important it is for each of us to take the message of this book seriously. Religions divide us. Race divides us. Gender divides us. Nationalities divide us. These are all traps for souls to fall into. If we are to see through the illusion of the Matrix and find our way out, we must detect the traps and avoid them. We must love one another in spite of our perceived differences. And rather than seeing those Rulers whose mission it is to create such differences as evil, we must understand that it is just their job. We can discern between the helpers and those who divide us by their teachings and their actions. If they teach unity and love, they are helpers. If they teach division and hate, they are dividers. Given this simple litmus test, let us take one last look at the core teachings of Jesus and other great mystics who sought to teach us unity and the dangers of believing in separation.

It is through these lessons that the soul achieves enlightenment:

*Love thy neighbor as thyself.*

*Devote your life to good works, because these works determine your soul's destiny.*

*Do not judge others. This includes your parents, your siblings, your children, your president (or former presidents), terrorists, serial killers, cockroaches, and even aliens. But most importantly, it includes you.*

*Love your enemies.*

*Forgive everyone who has ever trespassed against you.*

*Know that you are a part of God. God is within you and you can have your own personal revelations and contact with the divine.*

*Renounce the physical world as an illusion and focus your attention on the world beyond.*

*Know thyself.*

*Honor the female aspect of the divinity, as well as the male.*

*Accept that the real you is the immortal soul that animates your body. Your body is not the real you.*

*Live your life as if every thought you think and every action you take is being recorded, because it is.*

*You have many chances to attain enlightenment. Gaining spiritual maturity may take many lifetimes, but fewer lifetimes is better.*

*The ultimate goal in the journey of the soul is to reunite with the Source from which it came.*

*Tragic and negative events are part of God's plan to give us opportunities to learn the lessons of unconditional love and forgiveness.*

*Everyone has made a soul contract prior to incarnating into the flesh. It is our duty to discover what that contract involves, and then to live up to the agreement.*

*Everyone has a purpose in life. There is meaning everywhere; we just have to look for it.*

*Angelic beings, the sons of God, will be waiting for you to direct your soul's path when you die. It's a good idea to get ready now.*

These rules or principles of spiritual knowledge (gnosis) are not self-evident to most people. They do not represent religious dogma, but rather constitute immutable laws of the universe that must be learned through introspection. They could be seen as a blueprint or owner's manual for the soul that serves as a guide to help us maneuver through this labyrinth we call life on Earth. They cannot be changed, altered, or broken. That's just the way it is. Many readers may not be willing to accept that such rules exist, and that is inevitable. Consider what the world would be like if they were obvious to everyone. Would the world be a better place? Could they serve as guiding principles to help the religions of the world find some common ground? Perhaps that is why they have lain hidden in dark caves and in earthen jars for thousands of years. Perhaps the time is right for these truths to see the sunlight once again, and as a consequence, provide a means for bringing unity to a world torn apart by religious intolerance.

# Epilogue

IT WAS MANY YEARS after my first hypnotic regression that I finally dared to dig down into my soul and to face the indescribable emotions that overwhelmed me back in 1995. I was asked to speak at a conference in Denver in 2001, as one of many speakers from around the world on New Age issues dealing with everything from UFOs to crop circles. Among the speakers was Dr. Leo Sprinkle, a professor emeritus of counseling services at the University of Wyoming and a counseling psychologist in private practice. Dr. Sprinkle has worked with hundreds of patients with every sort of psychological problem, including many who had experienced contact with nonhuman entities. As with many psychologists today, Dr. Sprinkle uses hypnosis to achieve mental, spiritual, and physical healing with his patients.

Dr. Sprinkle is well known in the New Age community due to his courageous stance on the UFO issue in the face of persistent intolerance among the faculty and administration of his teaching institution. For years, he sponsored a national conference for persons having UFO encounters, and he helped countless individuals overcome their fears and come to grip with their life contracts. He is an avid believer that past-life regression therapy is a path toward physical, mental, and spiritual healing.

I asked Dr. Sprinkle if he would be so kind as to help me with my spiritual problem. I explained that I had never been able to break through the emotional block I encountered in my first attempt at past-life regression. He was happy to help, and we set up an appointment in my hotel room to conduct the session.

Once again, as we discussed my problem, the feelings of anxiety began to overwhelm me. I didn't know if I could go through with it. But gradually, he calmed me down and we began the session. Before long, my consciousness returned to those feelings of intense pain and sorrow I felt years before as I began to reach back in time to that faraway beach with the row of clay jars lined up neatly near the salty shores of the Dead Sea.

"Just go into the feeling," he suggested. "Go with it and let it take you where you need to go."

Then the tears began and the aching in my chest made it hard to breathe. My sobbing was uncontrollable, and I wasn't able to visualize anything more at that point. There was just agony.

"Just try to describe the feelings," he suggested.

"Grief," I finally said. "Horrible grief and sorrow."

"What else?" he asked, trying to get the full picture through my feelings.

"Guilt," I said, "guilt and shame. Also anger. A lot of anger at those animals who could do such a thing."

"Why the guilt?" he asked.

"Because I was a coward. We were all cowards! We ran and hid. We were terrified. No one would stand up for him. We let him go to the cross by himself, to be tortured and murdered. He was innocent. He had done nothing wrong. We should have done something, even if it meant dying along with him."

"And who was he?"

"Jesus," I said, resigned now to accept the truth.

"And who were you at that time?"

The tears came hard and fast as he asked that crucial question. "I don't know," I sobbed. The truth was I didn't want to know. I didn't want to own that information. I didn't want anyone else to know, either. Who was I to claim I knew the Master? I was nobody. And if it were true, whom would I tell? Who would believe me?

"What name comes to mind?" he pressed.

"I don't know. I don't want to say." My chest was heaving uncontrollably; I felt like I was going to explode. "All I know is that I feel as if I loved him like a brother. I loved him like a brother!" The implication of those words hit me like a ton of bricks and my sobbing grew in intensity. I could not speak.

I truthfully don't know if I was his brother, or if I just loved him like a brother. But this I do know: I have carried with me a burden throughout this lifetime—a burden from another place and another time long ago. I know it is my duty and obligation to help set the record straight about the true story of Jesus and the secrets and mysteries he described to his closest associates. And that is why this book exists. It represents part of my effort to fulfill my karmic contract. It is my duty, and it must be done. I only pray it is enough to atone for the sins of a life lived long ago.

# Bibliography

Barnstone, Willis, ed. *The Other Bible.* San Francisco: Harper, 1984.

Baigent, Michael and Richard Leigh. *The Dead Sea Scrolls Deception.* New York: Touchstone, 1991.

Baigent, Michael, Richard Leigh, and Henry Lincoln. *Holy Blood, Holy Grail.* New York: Dell, 1982.

Burrows, Millar. *The Dead Sea Scrolls.* New York: The Viking Press, 1955.

Cayce, Hugh Lynn, ed. *Edgar Cayce on Atlantis.* New York: Warner Books, 1968.

Cerminara, Gina. *Many Mansions: The Edgar Cayce Story.* New York: New American Library, 1967.

Charles, James H., ed. *Jesus and the Dead Sea Scrolls.* New York: The Anchor Bible Reference Library, 1992.

Charles, R.H., ed. *The Book of the Secrets of Enoch.* Oxford: Clarendon Press, 1896.

Churton, Tobias. *The Gnostics.* New York: Barnes & Noble, 1997.

Crick, Francis. *Life Itself.* New York: Simon and Schuster, 1981.

Cross, Frank M. *The Ancient Library of Qumran and Modern Biblical Studies.* Grand Rapids, Mich.: Baker Book House, 1980.

Davies, Paul. "The Harmony of the Spheres." *Time,* Feb. 6, 1996.

Doresse, Jean. *The Secret Books of the Egyptian Gnostics.* New York: MJF Books, 1958.

Eisenman, Robert, and Michael Wise. *The Dead Sea Scrolls Uncovered*. Rockport, Mass.: Element, 1992.

Eusebius. *The History of the Church*. London: Penguin Books, 1965.

"Evolution's Big Bang." *Time*, Dec. 4, 1995.

Fowler, Raymond E. *The Watchers II*. Newberg, Oreg.: Wild Flower Press, 1995.

Friedman, Richard Elliot. *Who Wrote the Bible?* San Francisco: HarperCollins, 1987.

Freke, Timothy and Peger Gandy. *The Jesus Mysteries*. New York: Three Rivers Press, 1999.

Furst, Jeffrey, ed. *Edgar Cayce's Story of Jesus*. New York: Berkley Books, 1976.

Gardner, Laurence. *Bloodline of the Holy Grail*. Shaftsbury, Dorset: Element, 1996.

Gardner, Laurence. *Genesis of the Grail Kings*. Boston: Element, 2000.

Gilbran, Kahlil. *The Prophet*. New York: Alfred A. Knopf, 1923.

Godden, Elaine, and Jutta Malnic. *Rock Paintings of Aboriginal Australia*. New Victoria, Australia: Reed Books, 1991.

Harner, Michael. *The Way of the Shaman*. New York: Harper and Row, 1980.

Haskins, Susan. *Mary Magdalene: Myth and Metaphor*. New York: Riverhead Books, 1993.

Head, Joseph, and Cranston, S. L. *Reincarnation: An East-West Anthology*. New York: The Julian Press, 1961.

Hendel, Ronald, S. "When the Sons of God Cavorted with the Daughter's of Men." In *Understanding the Dead Sea Scrolls*, edited by Herschel Shanks. New York: Random House, 1992.

The Holy Bible, King James Version.

Kersten, Holger. *Jesus Lived in India*. London: Penguin Books, 2001.

Kittler, Glenn, and Hugh Lynn Cayce, ed. *Edgar Cayce on the Dead Sea Scrolls*. New York: Paperback Library, 1970.

Larson, Edward J. *Trial and Error: The American Controversy Over Creation and Evolution*. New York: Oxford University Press, 2003.

Laurence, Richard. *The Book of Enoch the Prophet*. San Diego: Wizards Bookshelf, 1995.

Lewels, Joe. *The God Hypothesis: Extraterrestrial Life and Its Implications for Science and Religion*. 2d ed. Mills Spring, N.C. Wildflower Press, 2005.

Luna, Luis E., and Pablo Amaringo. *Ayahuasca Visions*. Berkeley, Calif.: North Atlantic Books, 1991.

Mack, Burton L. *The Lost Gospel of Q and Christian Origins*. New York: Harper Collins, 1994.

Mack, John E., M.D. *Abduction: Human Encounters with Aliens*. New York: Ballantine Books, 1995.

Mack, John E., M.D. *Passport to the Cosmos*. New York: Crown Publishers, 1999.

Maddex, Diane. *Scrolls from the Dead Sea*. Washington: Archetype Press, 1993.

Marrs, Jim. *Rule by Secrecy*. New York: HarperCollins, 2000.

Meurois-Givandan, Anne and Daniel. *The Way of the Essenes: Christ's Hidden Literature Remembered*. Rochester, Vt.: Destiny Books, 1993.

Milik, Joseph, ed. *The Books of Enoch*. Oxford: Clarendon Press, 1976.

Moore, David L. *The Christian Conspiracy*. Atlanta: Pendulum Press, 1994.

Narby, Jeremy. *The Cosmic Serpent.* New York: Jeremy P. Tarcher/Putnam, 1998.

The National Geographic Book Service. *Everyday Life in Bible Times.* National Geographic Society, 1967.

Pagels, Elaine. *The Gnostic Gospels.* New York: Random House, 1979.

Puryear, Herbert Bruce. Why Jesus Taught Reincarnation. Scottsdale, Ariz.: New Paradigm Press, 1992.

Radin, Dean. *Entangled Minds: Extrasensory Experiences in a Quantum Reality.* New York: Pocket Books, 2006

Rudoph, Kurt. *Gnosis.* New York: Harper, 1987.

Sagan, Carl. *The Dragons of Eden.* New York: Ballantine Books, 1977.

Shanks, Hershel, ed. *Understanding the Dead Sea Scrolls.* New York: Random House, 1992.

Silberman, Neil Asher. *The Hidden Scroll.* New York: Grosset/Putnam Book, 1994.

Sitchin, Zecharia. *Genesis Revisited.* New York: Avon Books, 1990.

Sitchen, Zecharia. *The Wars of Gods and Men.* New York: Avon Books, 1985.

Starbird, Margaret. *Magdalene's Lost Legacy.* Rochester, Vt.: Inner Traditions, 2003.

Starbird, Margaret. *The Woman with the Alabaster Jar: Mary Magdalene and the Holy Grail.* Rochester, Vt.: Inner Traditions, 2003.

Stearn, Jess. *Intimates Through Time: Edgar Cayce's Mysteries of Reincarnation.* New York: Signet Books, 1993.

Strassman, Richard. *DMT: The Spirit Molecule.* Rochester, Vt.: Park Street Press, 2001.

Talbot, Michael. *The Holographic Universe.* New York: Harper Perennial, 1998.

VanderKam, James C. "The Dead Sea Scrolls and Christianity." In *Understanding the Dead Sea Scrolls,* edited by Hershel Shanks. New York: Random House, 1992.

Watson, James. *DNA: The Secret of Life.* New York: Alfred Knopf, 2003.

Weiss, Brian. *Many Lives, Many Masters.* New York: Simon and Schuster, 1998.

Wigoder, Geoffrey, ed. *Illustrated Dictionary and Concordance of the Bible.* Jerusalem: G.G. The Jerusalem Publishing House, Ltd., 1986.

Wilson, Edmund. "The Dead Sea Scrolls." *The New Yorker,* May 1955.

Wise, Michael, Martin Abegg, Jr., and Edward Cook. *The Dead Sea Scrolls.* San Francisco: Harper, 1996.

Woodward, Mary Ann. *Edgar Cayce's Story of Karma.* New York: Berkley Books, 1972.

To order additional copies of this book,
please send full amount plus $5.00 for
postage and handling for the first book and
$1.00 for each additional book.

Send orders to:

## Galde Press, Inc.
PO Box 460
Lakeville, Minnesota 55044-0460

Credit card orders call 1–800–777–3454
Phone (952) 891–5991 • Fax (952) 891–6091
Visit our website at http://www.galdepress.com

Write for our free catalog.